LAWS AND LEGISLATION

AMERICAN RECOVERY AND REINVESTMENT ACT: HISTORY, OVERVIEW, IMPACT

LAWS AND LEGISLATION

Additional books in this series can be found on Nova's website at:

https://www.novapublishers.com/catalog/index.php?cPath=23_29&seriesp=Laws+and+Legislation

Additional e-books in this series can be found on Nova's website at:

https://www.novapublishers.com/catalog/index.php?cPath=23_29&seriespe=Laws+and+Legislation

LAWS AND LEGISLATION

AMERICAN RECOVERY AND REINVESTMENT ACT: HISTORY, OVERVIEW, IMPACT

PAUL G. TELLIS
EDITOR

Nova Science Publishers, Inc.

New York

For permission to use material from this book please contact us:
Telephone 631-231-7269; Fax 631-231-8175
Web Site: http://www.novapublishers.com

LIBRARY OF CONGRESS CATALOGING-IN-PUBLICATION DATA

American Recovery and Reinvestment Act : history, overview, impact / editor, Paul G. Tellis.
p. cm.
Includes index.
ISBN 978-1-61668-355-9 (hardcover)
1. Economic stabilization--Law and legislation--United States. 2. Economic development projects--Law and legislation--United States. 3. Tax incentives--Law and legislation--United States. 4. Federal aid--United States. 5. United States--Economic conditions--2009- I. Tellis, Paul G.
KF1570.A96 2010
343.73'0742--dc22

2010012178

Published by Nova Science Publishers, Inc. † New York

CONTENTS

PREFACE

On February 13, 2009, both the House and Senate passed the conference version of H.R. 1, the American Recovery and Reinvestment Act of 2009 (ARRA). The primary purposes of the ARRA focus on promoting economic recovery, assisting those most affected by the recession, improving economic efficiency by "spurring technological advances in science and health," investing in infrastructure, and stabilizing state and local government budgets. This book provides a brief overview of the key provisions of the ARRA including the agriculture, nutrition, and rural provisions; medicaid provisions; a summary and legislative history of the Act; and the estimated impact on employment and economic output as of September 2009.

Chapter 1 - On February 13, 2009, both the House and Senate passed the conference version of H.R. 1, the American Recovery and Reinvestment Act of 2009 (ARRA). The primary purposes of the ARRA focus on promoting economic recovery, assisting those most affected by the recession, improving economic efficiency by "spurring technological advances in science and health," investing in infrastructure, and stabilizing state and local government budgets. The House had previously passed its version of H.R. 1 (House-passed bill) on January 28, 2009, while the Senate passed S.Amdt. 570, an amendment in the nature of a substitute to H.R. 1 (Senate-passed bill), on February 10, 2009.

The ARRA provides funds to several existing workforce development programs administered by the U.S. Department of Labor (DOL), including programs authorized by the Workforce Investment Act (WIA).

This chapter provides a brief overview of the key provisions related to workforce development programs administered by DOL that were included in the ARRA under Division A, Title VIII, Department of Labor, and provides estimates of state grants for programs for which these estimates are relevant and for which data needed to produce the estimates are available. It also includes a discussion of relevant provisions that were included in the House- and Senate-passed versions of H.R. 1.

Chapter 2 features a letter to the U. S. House of Representatives.

Chapter 3 - On February 17, 2009, President Obama signed into law H.R. 1, the American Recovery and Reinvestment Act of 2009 (ARRA, P.L. 111-5). The ARRA is a response to the depth of the economic recession facing the United States (and the rest of the world) at the beginning of 2009. It is billed as an economic stimulus package to improve the situation of individuals and businesses. The ARRA boosts government spending on various infrastructure programs and government benefits programs, and offers individual and business tax benefits. The Congressional Budget Office (CBO) estimates that the ARRA will cost $787 billion over 10 years, although most of its budget authority is slated for two fiscal years (FY2009-FY2010).

Chapter 4 - The economy officially was considered in a recession in December 2008, but many forecasters had long recognized the downturn and some believed this economic contraction would be more severe than other post-World War II slowdowns. A combination of factors combined to present policymakers with difficult decisions on how best to stimulate the economy. Troubling instability in the housing and financial services sectors, weak auto manufacturing demand, and high energy costs earlier in 2008 had slowed growth dramatically and forced millions into unemployment. With declining tax revenue and increasing costs to provide unemployment and other benefits to unemployed workers, states were implementing measures to rein in spending, including restricting Medicaid eligibility and services.

Congress considered legislation aimed at stimulating economic activity in selected industrial sectors to save existing and create new jobs, reduce taxes, invest in future technologies, and fund infrastructure improvements. In addition to reducing some taxes and funding infrastructure projects, ARRA provisions were designed to provide: temporary support to families and individuals by increasing unemployment compensation benefits; financial assistance for individuals to maintain their health coverage under provisions in the Consolidated Omnibus Budget Reconciliation Act of 1985 (COBRA); temporary increases in Medicaid matching rates; and increases in disproportionate share hospital allotments.

The House approved the American Recovery and Reinvestment Act of 2009 (H.R. 1) on January 28, 2009. The Senate passed an amendment (S.Amdt. 570) as a replacement for the House- approved version of ARRA on February 10, 2009. ARRA was referred to a joint House and Senate conference committee. The joint Senate and House Conference Committee reached agreement, and ARRA was passed by the House and Senate on February 13, 2009. President Obama signed ARRA (P.L. 111-5) into law on February 17, 2009. This chapter is a summary of ARRA's Medicaid provisions.

Chapter 5 - President Barack Obama signed H.R. 1, the American Recovery and Reinvestment Act (ARRA) of 2009, into law on February 17, 2009, as P.L. 111-5 (123 Stat. 115-521). The act is seen as one of the most significant legislative responses made thus far to the current economic turmoil. This chapter provides a summary and legislative history of ARRA and identifies other resources that provide additional information regarding its content and implementation.

ARRA is a relatively lengthy and complex act, amounting to just over 400 pages (in slip law form) and melding together hundreds of billions of dollars in discretionary spending, mandatory spending, and revenue provisions encompassing the jurisdiction of several House and Senate committees. The act consists of two major divisions. Division A (Appropriations Provisions) includes supplemental appropriations for FY2009 (and later fiscal years) covering by separate titles all 12 of the regular appropriations acts, as well as four additional titles dealing with health information technology, a state fiscal stabilization fund, accountability and transparency, and general provisions. Division B (Tax, Unemployment, Health, State Fiscal Relief, and Other Provisions) consists of seven separate titles. Division A includes the discretionary spending provisions, but some significant substantive provisions as well; Division B includes the mandatory spending and revenue provisions, with some exceptions.

ARRA provides almost $800 billion through extensive discretionary spending, mandatory spending, and revenue provisions that the Administration estimates will save or create some 3.5 million jobs. Funding is provided for existing and some new programs in the 15 Cabinet-level departments and 11 independent agencies. Some of the funds are distributed to states, localities, other entities, and individuals through a combination of formula and competitive grants and direct assistance. In addition to new spending and tax provisions, new policies are created regarding unemployment compensation, health insurance, health information technology, broadband communications, and energy, among others.

Numerous oversight, accountability, and transparency provisions are contained in the act. They include various reporting requirements and funding for offices of inspector general, the Government Accountability Office, and a newly established Recovery Accountability and Transparency Board.

With regard to its specific impact on the budget, the act is estimated by the Congressional Budget Office to increase the deficit by $787.2 billion over the 11-year period covering FY2009-FY2019. The estimated deficit impact reflects spending increases of $575.3 billion (in outlays) and revenue reductions of $211.8 billion. The total spending increases consist of $311.2 billion in discretionary new budget authority (yielding $308.3 billion in outlays) and $269.5 billion in mandatory new budget authority (yielding $267.0 billion in outlays).

About 21% of total outlays ($120.1 billion) under ARRA are estimated to occur by the end of FY2009. By the end of FY2010, 59% of total outlays ($339.4 billion) are expected to occur, and by the end of FY2011, 81% of total outlays ($465.6 billion) are expected to occur. Revenue reductions occur more quickly, with reductions of $64.8 billion in FY2009 and $180.1 billion in FY2010, offset somewhat in later years by modest revenue increases.

Chapter 6 - In the wake of a rapidly deteriorating economic picture and year-long recession that the Congressional Budget Office has called the most severe since World War II, Congress passed the American Recovery and Reinvestment Act of 2009 (ARRA; P.L. 111-5). This chapter discusses ARRA's "general oversight provisions" and several related issues for Congress. For purposes of this chapter, the term "general oversight provision" means an oversight-related provision that addresses multiple programs, agencies, or appropriations accounts. Provisions that are specific to a single program or appropriation (e.g., appropriations set-asides and reporting requirements) are excluded from the report's scope.

The report includes tabular presentations of ARRA's general oversight provisions. The provisions provide for, among other things, establishment of a Recovery Accountability and Transparency Board, numerous reporting and evaluation requirements, and increased resources for agency Inspectors General (IGs) and the Government Accountability Office (GAO).

Even before considering experience with implementation, several broad issues related to ARRA oversight may be of interest to Congress. These include assessments of ARRA's role in achieving economic objectives. Typical objectives of a fiscal stimulus policy relate to increasing economic activity in the short term, compared to what would have happened without a stimulus. In addition, some stakeholders have emphasized that stimulating the economy in the short term alone is not a sufficient definition of "success." From this perspective, the manner in which spending, tax, and other public policies are implemented, and also the impacts of these policies, may be important.

All of these perspectives appear to have been included among the law's explicit purposes and "general principles concerning use of funds." Given ARRA's direction to "commenc[e] expenditures and activities as quickly as possible consistent with prudent management," difficult trade-offs among goals may be inevitable. Over time, Congress may consider whether existing management and oversight mechanisms, in combination with ARRA's additional provisions, adequately support effective management and oversight of ARRA implementation. The experience with ARRA also may offer lessons learned for the "normal," non-ARRA systems of oversight.

Beyond the immediate situation, additional oversight issues for Congress may relate to longer-term questions. These include how to build and monitor capacity within agencies to respond effectively to crises. Questions also may arise regarding how to build and monitor capacity in agencies and government overall to anticipate crises, mitigate their risks, and avoid preventable crises. This chapter analyzes these and other issues after reviewing how the oversight provisions were developed and providing an overview of the enacted provisions themselves, including related appropriations and reporting requirements.

Chapter 7 - Under the American Recovery and Reinvestment Act of 2009 (ARRA), also known as the economic stimulus package, certain recipients of funds appropriated in ARRA (most grant and loan recipients, contractors, and subcontractors) are required to report the number of jobs they have created or retained with ARRA funding since the law's enactment in February 2009. The law also requires the Congressional Budget Office (CBO) to comment on that reported number.[1]

Chapter 8 - The following list of authoritative resources is designed to assist in responding to a broad range of questions and concerns about the American Recovery and Reinvestment Act (ARRA), P.L. 111-5. Links to the full text of the act, Congressional Budget Office (CBO) estimates, White House fact sheets, and federal, state, and municipal government websites are included, along with other useful information. This list reflects information that is currently available on the Internet. It will be updated regularly as other relevant material becomes available.

In: American Recovery and Reinvestment Act: History… ISBN: 978-1-61668-355-9
Editor: Paul G. Tellis

Chapter 1

FUNDING FOR WORKFORCE DEVELOPMENT IN THE AMERICAN RECOVERY AND REINVESTMENT ACT (ARRA) OF 2009*

David H. Bradley and Ann Lordeman
Labor Economics
Social Policy

SUMMARY

On February 13, 2009, both the House and Senate passed the conference version of H.R. 1, the American Recovery and Reinvestment Act of 2009 (ARRA). The primary purposes of the ARRA focus on promoting economic recovery, assisting those most affected by the recession, improving economic efficiency by "spurring technological advances in science and health," investing in infrastructure, and stabilizing state and local government budgets. The House had previously passed its version of H.R. 1 (House-passed bill) on January 28, 2009, while the Senate passed S.Amdt. 570, an amendment in the nature of a substitute to H.R. 1 (Senate-passed bill), on February 10, 2009.

The ARRA provides funds to several existing workforce development programs administered by the U.S. Department of Labor (DOL), including programs authorized by the Workforce Investment Act (WIA).

This chapter provides a brief overview of the key provisions related to workforce development programs administered by DOL that were included in the ARRA under Division A, Title VIII, Department of Labor, and provides estimates of state grants for programs for which these estimates are relevant and for which data needed to produce the estimates are available. It also includes a discussion of relevant provisions that were included in the House- and Senate-passed versions of H.R. 1.

The report will be updated as warranted by legislative action.

---

* This is an edited, reformatted and augmented version of a CRS Report for Congress publication dated February 2009.

On February 13, 2009, both the House and the Senate passed the conference version of H.R. 1, the American Recovery and Reinvestment Act of 2009 (ARRA, hereafter referred to as the "conference version"). The primary purposes of the ARRA focus on promoting economic recovery, assisting those most affected by the recession, improving economic efficiency by "spurring technological advances in science and health," investing in infrastructure, and stabilizing state and local government budgets. The House had previously passed its version of H.R. 1 (hereafter referred to as the "House bill") on January 28, 2009, while the Senate passed S.Amdt. 570, an amendment in the nature of a substitute to H.R. 1 (hereafter referred to as the Senate bill), on February 10, 2009.

Under the House bill and the Senate bill, funds would have been provided to several existing workforce development programs administered by the U.S. Department of Labor (DOL), including programs authorized by the Workforce Investment Act (WIA). The conference version provides $4.81 billion in funding for these workforce development programs.[1]

This chapter provides a brief overview of the key provisions related to workforce development programs administered by DOL that were included in the conference version under Division A, Title VIII, Department of Labor. It also provides estimates of state grants for programs for which these estimates are relevant and for which data needed to produce the estimates are available. The estimates are shown in appendix tables that present state-by-state allocations for adult, youth, and dislocated worker programs.[2] It also includes a discussion of relevant provisions that were included in the House- and Senate-passed versions of H.R. 1.

Funding Overview

Under the House bill, an additional $5.0 billion would have been provided for existing workforce development and related programs administered by DOL; the Senate bill would have provided $3.93 billion for these same programs. The conference version provides $4.81 billion for workforce development programs. **Table 1** gives an overview of the specific funding provided under the House and Senate bills and the conference version. The remainder of this chapter provides a more detailed discussion of the specific funding provisions.

Table 1. Summary of Appropriations for Workforce Investment and Related Programs Included in H.R. 1

Program	Total Appropriation ($) House Bill	Total Appropriation ($) Senate Bill	Total Appropriation ($) Conference Version
Title I-B Grants to States for Adult Employment and Training Activities (WIA)	500,000,000	500,000,000	500,000,000
Title I-B Grants to States for Youth Activities (WIA)	1,200,000,000	1,200,000,000	1,200,000,000

Table 1. (Continued)

Program	Total Appropriation ($) House Bill	Total Appropriation ($) Senate Bill	Total Appropriation ($) Conference Version
Title I-B Grants to States for Dislocated Worker Employment and Training Activities (WIA)	1,000,000,000	1,000,000,000	1,250,000,000
Title I-D National Reserve Assistance for Dislocated Workers (WIA)	500,000,000	200,000,000	200,000,000
Title I-D YouthBuild Activities (WIA)	50,000,000	100,000,000	50,000,000
Title I-D Worker Training and Placement in High Growth and Emerging Industry Sectors (WIA)	750,000,000	250,000,000	750,000,000
Office of Job Corps	300,000,000	160,000,000	250,000,000
Community Service Employment for Older Americans	120,000,000	120,000,000	120,000,000
Employment Service Operations	500,000,000	400,000,000	400,000,000
Departmental Management	80,000,000	3,000,000	86,000,000
Total	5,000,000,000	3,933,000,000	4,806,000,000

Source: Table prepared by CRS, February 13, 2009, based on H.R. 1 as passed by the House of Representatives, January 28, 2009, S.Amdt. 570, released by the Senate Committee on Appropriations, February 9, 2009, and conference report to accompany H.R. 1. See footnote 2 for references to online versions.

FUNDING FOR WORKFORCE DEVELOPMENT

The House and Senate bills would have provided, and the Conference version did provide, funding for a number of existing workforce development programs, including the three state formula grant programs that provide funding for youth, adults, and dislocated workers—Title I-B of the WIA. Other programs authorized by the WIA will receive funding from the Conference version (and would have received funding under the House and Senate bills): National Reserve (WIA Title I-D, Section 173), YouthBuild (WIA Title I-D, Section 173A), and Pilot and Demonstration Programs (WIA Title I-D, Section 171). Additional workforce development programs provided for in the ARRA include state unemployment insurance and employment service operations, Title V of the Older Americans Act of 1965, and DOL management. Provisions applicable to each of these programs are discussed below.

WIA Title I Programs Included in the ARRA

The Workforce Investment Act of 1998 (P.L. 105-220) provides job training and related services to unemployed and underemployed individuals. WIA programs are administered by the DOL, primarily through its Employment and Training Administration (ETA). State and local WIA training and employment activities are provided through a system of One-Stop Career Centers. Authorization of appropriations under WIA expired in FY2003 but is annually extended through appropriations acts.[3]

WIA authorizes numerous job training programs, including:

- state formula grants for Youth, Adult, and Dislocated Worker Employment and Training Activities;
- Job Corps; and
- national programs, including the Native American Program, the Migrant and Seasonal Farmworker Program, the Veterans' Workforce Investment Program, Responsible Reintegration for Young Offenders, the Prisoner Reentry Program, Community-Based Job Training Grants, and YouthBuild.

In FY2008, programs and activities noted above were funded through the WIA at $5.2 billion, including $3.1 billion for state formula grants for adult, youth, and dislocated worker training and employment activities.

This section discusses WIA Title I programs that received additional funding through the ARRA. Where appropriate, appendix tables provide estimates of the amounts that states will receive.

Title I-B Grants to States for Adult Employment and Training

The adult program provides training and related services to individuals ages 18 and older through formula grants allocated to states, which in turn allocate funds to local entities. Any individual may receive "core" services (e.g., job search assistance). To receive "intensive" services (e.g., individual career planning and job training), an individual must have received core services and need intensive services to become employed or to obtain or retain employment that allows for self-sufficiency. To receive training services (e.g., occupational skills training), an individual must have received intensive services and need training services to become employed or to obtain or retain employment that allows for self-sufficiency.

Both the House and Senate bills would have provided an additional $500 million for Title I-B grants to states for adult employment and training activities, which would have been available for obligation on the date of enactment of the ARRA. The Senate bill would have required that priority for use of these funds be given to recipients of public assistance and other low-income individuals for intensive services and training. The House bill, however, did not indicate prioritization for use of funds under this section of the act.

The conference version provides an additional $500 million for Title I-B grants to states for adult employment and training activities. Similar to the Senate bill, the conference version requires that priority for use of these funds be given to recipients of public assistance and other low-income individuals for intensive services and training.

Funds for adult employment and training are allocated through the state grant formulas. Estimated state grants were calculated using these formulas after reserving 0.25% of the total appropriation for the outlying areas (as is done when making regular Title I-B allocations).

Appendix Table A1 details the results of these calculations.

Title I-B Grants to States for Youth Activities

The youth program provides training and related services to low-income youth ages 14-21 through formula grants allocated to states, which, in turn, allocate funds to local entities.

Both the House and Senate bills would have provided a total of $1.2 billion for grants for youth activities, including summer employment, which would be available for obligation on the date of enactment of the ARRA.[4] Each measure includes provisions affecting the expenditure of these funds:

- The House and Senate bills specified that no portion of this additional funding would be available for Youth Opportunity Grants.[5]
- The House and Senate bills would have changed the age for an "eligible youth" in these programs from 21 to 24.
- The House bill would have stipulated that the only performance measure to be used in assessing the effectiveness of summer jobs for youth is attainment of basic skills and, as appropriate, work readiness or occupational skills. The Senate bill would have required the use of the same performance indicator but would have applied it to all youth activities supported with funds from this section.

The conference version provides $1.2 billion for grants for youth activities and specifies that:

- no portion of this additional funding is available for Youth Opportunity grants;
- the age for an "eligible youth" in these programs from will increase from 21 to 24 years of age;
- the only performance measure to be used in assessing the effectiveness of summer employment for youth is attainment of basic skills and, as appropriate, work readiness or occupational skills; and
- the formula allocation for grants provided under this section is to remain the same as if the total allocation were less than $1 billion.[6]

Appendix Table A-2 provides estimated state grants under this program.

Title I-B and I-D Grants to States for Training and Employment of Dislocated Workers

A majority of WIA dislocated worker funds are allocated by formula grants to states (which in turn allocate funds to local entities) to provide training and related services to individuals who have lost their jobs and are unlikely to return to those jobs or similar jobs in the same industry. The remainder of the appropriation is reserved by DOL for a National Reserve account, which in part provides for National Emergency Grants to states or local entities (as specified under Section 173).

Both the House and Senate bills would have provided a total of $1.0 billion for formula grants to states for employment and training activities for dislocated workers, which would have been available for obligation on the date of enactment of the ARRA.

The House bill would have provided a total of $500 million for the Dislocated Workers National Reserve for grants to eligible entities serving areas of high unemployment or high poverty and experiencing major economic dislocations. Additionally, the House bill would have directed the Secretary of Labor to ensure that applicants for these funds demonstrate the manner in which supportive services (e.g. income support, child care) necessary for participation in job training would be provided.

The Senate bill would have provided a total of $450 million for the Dislocated Workers National Reserve, $200 million of which would have been for national emergency grants.[7] Additionally, the Senate bill would have directed the remaining $250 million for competitive grants to train workers for high growth and emerging industry sectors (see details in section on "Title I-D Grants for High Growth and Emerging Industry Sectors," below).

The conference version provides a total of $1.25 billion for formula grants to states for employment and training for dislocated workers. In addition, the conference version provides $200 million for the Dislocated Workers National Reserve, which is used for technical assistance, projects, and emergency grants.

Appendix Table A-3 provides estimated state grants under this program.

Title I-D Grants for YouthBuild

This competitive grant program funds projects that provide education and construction skills training for disadvantaged youth. Since its inception in 1992, the program was administered by the Department of Housing and Urban Development, but was moved to DOL by the YouthBuild Transfer Act (P.L. 109-281), effective for FY2007. Participating youth work primarily through mentorship and apprenticeship programs to rehabilitate and construct housing for homeless and low-income families.

Both the House and Senate bills would have provided additional funding for YouthBuild, which would be available for obligation on the date of enactment of the ARRA. The House bill would have provided $50 million for YouthBuild activities, but, unlike the Senate bill, did not specify any stipulations on expenditures. The Senate bill would have provided $100 million for YouthBuild grants. However, the Senate bill would have allowed, in program years 2008 and 2009, participation for individuals who have dropped out of high school and re-enrolled in an alternative school.[8] In addition, the Senate bill would have allowed a local YouthBuild board to award a training contract to an institution of higher education if such a choice would facilitate the training of multiple individuals in high-demand occupations.

The conference version provides $50 million for YouthBuild and, similar to the Senate bill, allows, in program years 2008 and 2009, participation for individuals who have dropped out of high school and re-enrolled in an alternative school, if that re-enrollment is part of a "sequential service strategy" (see footnote 8).

Title I-D Grants for High Growth and Emerging Industry Sectors

Funds for this program would be distributed by a competitive grant process to provide worker training and placement in high growth and emerging industry sectors.

The House bill would have provided a total of $750 million for these grants. Of the total proposed allotment in the House bill, $500 million would have been reserved for research, labor exchange, and job training projects that prepare workers for careers in the following energy efficiency and renewable energy industries:[9]

- energy-efficient building, construction, and retrofits industries;
- renewable electric power industry;
- energy-efficient and advanced drive train vehicle industry;
- biofuels industry;
- deconstruction and materials use industry;
- energy efficiency assessment industry serving the residential, commercial, or industrial sectors; and
- manufacturers that produce sustainable products using environmentally sustainable processes and materials.

In the House bill, the remainder of $250 million would have been allocated on the basis of priority for projects preparing workers for careers in the health care industry.

The Senate bill would have required the Secretary of Labor, in awarding the $250 million from the Dislocated Workers National Reserve, to give priority to projects that prepare workers for careers in the energy efficiency and renewable energy industries listed above and for careers in the health care sector.

The conference version provides $750 million for competitive grants for worker training in high- growth and emerging sectors. The conference version specifies that:

- of the $750 million, $500 million is reserved for research, labor exchange, and job training projects that prepare workers for careers in energy efficiency and renewable energy industries (listed above);
- the Secretary of Labor should give priority to projects in the health care industry when granting the remaining $250 million;
- a local workforce investment board may award a training contract to an institution of higher education if such a choice would facilitate the training of multiple individuals in high-demand occupations; and
- the $750 million is to remain available through June 10, 2010.

Job Corps

Job Corps is a residential job training program first established in 1964 that provides services to low-income individuals ages 16-24 primarily through contracts administered by DOL with corporations and nonprofit organizations. Currently, there are 122 Job Corps centers in 48 states, the District of Columbia, and Puerto Rico. On February 8, 2007, DOL announced that three new centers will open, including the first centers in each of the remaining two states, New Hampshire and Wyoming.

The House bill would have provided a total of $300 million to the Job Corps program, and the Senate bill would have provided $160 million for the Job Corps program. Both allocations would have been available for obligation on the date of enactment of the ARRA and would have remained available for obligation through June 30, 2010. While both the House and Senate bills would have allowed the Secretary of Labor to transfer up to 15% of the allocated funds for operational needs of Job Corps Centers, the House and Senate bills contained different stipulations:

- Funds provided in the House bill would have been available for construction, rehabilitation, and acquisition of Job Corps Centers; in the Senate bill, funds were to be used only for the construction, rehabilitation, or repair of facilities.
- The House bill would have allowed a partial exception to the requirement to close an account after five years, in order to give priority to projects that can begin construction within 120 days of enactment of the act.
- The House bill would also have given priority to activities that could start promptly and would have had the greatest impact on the energy efficiency of Job Corps facilities.
- The House bill would have required the Secretary of Labor to report to the Committee on Appropriations in the House and Senate on actual obligations, expenditures, and unobligated balances for each activity funded by this section. The initial report would have been due by September 30, 2009, and quarterly thereafter. The Senate bill would have required the Secretary of Labor, within 90 days of enactment of the bill, to provide to the Committee on Appropriations in the House and Senate an operating plan describing the uses of funds in this provision.

The conference version provides $250 million for the construction, rehabilitation, and acquisition of Job Corps Centers, with the following provisions:

- The funds will remain available for obligation through June 30, 2010.
- There will be a partial exception to the requirement to close an account after five years, in order to give priority to projects that can begin construction within 120 days of enactment of the act.
- The Secretary of Labor is permitted to transfer up to 15% of the allocated funds for operational needs of Job Corps Centers.
- The Secretary of Labor is required to provide to the Committee on Appropriations in the House and Senate an operating plan on the allocation of funds and a report on actual obligations, expenditures, and unobligated balances for each activity funded by this section. The initial report is due by September 30, 2009, and quarterly thereafter.

Additional Workforce Development Funding in the ARRA

In addition to adding funds to the job training programs in Title I of WIA, both the House and Senate bills would have provided additional funding for three related programs:

- The House bill would have allocated $500 million for state employment services operations, 50% of which would have been allocated for reemployment services for unemployment insurance claimants. In addition, the House bill would have altered the allocation formula for funds under this provision. The Senate bill would have allocated $400 million for these services, would have required that $250 million be allocated for reemployment services for unemployment insurance claimants, and would have required the Secretary of Labor to establish planning and reporting procedures to provide oversight of these funds.[10]
- Both the House and Senate bills would have allocated $120 million for the Community Service Employment for Older Americans program, which would have been allotted in proportion to grantees' PY2008 allocation within 30 days for the enactment of this legislation.
- The House bill would have provided $80 million for DOL Departmental Management for the enforcement of worker protection laws, oversight, and coordination activities related to the infrastructure and unemployment insurance investments in the ARRA. The Senate bill would have provided $3 million for the DOL Office of the Inspector General to provide oversight and audit of programs, grants, and projects funded under this act.

The conference version also provides additional funding for three workforce development-related programs:

- $400 million for state employment services operations, $250 million of which must be used for reemployment services for unemployment insurance claimants; it would also require the Secretary of Labor to establish planning and reporting procedures to provide oversight of these funds. The funds are to remain available to states through September 30, 2010.
- $120 million for the Community Service Employment for Older Americans program, which is to be allotted in proportion to grantees' PY2008 allocation within 30 days for the enactment of this legislation. Funds are to remain available through June 30, 2010.
- $80 million for DOL Departmental Management for the enforcement of worker protection laws, oversight, and coordination activities related to the infrastructure and unemployment insurance investments in the ARRA.
- $6 million for the DOL Office of the Inspector General to provide oversight and audit of programs, grants, and projects funded under this act.

APPENDIX. ESTIMATED STATE GRANTS FOR SELECTED PROGRAMS

Table A.1. Estimated Additional State Grants for Adult Activities (WIA Title I-B) Grants to States at an Appropriation Level of $500 Million

State	Estimated Additional State Grants		
	FY2009 ($) House bill	FY2009 ($) Senate bill	FY2009 ($) Conference Version
Alabama	5,155,000	5,155,000	5,155,000
Alaska	1,696,000	1,696,000	1,696,000
Arizona	7,693,000	7,693,000	7,693,000
Arkansas	5,124,000	5,124,000	5,124,000
California	80,927,000	80,927,000	80,927,000
Colorado	4,841,000	4,841,000	4,841,000
Connecticut	4,429,000	4,429,000	4,429,000
Delaware	1,247,000	1,247,000	1,247,000
District of Columbia	1,559,000	1,559,000	1,559,000
Florida	19,644,000	19,644,000	19,644,000
Georgia	13,252,000	13,252,000	13,252,000
Hawaii	1,247,000	1,247,000	1,247,000
Idaho	1,247,000	1,247,000	1,247,000
Illinois	26,051,000	26,051,000	26,051,000
Indiana	9,488,000	9,488,000	9,488,000
Iowa	1,571,000	1,571,000	1,571,000
Kansas	2,729,000	2,729,000	2,729,000
Kentucky	8,275,000	8,275,000	8,275,000
Louisiana	8,791,000	8,791,000	8,791,000
Maine	1,826,000	1,826,000	1,826,000
Maryland	4,959,000	4,959,000	4,959,000
Massachusetts	10,175,000	10,175,000	10,175,000
Michigan	31,169,000	31,169,000	31,169,000
Minnesota	7,022,000	7,022,000	7,022,000
Mississippi	7,851,000	7,851,000	7,851,000
Missouri	10,588,000	10,588,000	10,588,000
Montana	1,247,000	1,247,000	1,247,000
Nebraska	1,247,000	1,247,000	1,247,000
Nevada	3,426,000	3,426,000	3,426,000
New Hampshire	1,247,000	1,247,000	1,247,000
New Jersey	9,481,000	9,481,000	9,481,000
New Mexico	2,687,000	2,687,000	2,687,000
New York	31,834,000	31,834,000	31,834,000
North Carolina	10,442,000	10,442,000	10,442,000
North Dakota	1,247,000	1,247,000	1,247,000

Table A.1. (Continued)

State	Estimated Additional State Grants		
	FY2009 ($) House bill	FY2009 ($) Senate bill	FY2009 ($) Conference Version
Ohio	23,623,000	23,623,000	23,623,000
Oklahoma	3,687,000	3,687,000	3,687,000
Oregon	6,392,000	6,392,000	6,392,000
Pennsylvania	16,713,000	16,713,000	16,713,000
Puerto Rico	20,332,000	20,332,000	20,332,000
Rhode Island	2,128,000	2,128,000	2,128,000
South Carolina	10,522,000	10,522,000	10,522,000
South Dakota	1,247,000	1,247,000	1,247,000
Tennessee	10,945,000	10,945,000	10,945,000
Texas	34,692,000	34,692,000	34,692,000
Utah	1,816,000	1,816,000	1,816,000
Vermont	1,247,000	1,247,000	1,247,000
Virginia	5,280,000	5,280,000	5,280,000
Washington	9,792,000	9,792,000	9,792,000
West Virginia	2,434,000	2,434,000	2,434,000
Wisconsin	5,236,000	5,236,000	5,236,000
Wyoming	1,247,000	1,247,000	1,247,000
Subtotal to states, DC, and Puerto Rico	498,750,000	498,750,000	498,750,000
Outlying areas	1,250,000	1,250,000	1,250,000
Total	500,000,000	500,000,000	500,000,000

Source: CRS estimates based on analysis of FY2009 DOL data. Table prepared by CRS, February 13, 2009, based on H.R. 1 as passed by the House of Representatives, January 28, 2009, S.Amdt. 570, released by the Senate Committee on Appropriations, February 9, 2009, and conference report to accompany H.R. 1. See footnote 2 for references to online versions.

Notes: Funds were allocated through the WIA Adult Activities Grant formulas. Details may not add to totals due to rounding.

Notice: These are estimated grants only. These estimates are provided solely to assist in comparisons of the relative impact of alternative formulas and funding levels in the legislative process. They are not intended to predict specific amounts states will receive.

Table A.2. Estimated Additional State Grants for Youth Activities (WIA Title I-B) Grants to States at an Appropriation Level of $1.2 Billion

State	Estimated Additional State Grants		
	FY2009 ($) House bill	FY2009 ($) Senate bill	FY2009 ($) Conference Version
Alabama	11,765,000	11,765,000	11,765,000
Alaska	3,976,000	3,976,000	3,976,000
Arizona	18,011,000	18,011,000	18,011,000
Arkansas	12,187,000	12,187,000	12,187,000
California	188,507,000	188,507,000	188,507,000

Table A.2. (continued)

State	Estimated Additional State Grants		
	FY2009 ($) House bill	FY2009 ($) Senate bill	FY2009 ($) Conference Version
Colorado	11,995,000	11,995,000	11,995,000
Connecticut	11,146,000	11,146,000	11,146,000
Delaware	2,948,000	2,948,000	2,948,000
District of Columbia	4,010,000	4,010,000	4,010,000
Florida	43,306,000	43,306,000	43,306,000
Georgia	31,678,000	31,678,000	31,678,000
Hawaii	2,948,000	2,948,000	2,948,000
Idaho	2,948,000	2,948,000	2,948,000
Illinois	62,832,000	62,832,000	62,832,000
Indiana	23,917,000	23,917,000	23,917,000
Iowa	5,224,000	5,224,000	5,224,000
Kansas	7,194,000	7,194,000	7,194,000
Kentucky	17,889,000	17,889,000	17,889,000
Louisiana	20,214,000	20,214,000	20,214,000
Maine	4,337,000	4,337,000	4,337,000
Maryland	11,703,000	11,703,000	11,703,000
Massachusetts	25,089,000	25,089,000	25,089,000
Michigan	74,696,000	74,696,000	74,696,000
Minnesota	17,969,000	17,969,000	17,969,000
Mississippi	18,876,000	18,876,000	18,876,000
Missouri	25,657,000	25,657,000	25,657,000
Montana	2,948,000	2,948,000	2,948,000
Nebraska	2,974,000	2,974,000	2,974,000
Nevada	7,647,000	7,647,000	7,647,000
New Hampshire	2,948,000	2,948,000	2,948,000
New Jersey	21,045,000	21,045,000	21,045,000
New Mexico	6,299,000	6,299,000	6,299,000
New York	72,249,000	72,249,000	72,249,000
North Carolina	25,324,000	25,324,000	25,324,000
North Dakota	2,948,000	2,948,000	2,948,000
Ohio	56,726,000	56,726,000	56,726,000
Oklahoma	8,796,000	8,796,000	8,796,000
Oregon	15,220,000	15,220,000	15,220,000
Pennsylvania	41,058,000	41,058,000	41,058,000
Puerto Rico	42,886,000	42,886,000	42,886,000
Rhode Island	5,668,000	5,668,000	5,668,000
South Carolina	24,962,000	24,962,000	24,962,000
South Dakota	2,948,000	2,948,000	2,948,000
Tennessee	25,353,000	25,353,000	25,353,000
Texas	82,829,000	82,829,000	82,829,000

Table A.2. (continued)

State	Estimated Additional State Grants		
	FY2009 ($) House bill	**FY2009 ($) Senate bill**	**FY2009 ($) Conference Version**
Utah	5,118,000	5,118,000	5,118,000
Vermont	2,948,000	2,948,000	2,948,000
Virginia	13,114,000	13,114,000	13,114,000
Washington	23,682,000	23,682,000	23,682,000
West Virginia	5,397,000	5,397,000	5,397,000
Wisconsin	13,948,000	13,948,000	13,948,000
Wyoming	2,948,000	2,948,000	2,948,000
Subtotal for states, DC, and Puerto Rico	1,179,000,000	1,179,000,000	1,179,000,000
Outlying areas and Native Americans	21,000,000	21,000,000	21,000,000
Total	1,200,000,000	1,200,000,000	1,200,000,000

Source: CRS estimates based on analysis of FY2009 DOL data. Table prepared by CRS, February 13, 2009, based on H.R. 1 as passed by the House of Representatives, January 28, 2009, S.Amdt. 570, released by the Senate Committee on Appropriations, February 9, 2009, and conference report to accompany H.R. 1. See footnote 2 for references to online versions.

Notes: Funds were allocated through the WIA Youth Activities Grant formulas. Details may not add to totals due to rounding. As noted in footnote 4, the statutory formulas for state allotments for WIA Youth Activities stipulate that a total allotment in excess of $1 billion normally triggers a change in the allocation formula; however, the ARRA specifies the formula allocation is to remain the same as if the total allocation were less than $1 billion.

Notice: These are estimated grants only. These estimates are provided solely to assist in comparisons of the relative impact of alternative formulas and funding levels in the legislative process. They are not intended to predict specific amounts that states will receive.

Table A.3. Estimated Additional State Grants for Dislocated Worker Activities (WIA Title I-B) Grants to States at an Appropriation Level of $1.25 Billion

State	Estimated Additional State Grants		
	FY2009 ($) House bill	**FY2009 ($) Senate bill**	**FY2009 ($) Conference Version**
Alabama	10,635,000	10,635,000	13,294,000
Alaska	2,859,000	2,859,000	3,573,000
Arizona	14,028,000	14,028,000	17,535,000
Arkansas	6,060,000	6,060,000	7,575,000
California	178,870,000	178,870,000	223,588,000
Colorado	11,660,000	11,660,000	14,574,000
Connecticut	11,997,000	11,997,000	14,997,000
Delaware	1,644,000	1,644,000	2,055,000
District of Columbia	3,057,000	3,057,000	3,822,000
Florida	64,930,000	64,930,000	81,162,000
Georgia	35,307,000	35,307,000	44,134,000

Table A.3. (Continued)

State	Estimated Additional State Grants		
	FY2009 ($) House bill	FY2009 ($) Senate bill	FY2009 ($) Conference Version
Hawaii	1,742,000	1,742,000	2,178,000
Idaho	2,283,000	2,283,000	2,854,000
Illinois	55,242,000	55,242,000	69,053,000
Indiana	21,130,000	21,130,000	26,412,000
Iowa	4,212,000	4,212,000	5,265,000
Kansas	4,195,000	4,195,000	5,243,000
Kentucky	15,084,000	15,084,000	18,855,000
Louisiana	7,463,000	7,463,000	9,329,000
Maine	3,685,000	3,685,000	4,607,000
Maryland	9,072,000	9,072,000	11,340,000
Massachusetts	17,107,000	17,107,000	21,384,000
Michigan	63,237,000	63,237,000	79,046,000
Minnesota	16,898,000	16,898,000	21,122,000
Mississippi	11,454,000	11,454,000	14,318,000
Missouri	20,821,000	20,821,000	26,027,000
Montana	1,415,000	1,415,000	1,769,000
Nebraska	2,089,000	2,089,000	2,611,000
Nevada	11,536,000	11,536,000	14,420,000
New Hampshire	2,017,000	2,017,000	2,521,000
New Jersey	26,363,000	26,363,000	32,954,000
New Mexico	2,387,000	2,387,000	2,983,000
New York	53,497,000	53,497,000	66,871,000
North Carolina	35,805,000	35,805,000	44,756,000
North Dakota	739,000	739,000	923,000
Ohio	47,164,000	47,164,000	58,955,000
Oklahoma	4,855,000	4,855,000	6,069,000
Oregon	13,834,000	13,834,000	17,292,000
Pennsylvania	34,243,000	34,243,000	42,804,000
Puerto Rico	23,798,000	23,798,000	29,748,000
Rhode Island	6,405,000	6,405,000	8,006,000
South Carolina	19,914,000	19,914,000	24,892,000
South Dakota	769,000	769,000	961,000
Tennessee	22,870,000	22,870,000	28,587,000
Texas	43,341,000	43,341,000	54,176,000
Utah	2,851,000	2,851,000	3,564,000
Vermont	1,410,000	1,410,000	1,762,000
Virginia	11,378,000	11,378,000	14,222,000
Washington	17,848,000	17,848,000	22,310,000
West Virginia	2,885,000	2,885,000	3,607,000

Table A.3. (continued)

State	Estimated Additional State Grants		
	FY2009 ($) House bill	**FY2009 ($) Senate bill**	**FY2009 ($) Conference Version**
Wisconsin	12,945,000	12,945,000	16,181,000
Wyoming	471,000	471,000	588,000
Subtotal for states, DC, and Puerto Rico	997,500,000	997,500,000	1,246,875,000
Outlying areas	2,500,000	2,500,000	3,125,000
Total	1,000,000,000	1,000,000,000	1,250,000,000

Source: CRS estimates based on analysis of FY2009 DOL data. Table prepared by CRS, February 13, 2009, based on H.R. 1 as passed by the House of Representatives, January 28, 2009, S.Amdt. 570, released by the Senate Committee on Appropriations, February 9, 2009, and conference report to accompany H.R. 1. See footnote 2 for references to online versions.

Notes: The allocation formula for dislocated worker funding typically includes a set-aside for the National Reserve account. However, the ARRA includes a separate provision for this National Reserve; thus the full $1 billion is allocated for state grants in Table A-3. Details may not add to totals due to rounding. The allocation formula for Dislocated Worker grants uses a three-factor formula based on a state's relative share of total unemployed, excess unemployed, and long-term unemployed.

Notice: These are estimated grants only. These estimates are provided solely to assist in comparisons of the relative impact of alternative formulas and funding levels in the legislative process. They are not intended to predict specific amounts states will receive.

End Notes

[1] Relevant proposed statutory language is included in Title IX, Subtitle A, of H.R. 1; Title VIII of S.Amdt. 570; and Title VIII of the conference report for H.R. 1.

[2] Textual and data analysis of the ARRA is based on H.R. 1 as passed by the House of Representatives, January 28, 2009, available online at http://frwebgate.access.gpo.gov/cgi-bin/getdoc.cgi?dbname= 111_cong_bills&docid=f:h1ih.txt.pdf. Textual and data analysis of S.Amdt. 570 is based on the version released by the Senate Committee on Appropriations, February 9, 2009, available online at http://appropriations2009_02_09_Substitute_Amendment_to_HR1_%7BCollins_Nelson_ Amendment%7D.pdf?CFID=58 10469&CFTOKE N=89 153593. Textual and data analysis of conference report to accompany H.R. 1 is based on the version released by the House Committee on Rules, February 13, 2009, available online at http://www.house.gov/billtext/hr1_legtext_cr.pdf.

[3] For additional information about programs for Title I of WIA, see CRS Report RL33687, *The Workforce Investment Act (WIA): Program-by-Program Overview and Funding of Title I Training Programs*, by Blake Alan Naughton.

[4] As specified in the statutory formulas for state allotments for WIA Youth Activities, a total allotment in excess of $1 billion would trigger a change in the allocation formula; however, the ARRA specifies the formula allocation is to remain the same as if the total allocation were less than $1 billion.

[5] Although the ARRA specifically excludes funding for Youth Opportunity Grants, the most recent appropriation for these grants was FY2003.

[6] See footnote 4.

[7] Although it is not identified specifically in the legislation, the Senate Appropriations Committee Report indicates that these funds are to be used for grants authorized under WIA Section 173(a)(1), which refers to workers affected by major economic dislocations, such as plant closures or mass layoffs.

[8] The YouthBuild program includes an education component and occupational skills training component for youth ages 16 through 24. At least three-quarters of enrolled youth must be school dropouts and either low-income, in foster care (or have "aged out" of foster care), an offender, disabled, children of incarcerated parents, or migrants. S. 336 authorizes the program to serve youth who have dropped out of school and "re-enrolled in an alternative school, if that re-enrollment is part of a sequential service strategy." The accompanying report to S.

336 (S.Rept. 111-3) does not clarify whether these newly eligible youth could forgo participating in the educational component of the program and/or dually enroll in both YouthBuild's educational component and a separate alternative school. The report does not define the term "sequential service strategy."

[9] These industries are specified in WIA Section 171(e)(1)(B)(ii), as amended by the Green Jobs Act of 2007 (Title X of P.L. 110-140).

[10] Local employment service (ES) offices are known by different names, such as Employment Service, Job Service, One-Stop Career Center, and Workforce Development Center. These offices offer an array of services to job seekers and employers, including career counseling, job search workshops, labor market information, job listings, applicant screening, and referrals to job openings. States provide ES services through three tiers of service delivery: self-service, facilitated self-help, and staff-assisted. As the names of the tiers imply, progressively more active staff involvement is required as services range from internet job postings to career counseling. Funds for the ES are allocated to states by a formula using civilian labor force and unemployment data. This chapter will not provide a state-by-state estimate of the distribution of ES funds due to current limits on CRS modeling capacity for this program.

In: American Recovery and Reinvestment Act: History… ISBN: 978-1-61668-355-9
Editor: Paul G. Tellis

Chapter 2

SUMMARY OF ESTIMATED COST OF THE CONFERENCE AGREEMENT FOR H.R. 1, THE AMERICAN RECOVERY AND REINVESTMENT ACT OF 2009*

The House Committee on Rules

February 13, 2009

Honorable Nancy Pelosi
Speaker
U.S. House of Representatives
Washington, DC 20515

Dear Madam Speaker:

The Congressional Budget Office has reviewed the conference agreement for H.R. 1, the American Recovery and Reinvestment Act of 2009, as posted on the Web site of the House Committee on Rules. We have enclosed two tables with this letter: one that summarizes the estimated budgetary impacts of the legislation and another, more detailed table that shows the budgetary effects by title. Combining both spending and revenue effects, CBO estimates that enacting the conference agreement for H.R. 1 would increase federal budget deficits by $185 billion over the remaining months of fiscal year 2009, by $399 billion in 2010, by $134 billion in 2011, and by $787 billion over the 2009-20 19 period.

I hope this information is helpful to you. If you would like further details about this estimate, the CBO staff contact is Janet Airis.

Sincerely,

* This is an edited, reformatted and augmented version of a Congressional Budget Office publication dated February 2009.

Douglas W. Elmendorf

Douglas W. Elmendorf, Director
Enclosures
cc: Honorable John Boehner
Republican Leader

Honorable Steny Hoyer
Majority Leader

Honorable John M. Spratt Jr.
Chairman
Committee on the Budget

Honorable Paul Ryan
Ranking Member

Honorable David R. Obey
Chairman
Committee on Appropriations

Honorable Jerry Lewis
Ranking Member

Honorable Charles B. Rangel
Chairman
Committee on Ways and Means

Honorable Dave Camp
Ranking Member

Honorable Henry A. Waxman
Chairman
Committee on Energy and Commerce

Honorable Joe Barton
Ranking Member

Identical letter sent to the Honorable Harry Reid.

Table 1. Summary of Estimated Cost of The Conference Agreement for H.R. 1, the American Recovery and Reinvestment Act of 2009, as Posted on the Web Site of the House Committee on Rules

	By Fiscal Year, in Billions of Dollars											
	2009	2010	2011	2012	2013	2014	2015	2016	2017	2018	2019	2009-2019
DIVISION A—APPROPRIATIONS[a]												
Estimated Budget Authority	288.7	7.1	4.6	3.6	2.5	1.1	1.1	1.1	1.1	0.5	0	311.2
Estimated Outlays	34.8	110.7	76.3	38.1	22.9	12.8	7.0	3.1	1.6	0.8	0.1	308.3
DIVISION A—REVENUES												
Estimated Revenues	*	*	*	*	*	*	*	*	*	*	*	-0.1
DIVISION B—DIRECT SPENDING												
Estimated Budget Authority	90.3	107.6	49.0	7.6	7.3	15.1	4.7	-4.7	-4.1	-1.9	-1.4	269.5
Estimated Outlays	85.3	108.6	49.9	8.1	7.4	15.1	4.7	-4.7	-4.1	-1.9	-1.4	267.0
DIVISION B—REVENUES												
Estimated Revenues	-64.8	-180.1	-8.2	10.0	2.7	5.5	7.1	5.8	5.1	5.0	0.1	-211.8
NET IMPACT ON THE DEFICIT												
Net Increase or Decrease (-) in the Deficit	184.9	399.4	134.4	36.1	27.6	22.4	4.7	-7.3	-7.5	-6.1	-1.4	787.2

a. Most of the spending for Division A would stem from discretionary appropriations. The totals include about $29 billion in 2009-2019 changes to mandatory programs that are contained in Division A.

Notes: Components may not sum to totals because of rounding. * = revenue reductions of less than $50 million.

Sources: Congressional Budget Office and the Joint Committee on Taxation.

Table 2. Estimated Cost of the Conference Agreement for H.R. 1, the American Recovery and Reinvestment Act of 2009, As Posted on The Website of the House Committee on Rules

	By Fiscal Year, Millions of Dollars											
	2009	2010	2011	2012	2013	2014	2015	2016	2017	2018	2019	Total 2009 - 2019
Discretionary Spending 1/												
Division A Title I - Agriculture, Rural Development, Food and Drug Adminis-tration, and Related Agencies Distance Learning, Tele-medicine, and Broadband Program												
Budget Authority	2,500	0	0	0	0	0	0	0	0	0	0	2,500
Estimated Outlays	63	350	587	575	475	325	125	0	0	0	0	2,500
Supplemental Nutrition Assistance Program												
Estimated Budget Authority	4,859	6,056	4,317	3,115	1,639	5	0	0	0	0	0	19,991
Estimated Outlays	4,812	6,058	4,362	3,115	1,639	5	0	0	0	0	0	19,991
Other												
Budget Authority	3,971	4	0	0	0	0	0	0	0	0	0	3,975
Estimated Outlays	816	1,623	736	421	172	138	34	0	0	0	0	3,940
Subtotal, Title I												
Budget Authority	11,330	6,060	4,317	3,115	1,639	5	0	0	0	0	0	26,466
Estimated Outlays	5,691	8,031	5,685	4,111	2,286	468	159	0	0	0	0	26,431
Title II - Commerce, Justice, Science and Related Agencies Broadband Technology Opportunities Program												
Budget Authority	4,700	0	0	0	0	0	0	0	0	0	0	4,700
Estimated Outlays	84	756	860	1,250	1,210	390	150	0	0	0	0	4,700
State and Local Law Enforcement Assistance												
Budget Authority	2,765	0	0	0	0	0	0	0	0	0	0	2,765

Table 2. (Continued)

	By Fiscal Year, Millions of Dollars											
	2009	2010	2011	2012	2013	2014	2015	2016	2017	2018	2019	Total 2009 - 2019
	Discretionary Spending 1/											
Estimated Outlays	415	830	553	415	552	0	0	0	0	0	0	2,765
National Science Foundation												
Budget Authority	3,002	0	0	0	0	0	0	0	0	0	0	3,002
Estimated Outlays	342	1,266	794	349	162	63	12	0	0	0	0	2,988
Other												
Budget Authority	5,455	0	0	0	0	0	0	0	0	0	0	5,455
Estimated Outlays	1,697	2,148	654	521	298	39	0	0	0	0	0	5,357
Subtotal, Title II												
Budget Authority	15,922	0	0	0	0	0	0	0	0	0	0	15,922
Estimated Outlays	2,538	5,000	2,861	2,535	2,222	492	162	0	0	0	0	15,810
Title III – Depart-ment of Defense												
Budget Authority	4,555	0	0	0	0	0	0	0	0	0	0	4,555
Estimated Outlays	1,679	2,122	551	129	36	11	3	0	0	0	0	4,531
Title IV - Energy and Water Development Energy Efficiency and Renewable Energy												
Budget Authority	16,800	0	0	0	0	0	0	0	0	0	0	16,800
Estimated Outlays	445	2,045	3,340	3,715	3,300	2,540	1,048	267	100	0	0	16,800
Innovative Technology Loan Guarantee Program												
Budget Authority	6,000	0	0	0	0	0	0	0	0	0	0	6,000
Estimated Outlays	60	1,200	1,500	1,500	1,200	540	0	0	0	0	0	6,000
Other Energy Programs												
Budget Authority	15,935	175	275	475	875	1,050	1,050	1,050	1,050	490	0	22,425
Estimated Outlays	1,303	3,943	5,043	4,275	2,175	1,910	1,186	1,050	1,050	470	-30	22,375

Table 2. (Continued)

	By Fiscal Year, Millions of Dollars											
	2009	2010	2011	2012	2013	2014	2015	2016	2017	2018	2019	Total 2009 - 2019
	Discretionary Spending 1/											
Corps of Engineers												
Budget Authority	4,600	0	0	0	0	0	0	0	0	0	0	4,600
Estimated Outlays	1,171	1,701	980	378	270	100	0	0	0	0	0	4,600
Other, Title IV												
Budget Authority	1,000	0	0	0	0	0	0	0	0	0	0	1,000
Estimated Outlays	180	500	200	120	0	0	0	0	0	0	0	1,000
Subtotal, Title IV												
Budget Authority	44,335	175	275	475	875	1,050	1,050	1,050	1,050	490	0	50,825
Estimated Outlays	3,159	9,389	11,063	9,988	6,945	5,090	2,234	1,317	1,150	470	-30	50,775
Title V - Financial Services and and General Govern-ment Federal Buildings Fund												
Budget Authority	5,550	0	0	0	0	0	0	0	0	0	0	5,550
Estimated Outlays	400	900	1,000	1,100	1,000	500	300	150	50	0	0	5,400
Other												
Budget Authority	1,308	0	0	0	0	0	0	0	0	0	0	1,308
Estimated Outlays	220	662	339	67	19	0	0	0	0	0	0	1,307
Subtotal, Title V												
Budget Authority	6,858	0	0	0	0	0	0	0	0	0	0	6,858
Estimated Outlays	620	1,562	1,339	1,167	1,019	500	300	150	50	0	0	6,707
Title VI – Home-land Security												
Budget Authority	2,755	0	0	0	0	0	0	0	0	0	0	2,755
Estimated Outlays	506	591	857	457	230	93	10	0	0	0	0	2,744
Title VII - Interior, Environment, and Related Agencies Clean Water and Drinking Water State Revolving Funds												
Budget Authority	6,000	0	0	0	0	0	0	0	0	0	0	6,000
Estimated Outlays	180	1,380	1,800	1,240	600	320	120	68	36	42	0	5,786

Table 2. (Continued)

	By Fiscal Year, Millions of Dollars											
	2009	2010	2011	2012	2013	2014	2015	2016	2017	2018	2019	Total 2009 - 2019
	Discretionary Spending 1/											
Other												
Budget Authority	4,950	0	0	0	0	0	0	0	0	0	0	4,950
Estimated Outlays	988	2,118	897	531	183	9	9	9	9	6	0	4,759
Subtotal, Title VII												
Budget Authority	10,950	0	0	0	0	0	0	0	0	0	0	10,950
Estimated Outlays	1,168	3,498	2,697	1,771	783	329	129	77	45	48	0	10,545
Title VIII - Departments of Labor, Health and Human Services, and Education, and Related Agencies National Institutes of Health												
Budget Authority	10,000	0	0	0	0	0	0	0	0	0	0	10,000
Estimated Outlays	855	3,286	3,703	1,505	249	118	27	0	0	0	0	9,743
National Coordinator for Health Information Technology												
Budget Authority	2,000	0	0	0	0	0	0	0	0	0	0	2,000
Estimated Outlays	300	1,280	360	40	0	0	0	0	0	0	0	1,980
Other Department of Health and Human Services												
Budget Authority	9,897	0	0	0	0	0	0	0	0	0	0	9,897
Estimated Outlays	2,173	3,009	2,358	1,612	593	65	0	0	0	0	0	9,810
Budget Authority	4,470	0	0	0	0	0	0	0	0	0	0	4,470
Estimated Outlays	613	2,226	1,224	242	0	0	0	0	0	0	0	4,305
Department of Education Education for the Disadvantaged												
Budget Authority	13,000	0	0	0	0	0	0	0	0	0	0	13,000
Estimated Outlays	494	6,210	5,776	520	0	0	0	0	0	0	0	13,000

Table 2. (Continued)

	By Fiscal Year, Millions of Dollars											
	2009	2010	2011	2012	2013	2014	2015	2016	2017	2018	2019	Total 2009 - 2019
	Discretionary Spending 1/											
Special Education												
Budget Authority	12,200	0	0	0	0	0	0	0	0	0	0	12,200
Estimated Outlays	732	5,734	5,124	610	0	0	0	0	0	0	0	12,200
Student Financial Assistance												
Budget Authority	16,483	831	0	0	0	0	0	0	0	0	0	17,314
Estimated Outlays	917	14,572	1,056	15	0	0	0	0	0	0	0	16,560
Other Education												
Budget Authority	2,124	0	0	0	0	0	0	0	0	0	0	2,124
Estimated Outlays	207	1,078	624	203	12	0	0	0	0	0	0	2,124
Other, Title VIII												
Budget Authority	1,559	0	0	0	0	0	0	0	0	0	0	1,559
Estimated Outlays	540	324	283	237	155	4	4	2	0	0	0	1,549
Subtotal, Title VIII												
Budget Authority	71,733	831	0	0	0	0	0	0	0	0	0	72,564
Estimated Outlays	6,831	37,719	20,508	4,984	1,009	187	31	2	0	0	0	71,271
Title IX - Legislative Branch												
Budget Authority	25	0	0	0	0	0	0	0	0	0	0	25
Estimated Outlays	8	15	2	0	0	0	0	0	0	0	0	25
Title X - Military Construction and Veterans Affairs and Related Agencies												
Budget Authority	4,281	0	0	0	0	0	0	0	0	0	0	4,281
Estimated Outlays	448	1,564	1,229	638	241	93	33	0	0	0	0	4,246
Title XI - State, Foreign Operations and Related Programs												
Budget Authority	602	0	0	0	0	0	0	0	0	0	0	602
Estimated Outlays	96	180	162	114	50	0	0	0	0	0	0	602

Table 2. (Continued)

	By Fiscal Year, Millions of Dollars											
	2009	**2010**	**2011**	**2012**	**2013**	**2014**	**2015**	**2016**	**2017**	**2018**	**2019**	**Total 2009 - 2019**
	Discretionary Spending 1/											
Title XII – Trans-portation and Housing and Urban DevelopmentHigh-way Construction												
Budget Authority	27,500	0	0	0	0	0	0	0	0	0	0	27,500
Estimated Outlays	2,750	6,875	5,500	4,125	3,025	2,750	1,925	550	0	0	0	27,500
Other Transportation												
Budget Authority	20,620	0	0	0	0	0	0	0	0	0	0	20,620
Estimated Outlays	2,232	2,511	3,285	2,910	3,027	2,672	1,987	1,051	400	320	160	20,555
Public Housing Capital Fund												
Budget Authority	4,000	0	0	0	0	0	0	0	0	0	0	4,000
Estimated Outlays	80	1,200	1,200	800	640	40	40	0	0	0	0	4,000
Other Housing Assistance												
Budget Authority	9,662	13	0	0	0	0	0	0	0	0	0	9,675
Estimated Outlays	446	2,068	3,316	1,973	1,109	62	22	0	0	0	0	8,996
Subtotal, Title XII												
Budget Authority	61,782	13	0	0	0	0	0	0	0	0	0	61,795
Estimated Outlays	5,508	12,654	13,301	9,808	7,801	5,524	3,974	1,601	400	320	160	61,051
Title XIV - State Fiscal Stabilization Fund												
Budget Authority	53,600	0	0	0	0	0	0	0	0	0	0	53,600
Estimated Outlays	6,540	28,377	16,070	2,363	250	0	0	0	0	0	0	53,600
Subtotal, Division A												
Budget Authority	288,728	7,079	4,592	3,590	2,514	1,055	1,050	1,050	1,050	490	0	311,198
Estimated Outlays	34,792	110,702	76,325	38,065	22,872	12,787	7,035	3,147	1,645	838	130	308,338

Table 2. (Continued)

	By Fiscal Year, Millions of Dollars											
	2009	**2010**	**2011**	**2012**	**2013**	**2014**	**2015**	**2016**	**2017**	**2018**	**2019**	**Total 2009 - 2019**
Division A - Revenues												
Title XII – Trans-portation and Housing and Urban Development												
HOME, Low-income Housing Tax Credit Program	-1	-3	-8	-12	-14	-16	-17	-18	-18	-18	-18	-143
Net Increase or Decrease (-) in the Deficit, Division A	34,793	110,705	76,333	38,077	22,886	12,803	7,052	3,165	1,663	856	148	308,481
Direct Spending												
Division B												
Title I - Tax Provisions Refundable Tax Credits												
Estimated Budget Authority	1,528	32,027	30,105	726	706	686	666	646	634	622	610	68,955
Estimated Outlays	1,528	32,027	30,105	726	706	686	666	646	634	622	610	68,955
Other Provisions												
Estimated Budget Authority	3,580	844	434	21	10	0	0	0	0	0	0	4,889
Estimated Outlays	3,250	696	553	244	62	3	0	0	0	0	0	4,808
Subtotal, Title I												
Estimated Budget Authority	5,108	32,871	30,539	747	716	686	666	646	634	622	610	73,844
Estimated Outlays	4,778	32,723	30,658	970	768	689	666	646	634	622	610	73,763
Title II - Assistance for Unemployed Workers and Struggling Families Unemployment Compensation												
Estimated Budget Authority	16,981	20,460	470	295	140	135	140	145	150	155	160	39,231
Estimated Outlays	16,976	20,465	470	295	140	135	140	145	150	155	160	39,231
Economic Recovery Payments, TANF, and Child Support												
Estimated Budget Authority	19,530	962	-30	-12	-3	-1	0	0	0	0	0	20,447
Estimated Outlays	14,942	2,125	713	187	49	14	4	1	0	0	0	18,033
Subtotal, Title II												
Estimated Budget Authority	36,511	21,422	440	283	137	134	140	145	150	155	160	59,677

Table 2. (Continued)

	By Fiscal Year, Millions of Dollars											
	2009	2010	2011	2012	2013	2014	2015	2016	2017	2018	2019	Total 2009 - 2019
	Direct Spending											
Estimated Outlays	31,918	22,590	1,183	482	189	149	144	146	150	155	160	57,264
Title III - Health Insurance												
Assistance												
Estimated Budget Authority	14,302	9,206	1,493	67	0	0	0	0	0	0	0	25,069
Estimated Outlays	14,302	9,206	1,493	67	0	0	0	0	0	0	0	25,069
Title IV - Health Information												
Technology												
Estimated Budget Authority	438	178	4,741	6,469	6,463	14,231	3,848	-5,546	-4,990	-2,780	-2,233	20,819
Estimated Outlays	417	178	4,741	6,469	6,463	14,231	3,848	-5,535	-4,980	-2,780	-2,233	20,819
Title V - State Fiscal Relief												
Estimated Budget Authority	33,955	43,920	11,802	67	-8	33	44	56	57	59	59	90,044
Estimated Outlays	33,881	43,923	11,847	88	-6	35	44	56	57	59	59	90,042
Subtotal, Direct Spending												
Estimated Budget Authority	90,314	107,597	49,015	7,633	7,308	15,084	4,698	-4,699	-4,149	-1,944	-1,404	269,454
Estimated Outlays	85,295	108,619	49,922	8,076	7,414	15,104	4,702	-4,687	-4,139	-1,944	-1,404	266,958
Title I - Tax Provisions	-64,792	-179,893	-8,194	9,949	2,506	5,228	6,670	5,313	4,562	4,495	-408	-214,576
Title II - Assistance for Unemployed Workers and Struggling Families	-44	-261	-186	-263	-225	-139	-81	34	65	105	115	-879
Title III - Health Insurance Assistance	0	52	86	93	75	46	29	10	1	0	0	392
Title IV - Health Information Technology	0	0	120	250	360	410	435	435	425	415	410	3,260
Subtotal, Revenues	-64,836	-180,102	-8,174	10,029	2,716	5,545	7,053	5,792	5,053	5,015	117	-211,803
Net Increase or Decrease (-) in the Deficit, Division B	150,131	288,722	58,096	-1,953	4,698	9,558	-2,351	-10,480	-9,192	-6,959	-1,521	478,761
	Net Impact on the Deficit											
Net Increase or Decrease (-) in the Deficit	184,924	399,427	134,429	36,124	27,584	22,361	4,701	-7,315	-7,529	-6,103	-1,373	787,242

Table 2. (Continued)

	By Fiscal Year, Millions of Dollars											
	2009	2010	2011	2012	2013	2014	2015	2016	2017	2018	2019	Total 2009 - 2019
	Net Impact on the Deficit											
Memorandum												
On-Budget												
Estimated Budget Authority	379,042	114,676	53,618	11,248	9,857	16,176	5,787	-3,609	-3,086	-1,440	-1,391	580,879
Estimated Outlays	120,087	219,321	126,258	46,166	30,321	27,928	11,776	-1,500	-2,481	-1,092	-1,261	575,523
Revenues	-64,821	-180,075	-8,218	9,927	2,577	5,389	6,886	5,624	4,890	4,857	-41	-213,017
Net Impact on the Deficit	184,908	399,396	134,476	36,239	27,744	22,539	4,890	-7,124	-7,371	-5,949	-1,220	788,540
Off-Budget												
Estimated Budget Authority	0	0	-11	-25	-35	-37	-39	-40	-13	-14	-13	-227
Estimated Outlays	0	0	-11	-25	-35	-37	-39	-40	-13	-14	-13	-227
Revenues	-16	-30	36	90	125	140	150	150	145	140	140	1,071
Net Impact on the Deficit	16	30	-47	-115	-160	-177	-189	-190	-158	-154	-153	-1,298
Unified Budget												
Estimated Budget Authority	379,042	114,676	53,607	11,223	9,822	16,139	5,748	-3,649	-3,099	-1,454	-1,404	580,652
Estimated Outlays	120,087	219,321	126,247	46,141	30,286	27,891	11,737	-1,540	-2,494	-1,106	-1,274	575,296
Revenues	-64,837	-180,105	-8,182	10,017	2,702	5,529	7,036	5,774	5,035	4,997	99	-211,946
Net Impact on the Deficit	184,924	399,427	134,429	36,124	27,584	22,361	4,701	-7,315	-7,529	-6,103	-1,373	787,242

Source: Congressional Budget Office and Joint Committee on Taxation.

Notes: TANF = Temporary Assistance for Needy Families.

Estimates in this table reflect an assumed enactment date in mid - February, 2009. Outlays projected for 2009 would occur over a 7 1/2 month period.

Positive revenue numbers reflect decreases in the deficit; negative revenue numbers reflect increases in the deficit.

Positive numbers for "net impact on the deficit" reflect an increase in the deficit; negative numbers reflect a decrease in the deficit.

Components may not sum to totals because of rounding.

1. Includes estimates for changes to mandatory programs contained in Division A.

In: American Recovery and Reinvestment Act: History... ISBN: 978-1-61668-355-9
Editor: Paul G. Tellis

Chapter 3

AGRICULTURE, NUTRITION, AND RURAL PROVISIONS IN THE AMERICAN RECOVERY AND REINVESTMENT ACT (ARRA) OF 2009*

Jim Monke, Joe Richardson, Megan Stubbs, Taklock Cowan, Ralph M. Chite, Geoffrey S. Becker and Remy Jurenas
Agricultural Policy
Social Policy
Agricultural Conservation and Natural Resources Policy
Natural Resources and Rural Development
Section Research Manager

SUMMARY

On February 17, 2009, President Obama signed into law H.R. 1, the American Recovery and Reinvestment Act of 2009 (ARRA, P.L. 111-5). The ARRA is a response to the depth of the economic recession facing the United States (and the rest of the world) at the beginning of 2009. It is billed as an economic stimulus package to improve the situation of individuals and businesses. The ARRA boosts government spending on various infrastructure programs and government benefits programs, and offers individual and business tax benefits. The Congressional Budget Office (CBO) estimates that the ARRA will cost $787 billion over 10 years, although most of its budget authority is slated for two fiscal years (FY2009-FY2010).

Agriculture programs—including nutrition assistance, rural development, farmer assistance, and conservation—would receive about $26.6 billion of the $787 billion in the enacted ARRA (about 3.4%). The $26.6 billion is allocated as follows:

* This is an edited, reformatted and augmented version of a CRS Report for Congress publication dated February 2009.

- Nutrition assistance programs receive $20.8 billion (78% of the total amount for agriculture). Food stamp benefits and eligibility in the newly renamed Supplemental Nutrition Assistance Program (SNAP) represent the largest single increase (nearly $20 billion); benefits rise 20% on average from current levels.
- Rural development receives a sizeable increase of $4.4 billion over two years (compared to a regular annual appropriation of about $2.5 billion). Rural broadband receives $2.5 billion of this, an amount that allows outlays through FY2015 that are 20-30 times more than recent annual appropriations.
- Assistance for farmers totals $744 million, including crop insurance/disaster programs ($674 million), aquaculture feed cost assistance ($50 million), and farm loan programs ($20 million).
- Conservation programs receive $348 million for watershed flood prevention ($290 million) and dam rehabilitation projects ($50 million).
- USDA receives $250 million for its own facilities maintenance ($200 million) and computer infrastructure ($50 million).
- The USDA Office of Inspector General receives $23 million for increased oversight and audits of these supplemental spending programs.
- Trade Adjustment Assistance for Farmers is reauthorized.

This chapter analyzes the agriculture, nutrition, and rural provisions in the ARRA.

BACKGROUND ON THE AMERICAN RECOVERY AND REINVESTMENT ACT OF 2009

On February 17, 2009, President Obama signed into law H.R. 1, the American Recovery and Reinvestment Act of 2009 (ARRA, P.L. 111-5). The House passed the conference agreement on February 13 by a vote of 246-183, and the Senate the same day by a vote of 60-38. Prior to the conference agreement, the House passed its bill on January 28, 2009, by a vote of 244-188. The Senate passed its version on February 10 by a vote of 61-37.

The Congressional Budget Office (CBO) estimates that the ARRA will cost $787 billion over 10 years,[1] although most of its budget authority is slated for two fiscal years (FY2009-FY2010). Outlays and economic effects may occur in some programs over a longer period of time.[2]

The ARRA is a further response to the depth of the economic recession facing the United States (and the rest of the world) at the beginning of 2009. Both the Obama Administration and many Members of Congress had called for an economic stimulus package to follow the Troubled Asset Relief Program (TARP) that was enacted in October 2008 (P.L. 110-343, Emergency Economic Stabilization Act of 2008). The TARP was focused primarily on the recovery of financial institutions.[3] The ARRA—billed as an economic stimulus package—is focused on stimulating the economy via individual and business economic activity. The package boosts government spending on various infrastructure programs[4] and certain government benefits programs. It also offers tax incentives and benefits for individuals and businesses.[5]

The enacted ARRA's cost is less than either the House- or Senate-passed versions, $820 billion[6] and $838 billion,[7] respectively. Of the ARRA's $787 billion

, $308 billion (39%) is appropriations—mostly discretionary spending for government agencies to use on various forms of infrastructure development, benefits programs, and government loan and grant programs. The stimulus spending will be tracked online at http://www.recovery.

This chapter analyzes the agriculture, nutrition, and rural provisions in the ARRA.

AGRICULTURE, NUTRITION, AND RURAL PROGRAMS

Agriculture, nutrition, and rural programs—including food assistance, rural development, farmer assistance, conservation, and other related programs (a few of which are administered outside the U.S. Department of Agriculture (USDA))—would receive about $26.6 billion of the $787 billion in the enacted ARRA (about 3.4%, **Figure 1**). This is a compromise between the $27.2 billion for comparable programs in the House-passed bill and $24.5 billion in the Senate-passed bill (**Table 1**). These amounts are to supplement existing programs funded by the appropriations committee. They do not include amounts that farmers or rural areas might receive along with the rest of the country under other areas of the stimulus package—such as transportation, bio-energy, health, and education programs—that are unspecified in their geographic or rural distribution.

The $26.6 billion for agriculture, nutrition, and rural programs is allocated as follows (**Figure 2**, **Table 1**):

- Nutrition assistance programs receive $20.8 billion. Food stamp benefits in the newly renamed Supplemental Nutrition Assistance Program (SNAP) represent the largest single increase and rise 20% on average from current levels.
- Rural development receives a sizeable increase of $4.4 billion over two years (compared to a regular annual appropriation of about $2.5 billion). Rural broadband receives $2.5 billion of this, an amount that allows outlays through FY2015 that are 20-30 times more than recent annual appropriations.
- Assistance for farmers totals $744 million, including crop insurance/disaster programs ($674 million) and farm loan programs ($20 million).
- Conservation programs receive $348 million for watershed flood prevention ($290 million) and dam rehabilitation projects ($50 million).
- USDA receives $250 million for its own facilities maintenance ($200 million) and computer infrastructure ($50 million).
- The USDA Office of Inspector General receives $23 million for increased oversight and audits of these supplemental spending programs.
- Trade Adjustment Assistance for Farmers is reauthorized.

The conference agreement generally follows the House-passed bill for the biggest nutrition programs, while picking up a few provisions from the Senate bill and omitting a House provision for an after-school feeding program. The rural broadband and conservation provisions generally follow the House bill, while amounts for these and other rural development programs are reduced to accommodate the smaller Senate bill. This is particularly important for rural broadband, since the Senate bill would have given all broadband money to the Department of Commerce with a carve-out for rural areas. Amounts for USDA facilities and computer infrastructure follow Senate- passed levels rather than higher House-passed amounts, which was a particularly large reduction for requested Farm Service Agency computer improvements. The farmer assistance programs, originally only in the Senate-passed bill, remained in the enacted law. But the supplement for farm loan programs was reduced, despite the increased demand for USDA farm loans as a lender of last resort in the financial crisis.

The enacted ARRA does not fund a USDA biorefinery program, the Rural Energy for America Program, or agricultural research grants. It also did not retain language about “downer” cattle.

Nutrition Assistance

The enacted ARRA includes nine items that substantially increase spending on domestic food assistance programs. The Congressional Budget Office (CBO) estimates total new spending on these initiatives at $11.5 billion in the first two years (FY2009-FY2010) and $20.8 billion over ten years (through FY2019). The lion’s share would go to pay for added benefits, loosened eligibility standards, and administrative costs under the Supplemental Nutrition Assistance Program (SNAP, formerly the Food Stamp program), as well as more money for nutrition assistance grants to Puerto Rico and American Samoa (these grants operate in lieu of the SNAP). Other nutrition programs in the ARRA include the Special Supplemental Nutrition Program for Women, Infants, and Children (the WIC program), Older Americans Act nutrition programs for seniors, equipment assistance for school meal programs, The Emergency Food Assistance Program (TEFAP), and the Food Distribution Program on Indian Reservations (FDPIR).

The House-passed version of the new law included eight items that would have increased spending on domestic food assistance programs. CBO estimated total new spending on these initiatives at $11.4 billion in the first two years (FY2009-FY2010) and $21.2 billion over ten years (through FY2019). As with the final law, the majority of spending would have gone to added benefits, loosened eligibility standards, and administrative costs under the SNAP, along with more funding for nutrition assistance grants for Puerto Rico and American Samoa. Other programs included in the House bill were management information system support for the WIC program, Older Americans Act nutrition programs, child nutrition after-school efforts, and TEFAP.

Although its provisions differed, the Senate-approved version covered seven of the eight areas touched on by the House (it did not include money for after-school programs) and added three new items affecting equipment assistance for school meal programs, contingency funding for the WIC program, and the new money for the FDPIR. Preliminary CBO estimates indicated that total new spending under the Senate’s proposals would have been $13.8 billion in the first two years (FY2009-FY2010) and $17.5 billion over ten years (through FY2019).

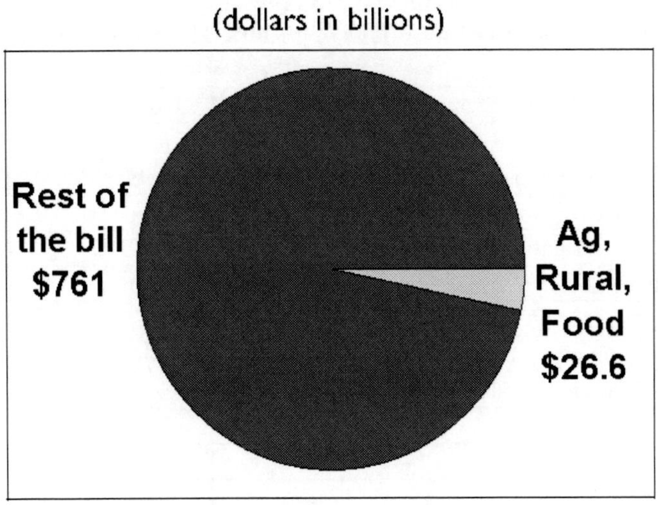

Source: CRS, from CBO estimates.

Figure 1. Agriculture, Nutrition, and Rural Share of the ARRA

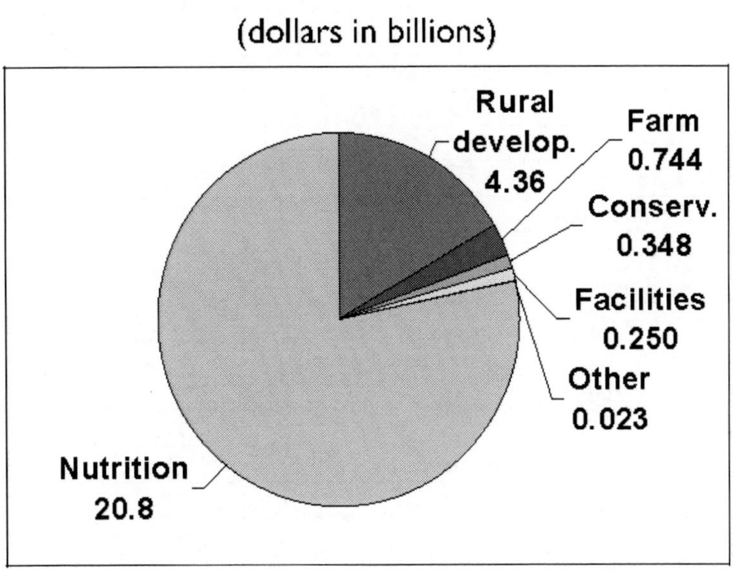

Source: CRS, from CBO estimates.

Figure 2. Agriculture, Nutrition, and Rural Programs in the ARRA

Table 1. Agriculture, Nutrition, and Rural Provisions in the American Recovery and Reinvestment Act of 2009 (P.L. 111-5)
(budget authority in millions of dollars, 10-year CBO scores)

Agricultural Program	House	Senate	Enacted
Nutrition Assistance			
SNAP (formerly Food Stamps)[a]	19,991	16,557	19,986
WIC benefits contingency fund	—	380	400
WIC management information systems	100	120	100
Emergency food assistance	150	150	150
Seniors nutrition programs[b]	200	100	100
School lunch program equipment assistance	—	100	100
Food Distribution Program on Indian Reservations	—	5	5
After-school feeding program	726	—	—
Subtotal, Nutrition Assistance	**21,167**	**17,412**	**20,841**
Rural Development			
Rural broadband infrastructure development	2,825	3,325[c]	2,500
Rural water and waste disposal program	1,500	1,375	1,380
Rural housing service	500	200	200
Rural community facilities program	200	127	130
Rural business program	100	150	150
Distance learning and telemedicine program	—	100	—
Biorefinery program	—	200	—
Salaries and expenses	—	80	—
Rural Energy for America program	—	50	—
Subtotal, Rural Development	**5,125**	**5,607**	**4,360**
Farmer Assistance			
Agricultural crop disaster assistance	—	674	674
Aquaculture feed cost assistance	—	50	50
FSA farm loan program (including emergency loans)	—	71	20
Subtotal, Farmer Assistance	**—**	**794**	**744**
Conservation			
NRCS watershed and flood prevention	175	275	145
NRCS floodplain easements	175		145
NRCS watershed rehabilitation program	50	65	50
Farm bill administration (conservation technical assistance)	—	34	8
Subtotal, Conservation	**400**	**374**	348
USDA facilities infrastructure			
USDA for facilities infrastructure	—	200	—
ARS facilities deferred maintenance	209	—	176
USDA headquarters repair and improvements	44	—	24
FSA information technology / administration	245	54	50
Subtotal, USDA facilities infrastructure	**498**	**254**	**250**

Table 1. (Continued)

Agricultural Program	House	Senate	Enacted
Other			
USDA Office of Inspector General	23	23	23
CSREES competitive research grants	—	50	—
Subtotal, Other	**23**	**73**	**23**
Total, Agriculture, Nutrition, and Rural Provisions	**27,213**	**24,514**	**26,566**

Source: CRS compilation from H.R. 1, H.Rept. 111-4, S.Rept. 111-3, H.Rept. 111-16, and CBO estimates. Includes rural and nutrition programs elsewhere in the bill that are not in the U.S. Department of Agriculture.

Notes: In general, budget authority in the stimulus bill is for two years (FY2009-FY2010, with the exception of certain nutrition programs described in the text), but outlays may be spread over a longer period.

a. Amounts for SNAP in this table include increased SNAP benefits, suspension of time limits for able-bodied adults without dependents, larger nutrition assistance block grants for Puerto Rico and American Samoa, and additional payments for SNAP administrative costs.

b. The seniors nutrition program authorized by the Older Americans Act is operated by the Administration on Aging in the Department of Health and Human Services, not the U.S. Department of Agriculture.

c. Senate-passed H.R. 1 states that the budget authority for rural broadband is 50% of the $6.65 billion specified for the Department of Commerce National Telecommunications and Information Administration, inferred in the bill as follows: "50% of the funds ... shall be used to support projects in rural communities, which in part may be transferred to the Department of Agriculture for administration through the Rural Utilities Service if deemed necessary and appropriate by the Secretary of Commerce."

Supplemental Nutrition Assistance Program Provisions

Under the ARRA, Supplemental Nutrition Assistance Program (SNAP, formerly the Food Stamp program) benefits will be increased significantly, and time limits on eligibility for able-bodied adults without dependents will, in most cases, be suspended. Moreover, state agencies operating SNAP will receive extra administrative funding.

- SNAP benefits add to eligible low-income households' ability to cover their food costs out of their own income. Monthly allotments are based on the estimated cost of a minimally adequate diet. This means that the benefit for any recipient household equals the inflation-indexed cost of USDA's "Thrifty Food Plan" (its least costly diet calculation, the maximum benefit) varied by household size and adjusted for household income. In recognition of relatively rapid food-price inflation (benefits were last adjusted in October 2008), the new law substantially raises SNAP benefits (based on provisions in the House bill).
- The ARRA provides an immediate (effective in April 2009) across-the-board increase in SNAP benefits. This add-on is accomplished by raising by 13.6% the base Thrifty Food Plan amounts normally used to calculate benefits. This effectively boosts each recipient household's monthly benefit by an amount equal to 13.6% of the maximum (Thrifty Food Plan) benefit for its household size. For a one-person

household, the added benefit will be $24 a month; for two persons, $44 a month; for three persons (the typical household) $63 a month; for four persons, $80 a month; and for larger households, higher amounts. As a result, the ARRA benefit will provide new support boosting present average household benefits by about 20%.

- The new law also will increase present nutrition assistance grants for Puerto Rico and American Samoa by 13.6%, enabling them to raise benefit levels and cover higher administrative costs. SNAP benefit and the grants for Puerto Rico and American Samoa will continue at the new, higher levels set by the ARRA until normal annual indexing rules provide benefits/grants that surpass the value of the new add-on.
- Finally, states are protected from federal financial penalties under SNAP "quality control" rules for most of the mistakes they or recipients may make under the new benefit provisions (as proposed in the Senate bill). CBO estimates that new SNAP benefits will cost $9.9 billion for FY2009-FY2010, noticeably increasing the $100 billion anticipated under pre-ARRA law. Added spending for Puerto Rico and American Samoa is expected to equal some $375 million for FY2009- FY2010.
    - The House effectively provided the same increase in SNAP benefits and new money for Puerto Rico and American Samoa set out in the final law.
    - On the other hand, the Senate would have immediately increased the base Thrifty Food Plan amounts used to calculate SNAP benefits by 85% for one month. For the remainder of FY2009, it would have boosted benefits by 12%. In FY2010 and FY2011, basic benefits would have remained 12% higher, until normal indexing rules caught up (similar to policy followed in the final law and the House bill). Nutrition assistance grants for Puerto Rico would have been increased by 12% through FY2011 (or until normal inflation indexing caught up). In FY2009 and FY20 10, the Senate initiatives (including those for Puerto Rico and American Samoa) were expected to cost $12.5 billion, significantly more than the House provisions.
- SNAP eligibility for most able-bodied adults without dependents (ABAWDs) who are not working at least half-time is limited to 3 months out of every 36 months (without regard to their financial status). States have the option to waive this requirement in a number of circumstances, and most states take advantage of this option. Reacting to high unemployment rates, the ARRA (as in the House bill) effectively suspends this requirement for those who cannot find a job through FY2010. In the Senate version, the suspension would have lasted through FY2011. CBO estimates the cost of this suspension in the final bill at $300 million through FY2010.
- While SNAP benefit costs are entirely a federal responsibility, states operating SNAP share administrative costs with the federal government. Approximately half of administrative costs are picked up by states—estimated at between $2.5 and $3 billion in FY2008. Participation in the SNAP is rising dramatically, leading to higher administrative costs. Closely following provisions in both the House and Senate bills, the new law provides $145 million (FY2009) and $150 million (FY2010) in additional federal money for SNAP administrative costs, distributed based on state SNAP participation levels (including measures for recently increasing caseload burdens) and without requiring normal state matching funds. A small amount ($4.5

million) of this is set aside for federal oversight, monitoring, and evaluation of the effects of the new SNAP benefit and eligibility rules.

Women, Infants, and Children Program Provisions

The Special Supplemental Nutrition Program for Women, Infants, and Children (the WIC program) provides special vouchers for food purchases to lower-income pregnant/postpartum women, infants, and children judged to be at "nutritional risk"; it also offers nutrition education, medical referral, and breastfeeding initiatives. State agencies implementing the WIC program have consistently called for added support for implementing new or upgraded "management information systems" to improve their ability to deliver benefits more efficiently. Moreover, changing economic conditions and food-price inflation have made existing projections of the need for WIC funding increasingly uncertain.

The ARRA provides $400 million for a contingency reserve to support participation or food costs that exceed current budget estimates in the next two years. It also makes available an additional $100 million for WIC state agencies' management information system expansions/upgrades.

Both the House and Senate included funding for WIC management information systems (although they differed slightly in the dollar amount); the extra money for a contingency fund is derived from the Senate proposal.

Older Americans Act Nutrition Provision

Older Americans Act nutrition programs provide federal payments for meals served to seniors in congregate meal settings (e.g., senior citizens centers) and to those served with home-delivered meals ("meals-on-wheels"). For FY2009, approximately $800 million is available. In recognition of higher food and other costs faced by these programs, the ARRA (as in the Senate proposal) provides an immediate infusion of $100 million. The funds are to be allocated as follows: $65 million for congregate meal services, $32 million for home-delivered meal services, and $3 million for Native American nutrition services. The House bill would have made a total of $200 million available ($100 million for FY2009 and FY2010). This program, unlike other nutrition programs, is administered by the Administration on Aging in the Department of Health and Human Services and does not appear in the regular Agriculture Department appropriations.

The Emergency Food Assistance Program

The Emergency Food Assistance Program (TEFAP) buys federally purchased food commodities for emergency food assistance providers (like food banks and soup kitchens) tapped by states as regional and local sponsors. TEFAP also makes grants for distribution and storage costs incurred by sponsors. In FY2009, TEFAP is budgeted at $250 million in commodities and $50 million for distribution/storage costs. As in both the House and Senate bills, the ARRA makes an additional $150 million available through FY2010: $100 million for commodity acquisitions and $50 million for distribution/storage costs.

School Equipment Grants

Child nutrition programs do not provide direct assistance to schools covering costs related to the equipment used to provide meals. Drawing from the Senate bill, the new law makes $100 million available to states for use in making competitive grants to schools (based on need) for school food service equipment. The House bill did not contain a comparable amendment and a Senate provision allowing for a specific reserve of money for enhancement to states' commodity distribution agencies' ordering and management systems was not included.

Food Distribution Program on Indian Reservations

At the discretion of individual tribes, the Food Distribution Program on Indian Reservations (FDPIR) provides monthly food packages in lieu of SNAP benefits; federal support includes the cost of commodities included in the food packages and administrative/distribution expenses. Spending on this program typically totals $80-$90 million a year. Closely tracking the Senate bill, the enacted ARRA makes an extra $5 million available for FDPIR costs related to facility improvements and equipment upgrades that make commodities more accessible to participants. The House bill did not include a comparable provision.

After-School Program Proposal

Child nutrition law (through the Child and Adult Care Food program and the School Lunch program) provides federal subsidies for snacks served by sponsors (like schools) of after-school programs. In eight states, after-school sponsors also may receive federal payments for suppers that they serve free to lower-income children—Delaware, Illinois, Michigan, Missouri, New York, Oregon, Pennsylvania, and West Virginia. The House would have expanded this rule to make after-school sponsors in all states eligible to receive federal subsidies for suppers, at an initial cost of some $50 million over FY2009 and FY2010 (more than $700 million through FY2019). The Senate bill contained no comparable proposal, and neither does the new law.

Longer-Term Effects

About 55% of the estimated new spending on ARRA's nutrition assistance provisions is expected to occur in FY2009 and FY2010. This is effectively the same proportion as under the House bill, but much lower than the 79% in the Senate. There is likely to be new spending beyond FY2010 for several reasons. Most important, the across-the-board percentage boosts in SNAP benefits and nutrition assistance grants for Puerto Rico and American Samoa may very well continue to have an effect on spending (causing budget outlays above currently expected levels, the CBO "baseline") if normal inflation indexing does not catch up with the new law's add-on percentage increases. Second, the terms of the ABAWD rule suspension will probably have effects beyond FY2010 because months receiving SNAP benefits during the suspension period will not be counted when the pre-ARRA rules come back into place. Third, while several provisions make new funding "available" through FY2010 (e.g., equipment assistance grants, WIC management information systems aid), significant outlays are probable beyond FY2010.

Finally, it should be noted that most of the documents accompanying the House, Senate, and final-law nutrition assistance packages, as well as the table included in this chapter, present estimates of total costs (through FY2019), whereas the discussion above differentiates spending by time periods and concentrates on spending through FY2010.

Rural Development

The enacted ARRA authorizes $4.36 billion in supplemental budget authority over two years for various rural development loan and grant programs. This is $1.25 billion less than the Senate measure and $765 million less than the House bill. The enacted law will support a total program level (direct and guaranteed loans and grants) of $24.37 billion (**Table 2**). These basically two- year amounts represent a sizeable increase compared to a regular annual appropriation of about $2.5 billion for all USDA Rural Development loan and grant programs and regular annual loan and grant level of about $16 billion.

Rural broadband and rural water projects account for 89% of the budget authority and 36% of the program level of rural development programs in the ARRA. Rural housing accounts for about half of the program level. The various loan and grant provisions are discussed below.

Broadband, Distance Learning, and Telemedicine Support

The enacted ARRA authorizes $2.5 billion for rural broadband loans and grants, $825 million less than the Senate measure and $325 million less than the House bill. The funds would be administered by the Rural Utilities Service (RUS).

The Senate bill authorized a Technology Opportunities Program (TOP) within the U.S. Department of Commerce and proposed a total of $6.50 billion in broadband funding for TOP, half of which would have been used to support projects in rural areas. All the Senate funding, however, was to be administered by TOP rather than by RUS. The House bill proposed $2.8 billion in supplemental budget authority to be administered by RUS. The House bill's proposed funding supported both broadband loans and grants, while the Senate bill supported broadband grants.

Report language for the ARRA states that the funding will be available for broadband infrastructure in any area of the United States, rather than to the more restricted rural definition in the statutory language of Title VI of the Rural Electrification Act of 1936.[8] At least 75% of the area to be served by rural broadband projects, however, must be in rural areas without sufficient access to high speed broadband to facilitate economic development. Priority in applications will go for projects (1) that will deliver end users a choice of more than one service provider; (2) that provide broadband service to the largest proportion of rural residents without access to broadband service; (3) that are from borrowers or former borrowers under the rural telephone loan programs; and (4) that can begin promptly after approval. Unlike the Senate bill, the ARRA does not require a 20% matching amount from applicants.

Table 2. Rural Development in the American Recovery and Reinvestment Act of 2009: Budget and Program Levels (dollars in millions; amounts in H.R. 1 reflect 10-year scores)

Rural Development Programs	P.L. 110-161		American Recovery and Reinvestment Act of 2009					
	FY2008 or Baseline		House		Senate		Enacted (P.L. 111-5)	
	Budget Authority	Program Level	Budget Authority	Program Level	Budget Authority	Program Level	Budget Authority	Program Level
Rural broadband infrastructure development	20	298	2,825	5,500	3,325	3,325[a]	2,500	4,867[d]
Rural water and waste disposal program	559	1,097	1,500	3,836	1,375	3,783	1,380	3,788
Rural housing fund program	207	5,567	500	22,129	200	11,472	200	11,472
Rural community facilities program	68	501	200	1,239	127	1,546	130	1,234
Rural business program	87	993	100	2,013	150	3,010	150	3,010
Distance learning and telemedicine program	35	35	—	—	100	497[e]	—	—
Biorefinery program	75[b]	—[c]	—	—	200	—[c]	—	—
Rural Energy for America program	55[b]	—[c]	—	—	50	—[c]	—	—
Salaries and expenses	169	—	—	—	80	—	—	—
Other rural development programs	1,060	8,049	—	—	—	—	—	—
Subtotal, Rural Development	**2,334**	**16,540**	**5,125**	**34,717**	**5,607**	**23,633**	**4,360**	**24,371**

Source: CRS compilation from H.R. 1, H.Rept. 111-4, and S.Rept. 111-3, H.Rept. 111-16. Amounts for FY2008 are from S.Rept. 110-426 (S. 3289) or P.L. 110-246.

Notes: *Budget authority* reflects the cost to an agency of salaries, expenses, and the costs of making loans and grants such as interest subsidies and projected non-repayment of loans. Program level reflects the benefits derived by recipients, such as the sum of grants, direct loans, and loans guaranteed.

a. Senate budget authority for the rural broadband amount is 50% of the $8.65 billion specified for the Department of Commerce National Telecommunications and Information Administration, inferred in the bill as follows: "50% of the funds...shall be used to support projects in rural communities, which in part may be transferred to the Department of Agriculture for administration through the Rural Utilities Service if deemed necessary and appropriate by the Secretary of Commerce."

b. Mandatory funding specified in the 2008 farm bill. However, the FY2009 Senate-reported agriculture appropriations bill (S. 3289, S.Rept. 110-426) would reduce the biorefinery program's $75 million to $72 million, and the Rural Energy for America program's $55 million to zero.

c. Not specified in the bill or report language.

d. Not specified in the bill or report language. Computed assuming the ratio of program level to budget authority in the House bill.

e. The original Senate bill (S.Amdt. 98) provided $200 million budget authority for $993 million program level. The Senate-passed bill cut the budget authority by half.

The House committee report stated an estimated program level of $5.5 billion in competitive grants and loans for rural broadband development.[9] Based on the loan and grant amount in the House bill, the enacted ARRA may support about $4.9 billion in loans and grants. The House committee report also projected that new service would be provided to 7,600 rural communities and 3.6 million rural residents and businesses, with 119,000 jobs created.

As part of the TOP funding in the Department of Commerce, the enacted ARRA adopts Senate provisions to target $200 million to expand public computing capacity at community colleges and libraries, provide $250 million for grants to encourage adoption of broadband services, and provide $350 million for the National Telecommunications and Information Administration (NTIA) to carry out a broadband mapping project. While part of TOP, these targeted funds could benefit rural areas. The ARRA also adopts Senate language to provide an additional $650 million for NTIA's Digital Television (DTV) converter box program, funding that might also benefit rural businesses and residences.

CBO estimates that rural broadband outlays will occur primarily from FY2010 to FY20 15, generally ranging from $300 million to $600 million in budget authority annually (see footnote 1). Even after accounting for spreading the stimulus budget authority over a longer period than two years, the level of support in the enacted law, as it was in the House and Senate bills, is about 20-30 times more than the rural broadband program has received in recent years. In FY2008, the program received about $20 million in budget authority to support about $313 million in loans and grants.

Given the large proposed increases in funding for broadband development (both rural and nonrural), questions may arise regarding the capacity of the designated federal agencies to effectively manage the grant and loan application and oversight process. USDA's RUS has many years of successful management of telecommunication loans and grants, but the sheer size of the proposed expansion and the speed of implementation could prove challenging even for this agency. Moreover, it was concern with RUS's difficulties implementing Enhanced

Access to Rural Broadband in the 2002 farm bill that led to the Senate bill putting the rural broadband stimulus funding in the Department of Commerce. That 2002 farm bill provision authorized loan guarantees under conditions that broadband service providers have capital reserve requirements, matching funding, and preparation of a sophisticated business plan, among other requirements. After making some initial loan guarantees and reviewing the quality of applications for funding under the Enhanced Access program, RUS determined that they needed to initiate an education program for would-be providers and reconsider the original program requirements before approving new loan guarantees—fulfilling the agency's due diligence obligations. The program's regulations were substantially revised, and a revised program was reauthorized in the 2008 farm bill (P.L. 110-246).

The appropriation to the TOP in U.S. Department of Commerce's NTIA could prove even more of a challenge for oversight and administration than for RUS. The TOP has not been funded since 2004. Between 1994 and 2004, TOP managed a relatively small grants program (610 grants totaling $233.5 million) that supported demonstrations of new telecommunications and information technologies. The new $4.7 billion program of loans and grants will be a major undertaking for TOP and the NTIA.

The enacted ARRA does not provide the broadband investment tax credits that were proposed in the Senate bill. Tax credits in the Senate bill were valued at 10%-20% of broadband expenditures in the respective tax year. The amount of the tax credit was based on a company's expenditures for "current generation" broadband technologies and "next generation technologies," with the latter receiving larger credits for expenditures.[10]

The ARRA also does not authorize funding for the rural distance learning and telemedicine (DLTM) program administered by RUS. The Senate bill proposed $100 million in supplemental budget authority for the DLTM program, which supported a program level of $497 million in loans and grants for the DLTM program.

Rural Water and Waste Water Assistance

The ARRA authorizes $1.380 billion for the USDA water and waste water loan and grant program, $5 million more than the Senate bill and $120 million less than the House bill. The enacted funding will support a program level of $3.8 billion ($2.8 billion in direct loans and $968 million in grants).

Rural water and waste water disposal loans and grants are administered by USDA's Rural Utilities Service (RUS). Funds support construction of and improvements to community drinking water and wastewater treatment projects serving rural households and businesses. On an annual basis, the enacted funding is more than double the regular annual appropriations for RUS water and waste water programs, which in FY2008 received about $560 million in budget authority to support about $1.2 billion of loans. Similar to the backlog in other rural development programs, $2.4 billion in applications for water and waste loans and $990 million for water and waste grants went unfunded in FY2008.

Rural Housing Assistance

The enacted ARRA authorizes $200 million in supplemental budget authority for rural housing, the same as proposed by the Senate bill. The House-passed bill proposed $500 million. The ARRA's $200 million of budget authority will support a program level of $11.5 billion of direct and guaranteed loans. Within this loan authorization level, $10.5 billion is for

Section 502 guaranteed single-family home loans, and $1.0 billion is for Section 502 direct single-family home loans. In the House bill, $18 billion was proposed for loan guarantees and $4 billion for direct loans.

The Section 502 single family housing loan program is the largest part of the RHS portfolio. Section 502 loans are primarily used to help low-income individuals or households purchase modest homes in rural areas. Funds can be used to build, repair, renovate, or relocate a home, or to purchase and prepare sites, including providing water and sewage facilities. In 2008, there was a $2.6 billion backlog of unfunded applications for the Section 502 housing program.

The enacted ARRA does not include the House measure for rural housing assistance ($10 million) under the Self-Help and Assisted Homeownership Opportunity Program (SHOP) funded through the Department of Housing and Urban Development. This program supports eligible local and regional nonprofit housing organizations to develop or rehabilitate low-income rural housing.

Rural Community Facilities

USDA's Rural Housing Service (RHS) administers the Community Facilities loan and grant program. This program provides support for "essential" community facilities in rural communities (e.g., public safety, libraries, education, community centers, day care, and rural medical clinics). The enacted ARRA authorizes $130 million in supplemental budget authority to support a program level of $1.23 billion ($1.17 billion for direct loans and $63 million for grants). Although the enacted budget authority is $70 million less than that proposed in the House measure, the authorized funding would support nearly the same in program funding as the House bill and about $310 million less than the Senate measure due to the allocation of loans versus grants.

In FY2008, the community facilities account received about $68 million of budget authority. Like most rural development programs, applications for the community facilities exceed the regular annual appropriations to support the various projects. Currently, there are approximately $1.2 billion in pending loan and grant applications.

Rural Business Development

Rural business development is supported by USDA's Rural Business-Cooperative Service (RBS). The enacted law authorizes $150 million in budget authority to support a program level of $3 billion in Business and Industry Guaranteed loans and Rural Business Enterprise Grants. This is the same as proposed by the Senate bill and 50% more than the House bill.

Rural businesses can often be at a disadvantage in borrowing, especially in the current period of high demand and tightened credit. Private sector loans to rural businesses backed by federal guarantees (e.g., the Business and Industry Guaranteed loan program) have become increasingly important sources of capital to rural businesses.

Other Rural Funding

The ARRA authorizes no funding for biorefinery loans and grants or for the Rural Energy for America Program (REAP). The Senate bill proposed funding of $200 and $50 million respectively for these programs. Both programs are slated to receive mandatory funds in the 2008 farm bill, but the Senate-reported FY2009 agriculture appropriations bill would reduce the mandatory funding levels.[11] REAP provides loans and grants to promote energy efficiency and renewable energy development for agricultural producers and rural small businesses.

Funding proposed in the bills for other programs might also affect rural areas, although the funds are not explicitly targeted to rural areas nor are they administered by USDA Rural Development agencies. Tax reductions to businesses, small business tax credits, economic development assistance, funds to modernize roads and bridges, school construction, and health care facilities could also provide new assistance to rural areas.

Farmer Assistance

The enacted ARRA contains $744 million to directly assist farmers, including $674 million for crop disaster programs (primarily the supplemental revenue assistance program (SURE)), $50 million for aquaculture feed price assistance, and $20 million for the USDA Farm Service Agency farm operating loan program.

Supplemental Revenue Assistance Program Eligibility and Payments

The new supplemental revenue assistance payment (SURE) program in the 2008 farm bill may have greater participation because the enacted ARRA allows producers who did not enroll in the federal crop insurance or the noninsured crop disaster program—normally a requirement for participating in SURE—to still participate in SURE for 2008. It also allows potentially higher SURE payments than producers otherwise would have received. Thus, while not an ad hoc disaster program, the ARRA provision is a one-year modification of this new and permanent agriculture disaster program.

CBO estimates that these provisions would cost about $674 million. About $100-$150 million of this amount would be for the cost of higher crop insurance subsidies, and $500-$600 million would be for higher SURE program benefits.

Regarding the origins of SURE, Congress has provided ad hoc disaster assistance to farmers and ranchers experiencing significant weather-related production losses in virtually every crop year between 1988 and 2007. The 2008 farm bill (P.L. 110-246) authorized a new $3.8 billion trust fund to cover the cost of making agricultural disaster assistance available over a four-year period (FY2008-FY2011) through an array of new programs. The largest of these programs is the SURE program for crop producers, which is designed to supplement payments made by two ongoing federal programs—the federal crop insurance program and the noninsured crop disaster assistance program (NAP).[12]

Although enrollment in crop insurance and NAP is a prerequisite for receiving a SURE payment, the enacted ARRA would allow crop producers who did not enroll in either program for 2008 to participate in the SURE program, as long as the producer pays a $100 administrative fee normally paid for the lowest level of crop insurance coverage or NAP assistance. The 2008 farm bill made a similar exception for those not enrolled in crop insurance or NAP for 2008, but the buy-in fee had to be paid by September 16, 2008. Under the ARRA, the producer would be required to pay the fee within 90 days of enactment of the conference agreement (by about May 18, 2009), and would have to commit to purchasing a crop insurance policy or NAP coverage for the next available crop year.

Additionally, the enacted law would allow all producers to receive potentially higher SURE payments than they otherwise would have received by altering the payment formula.

Aquaculture Grant

The enacted ARRA authorizes a new $50 million grant program for aquaculture producers to compensate them for their share of high feed prices in 2008. There is no feed cost support in the ARRA for producers other than aquaculture.

Feed costs for livestock, poultry, and aquaculture producers reached high levels in 2008, when the cost of soybean- and corn-based ingredients reached record levels. The costs of these particular ingredients have moderated recently given the general drop in commodity prices during the fall of 2008 and the global financial crisis.

Grants would be made by USDA to the states within 120 days of enactment, prorated by the amount of aquaculture feed used by each state in 2007. A recipient state must demonstrate to USDA that it will provide the grants to eligible recipients within 60 days of receiving the funds, and then file a report to USDA on how the assistance was provided within 30 days after disbursement.

Any aquaculture producer who receives a grant under this provision would be ineligible for disaster assistance under the 2008 farm bill-authorized Emergency Assistance for Livestock, Honey Bees, and Farm Raised Fish program (a livestock counterpart to the SURE program) that provides up to $50 million to compensate these producers for disaster losses not covered under other disaster programs.

Farm Loan Programs

The enacted ARRA includes $20 million in budget authority (loan subsidy) for the USDA Farm Service Agency (FSA) to support $173 million in direct farm operating loans. This is 80% less than the $850 million in loan authority that the Senate-passed bill would have provided for direct and guaranteed farm operating, farm ownership, and emergency loans. The House-passed version had no funding for farm loans (**Table 3**).

FSA lends to farmers and ranchers who are not able to obtain credit from commercial lenders. It makes direct loans and services them, and guarantees some loans made by commercial lenders to farmers. As such, it is often referred to as a "lender of last resort." FSA's regular annual budget for farm loans is usually about $150 million to support $3.5 billion in loans.[13]

The loans supported by the stimulus are targeted to direct farm operating loans because the demand for FSA direct loans is increasing much faster than the demand for guaranteed loans in the current financial environment.[14] The demand for direct farm operating loans (the loans farmers use to buy seed, fertilizer, and fuel to plant a crop), in particular, is up about 200% or more from this time last year, according to agency officials. Thus, FSA is expecting—and is already experiencing—significantly higher demand for its loans in FY2009. However, funding for these loans is nearly constant under both the continuing resolution and the Senate-reported agriculture appropriations bill for FY2009. Consequently, FSA was expecting to not have enough funding available for the increased demand for farm loans in FY2009. The stimulus funding will satisfy some, but likely not all, of this demand.

Table 3. Farm Loans in the American Recovery and Reinvestment Act of 2009: Budget and Loan Authority (dollars in millions)

FSA Farm Loan Program	American Recovery and Reinvestment Act of 2009							
	FY2008 (P.L. 110-161)		House		Senate		Enacted (P.L. 111-5)	
	Budget Authority	Loan Authority	Budget Authority	Loan Authority	Budget Authority	Loan Authority	Budget Authority	Loan Authority
Farm ownership loans								
Direct	9.9	222	—	—	17.2	300	—	—
Guaranteed	5.0	1,239	—	—	0.3	100	—	—
Farm operating loans								
Direct	73.0	575	—	—	23.6	200	20	173
Guaranteed (unsubsidized)	24.6	1,017	—	—	1.3	50	—	—
Guaranteed (interest assistance)	36.0	270	—	—	0.0	0	—	—
Emergency loans	0[a]	0[a]	—	—	28.4	200	—	—
Subtotal, loan sub-sidies and authorities	**148.5**	**3,324**	**0**	**0**	**70.9**	**850**	**20**	**173**
Salaries and expenses	**309.1**	—	—	—	—	—	—	—
Subtotal, FSA Farm Loan Program	**457.6**	**3,324**	**0**	**0**	**70.9**	**850**	**20**	**173**

Source: CRS compilation from H.R. 1, and S.Rept. 111-3. Amounts for FY2008 are from S.Rept. 110-426 (S. 3289).

Notes: *Budget authority* reflects the cost of making loans, such as interest subsidies and projected non-repayment of loans. Loan authority reflects the amount of loans that the agency may make or guarantee.

a. No new money has been appropriated for several years given availability of carryover funds. At the end of 2008, the emergency loan program had about $84 million in unobligated loan authority.

While the global financial crisis has been slower to affect the balance sheets of farmers and agricultural lenders than the housing market, it has begun to take its toll.[15] Farm commodity prices have fallen since last summer with the rest of the market, reducing expectations for farm income in 2009. USDA expects net farm income to decline 20% in 2009,[16] and this may reduce some farmers' ability to repay loans later in the year. And while default rates have been historically low in recent years for all farm lenders, they appear to have bottomed out and begun to rise since the middle of 2008. For example, Farm Credit

System nonperforming loans more than tripled (albeit from historically low levels) in 2008, rising from 0.43% to 1.5%,[17] a level not seen since the mid-1990s, when the system had finally recovered from the farm financial crisis of the 1980s (**Figure 3**). The Kansas City Federal Reserve Bank also notes a rise in agricultural loan delinquency in the first three quarters of 2008, from 1.08% to 1.23% (**Figure 4**).

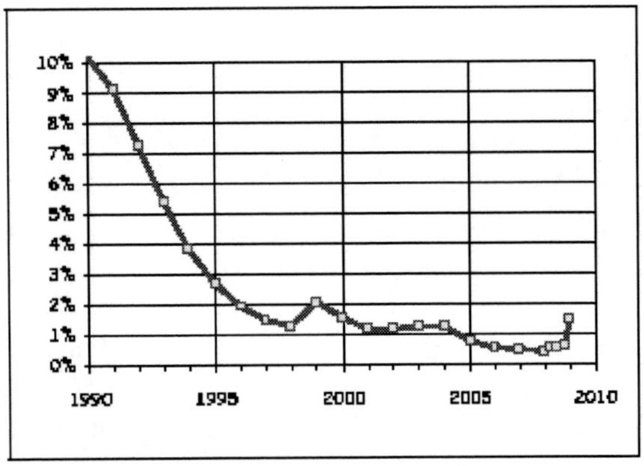

Source: CRS, using Farm Credit System data

Notes: Nonperforming loans include nonaccrual loans, accruing restructured loans, and accruing loans 90 days or more past due.

Figure 3. Farm Credit System Nonperforming Loans

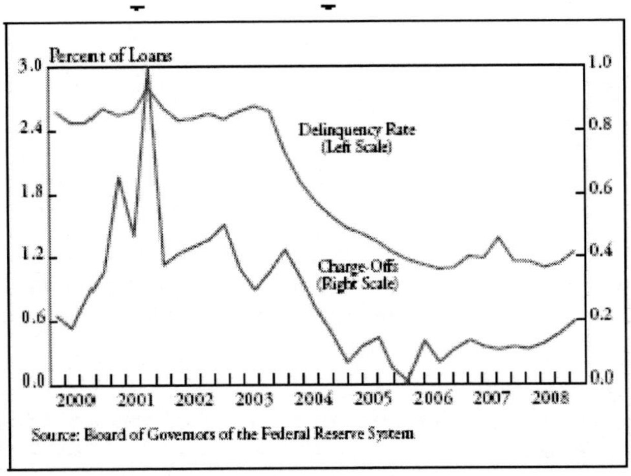

Source: Federal Reserve Bank of Kansas City, *Main Street Economist*, Issue I, February 2009.

Figure 4. Delinquency Rate and Charge-Offs on Agricultural Loans

On the lenders' side, agricultural lenders face challenges not unlike other banks in accessing capital. While some independent rural banks may be less affected than urban money center banks, the rural banks are not immune to the financial crisis. For example, the Farm Credit System (FCS)—a private entity but still a government-sponsored enterprise—is very dependent on the bond market and has felt the shock of the financial crisis in its ability to sell bonds to fund its loans. Although its bonds are still credit-worthy and able to be sold, the terms of FCS's recent bond sales reflect the change and turmoil in the financial markets.

As a consequence of the global financial crisis, agricultural lenders are expected to tighten credit standards this year—at a minimum requiring more documentation and oversight of loans, and possibly making or having less credit available to producers.[18]

Conservation Programs

USDA conservation programs administered by the Natural Resources Conservation Service (NRCS) receive $348 million in the enacted ARRA, which is $52 million less than the House bill and $26 million less than the Senate version.

Most is for watershed and flood prevention projects or easements. The conference agreement would provide $290 million for watershed and flood prevention divided in half, with $145 million for watershed and flood prevention construction projects and $145 million to purchase floodplain easements. For dam rehabilitation, the conference agreement would provide $50 million. It also provides $8 million in mandatory funding for technical assistance to implement 2008 farm bill programs.

The ARRA does not include language in the Senate bill that would have allowed state and local governments to once again receive benefits in the Conservation Reserve Program (CRP).

Watershed and Flood Prevention Operations

The enacted ARRA provides $145 million for Watershed and Flood Prevention Operations to fund financial and technical assistance to plan[19] and install projects on private lands (such as improvements for soil conservation and the utilization and disposal of water). The House version would have provided $30 million more than enacted, and the Senate-passed version $130 million more than enacted (**Table 1**). The watershed project costs are shared with local sponsors, states, and/or other public agencies. The new funds must be obligated by September 30, 2010; management and oversight expenses are not limited.

Regular appropriations for the program reached a high of $200 million in FY2002 and have declined steadily to $30 million in FY2008.[20] As appropriated funding decreased, the number of earmarks increased, reaching 85% of appropriated funding in FY2006.

Once a locally sponsored project completes required planning and environmental assessments, and signs an agreement with NRCS, it is considered an authorized watershed project and is eligible for funding. Currently there are over 300 unfunded authorized watershed projects totaling $1.28 billion. The $145 million in ARRA will alleviate only a small portion of the unfunded projects, but it will still provide greater funding than recent years' appropriations.

Floodplain Easements

The remaining $145 million of the total $290 million for watershed protection would be used to purchase floodplain easements under the authority of the Emergency Watershed Protection (EWP) program. The House-passed bill would have provided $30 million more than enacted, but the Senate bill did not have funding for the easement program.

Under a floodplain easement, a landowner voluntarily offers to sell NRCS a permanent conservation easement that provides NRCS with full authority to restore and enhance the floodplain's functions and values.

NRCS maintains a list of easement offers totaling over $250 million in nine states that meet basic eligibility criteria. The conference committee report directs NRCS to conduct open enrollment nationwide and prioritize projects based on cost-effectiveness in providing the greatest public safety, flood protection, economic, and environmental benefit.[21]

Watershed Rehabilitation Program

The enacted ARRA provides $50 million to NRCS for the Watershed Rehabilitation Program, the same as the House-passed bill but $15 million less than the Senate-passed bill.

NRCS provides technical and financial assistance to watershed project sponsors to rehabilitate aging dams. In FY2007, 775 watershed dams previously built with NRCS assistance reached the end of their designated life span. By 2015, USDA estimates this number will exceed 4,300. If a dam should fail, a serious threat would be posed to the health and safety of those living downstream.

The 2008 farm bill authorizes $100 million of one-time mandatory funding for the program in FY2009. The program was appropriated $20 million in discretionary funds in FY2008. According to NRCS, 28 states requested $42 million for 95 projects for FY2009, including 37 new projects and assessments of 102 dams.[22] The level funding in ARRA combined with annual appropriations and mandatory funding would cover the proposed projects as well as dam assessments. However, mandatory program funding in FY2009 is not guaranteed given limitations placed on spending in recent appropriations acts (including limitations in the Senate-reported FY2009 agriculture appropriations bill).[23] The number of dams reaching the end of their designed life span will only increase in future years.

Use of CCC for Farm Bill Administration

The enacted ARRA allows mandatory funds of the Commodity Credit Corporation (CCC) to be used for administrative expenses and technical assistance in the 2008 farm bill (Section 103). Similar language was in the Senate-passed bill, but clarifying language was added. The House bill did not include this section.

Since 1996, statute has prohibited or limited the use of CCC funds for certain administrative and information management activities. The provision would benefit conservation programs, because it states the allowance is not for Title I (farm commodity) programs. CBO estimates the cost of this provision at a total of $8 million for FY2009-FY2010 (the same as the Senate-passed bill for FY2009-FY2010, except that the Senate bill also applied to FY2011-FY2019 at an additional cost of $26 million).

Conservation Reserve Program (CRP)

The enacted ARRA does not have a provision that was in the Senate bill to allow a state, local government, political subdivision, or agency of the government to receive Conservation Reserve Program (CRP) payments.

Prior to the 2008 farm bill, state and local government entities (including public schools) were eligible to receive CRP payments, but Section 1603 of the 2008 farm bill, in amending payment limits, prohibited these public entities from receiving farm commodity subsidies and conservation program benefits. The Senate stimulus bills would have exempted CRP alone from this farm bill limitation and allowed state and local government entities to again receive CRP benefits.

USDA Facilities Infrastructure

The enacted ARRA has three provisions totaling $250 million that fund infrastructure maintenance or development within USDA, $4 million less than the Senate bill and $248 million less than the House bill. Some of the infrastructure outlays will remain at the USDA headquarters in Washington, DC, and some will be distributed by USDA to the department's research facilities throughout the country.

The conference agreement includes $176 million for Agricultural Research Service facilities maintenance and $24 million for USDA headquarters facilities improvements. When combined, this $200 million is the same as the Senate-passed amount for these types of facilities repairs, although the Senate bill would have given the Secretary discretion as to how it would be allocated. Comparing it to the House-passed bill, the $176 million for ARS facilities in the enacted law is $33 million less than in the House bill, and the $24 million for headquarters improvements is $20 million less than the House bill.

The conference agreement also includes $50 million for "maintaining and modernizing the information technology system" of the Farm Service Agency (FSA). This amount is $4 million less than the Senate-passed amount and $195 million less than the House version.

These projects are an ongoing need and have been difficult to fund in prior regular appropriations bills because of competing funding priorities and their relatively high cost given other choices. Funding them may be stimulative insofar as they require contracts with private construction companies for durable facilities repairs or purchases of computer equipment. They are intended to improve the ability of USDA to continue to serve its farmer clients, efficiently and safely house its employees, and continue to conduct its research mission.

Farm Service Agency Information Technology

The enacted ARRA provides $50 million to the Farm Service Agency (FSA) for maintaining and modernizing its information technology (computer) systems. The Senate-passed bill would have allowed $54 million and the House-passed bill considerably more, $245 million.

The enacted amount may allow USDA to address only the "stabilization" of the existing, outdated USDA mainframe system in FY2009. Stabilization for FY2010 and modernization plans through FY2011 will need future appropriations of about $340 million according to USDA's plans, some of which would have been funded in the House-passed bill.

For many years, FSA has had problems with an outdated mainframe computer system. FSA is the agency that administers the farm commodity subsidy programs. Its service to farmers—particularly through its network of county offices where enrollment and verification occurs—has been jeopardized by computer malfunctions. At one time in 2007, the computer system would fail daily or county offices would be rationed in the amount of time they would be allowed to use or access their computers because of overloading the system. Data processing requirements are increasing with each farm bill, and the 2008 farm bill's new Average Crop Revenue Election (ACRE) and adjusted gross income limits are expected to further stress the antiquated computer system. For many years, FSA has sought increased funding for computers, and to some extent partial funding has been appropriated through annual appropriations bills, but the computer problems have continued.

Following the 2007 computer system failures, USDA developed a "stabilization and modernization" plan in consultation with industry experts. The stabilization plan is meant to shore up the current computer system while upgrades are implemented and prepare it for migration to the new system. The modernization plan (called MIDAS, "modernize and innovate the delivery of agricultural systems") would replace antiquated mainframe hardware that relies on the outdated COBOL computer language with a modern Web-based system.

In August 2008, FSA estimated that the stabilization plan needed $87 million in additional funding through its duration of FY2010. For the modernization plan, the development and initial implementation of MIDAS was estimated to cost $305 million over a three-year period (FY2009- FY2011).[24] In August 2008, the Bush Administration made a supplemental FY2009 budget request for $172 million for FSA computers, including $51 million for stabilization, $66 million for MIDAS costs in FY2009, and $55 million for costs to implement the 2008 farm bill.

Based on figures in USDA's stabilization and modernization plan, the $245 million in House- passed H.R. 1 would have funded the $87 million stabilization plan through FY2010 and the estimated costs of MIDAS in FY2009-FY2010 (about half of MIDAS implementation costs). The enacted $50 million will address only the FY2009 stabilization requirements.

Agricultural Research Service Facilities Maintenance

The Agricultural Research Service (ARS) is USDA's in-house science agency that conducts long-term basic and applied research on subjects of national and regional importance. Its annual budget consists of about $1 billion for salaries and expenses for personnel to conduct experiments and maintain facilities, and a much smaller amount for the construction of new facilities. Over time, the maintenance of various USDA-owned facilities has lagged.

The enacted ARRA provides $176 million for work on critical deferred maintenance projects. ARS has identified $315 million worth of deferred maintenance projects at its facilities all over the country. The House committee report stated that the $209 million in the House-passed bill would fully fund the list of "critical" maintenance needs (footnote 9). Presumably, the maintenance program would require contracts with local construction companies to perform the work.

USDA Headquarters Repair and Improvements

The enacted ARRA provides $24 million for construction, repair, and improvement projects at USDA's headquarters complex in Washington, D.C. The conference report states that the funding is for "priority maintenance, repair, and modernization investments in USDA's headquarters buildings and facilities" (footnote 21) on Independence Avenue in

Washington, DC. The House committee report used similar language, citing "long-delayed modernization and security improvements" (footnote 9).

Office of Inspector General

The enacted ARRA provides $22.5 million of additional funding for the USDA Office of Inspector General (OIG), part of supplemental funding for OIG's throughout the government. The purpose of the funding is to allow for additional oversight and audit activities related to the spending in the stimulus package. The funding remains available until the end of FY2013. Both the House and Senate versions of the bill would have provided basically the same amount, although the duration in the Senate bill was only through FY2011. In FY2008, the USDA Office of Inspector General received $79 million. If the supplemental funding is divided equally over five fiscal years, it represents about a 6% increase for the USDA OIG.

Trade Adjustment Assistance for Farmers

The enacted ARRA temporarily amends the Trade Adjustment Assistance for Farmers (TAAF) program and authorizes funding through December 31, 2010 (Sections 1881-1887). TAAF's objective is to assist agricultural producers who have experienced a decline in prices of a commodity that they produce caused in large part by increased imports. Support has been available in the form of cash payments and technical assistance. Eligible producers of raw and natural agricultural commodities (crops, livestock, farm-raised aquatic products, and seafood that competes with aquaculture products), including fishermen, must follow a two-part process to qualify for TAAF benefits. The enacted changes make it easier for producers to qualify for assistance. But instead of automatically receiving cash payments under a formula, a producer now only becomes eligible for financial assistance upon completing training intended to help him become more competitive in producing the same or another commodity. Such assistance is to be used to implement a business adjustment plan.[25]

Competitive Research Grants

The enacted ARRA does not contain any money for competitive research grants at USDA, unlike the Senate-passed bill, which included $50 million of such funding. The Senate bill would have supplemented competitive research grants to universities under the Agricultural and Food Research Initiative (AFRI). The supplemental grants would have been limited to research on "renewable fuels and emerging agricultural production technologies," both areas that the Senate committee believed would have stimulated future economic activity. The House bill did not include any such funding.

Ban on Inspection of "Downer" Cattle

A provision in the Senate stimulus measure, deleted by House-Senate conferees, raised an issue of longstanding priority for many animal activists—what they view as mistreatment of animals at livestock markets and slaughterhouses. In particular, these activists have sought legislation for years to ban "downers" or nonambulatory animals from being used for food and/or to require that they be humanely euthanized, as an incentive for better treatment. Some food safety advocates also have supported such measures as a means of keeping diseased animals out of the food supply. Most animal producers have opposed these bills as misguided; they argue, among other things, that their industry has largely eliminated this problem.

Section 104 of the Senate bill would have permanently prohibited the use of federal funds to pass any nonambulatory disabled cattle for use as human food through USDA inspection, regardless of the reason or time the animal became nonambulatory. (The provision did not have a budgetary score.) Because cattle must pass USDA inspection before they can be processed into human food, such a provision would have removed an economic incentive to slaughter downers.

This provision, which was not in the House-passed version of the stimulus package, generally would have written into statute what USDA has promulgated through regulatory action. Specifically, USDA's meat inspection regulations define nonambulatory disabled livestock as those "that cannot rise from a recumbent position or that cannot walk, including, but not limited to, those with broken appendages, severed tendons or ligaments, nerve paralysis, fractured vertebral column, or metabolic condition." These regulations were adopted several years ago primarily to ensure that any cow affected with bovine spongiform encephalopathy (BSE, or "mad cow disease") does not enter the food supply. However, the Senate language would have exempted from the ban cattle under 500 pounds or less than five months old—essentially, veal calves.[26]

End Notes

[1] Congressional Budget Office, "Estimated Cost of the Conference Agreement for H.R. 1, the American Recovery and Reinvestment Act of 2009," February 13, 2009, at http://www.cbo.gov/ftpdocs/99xx/doc9989/hr1conference.pdf.

[2] Congressional Budget Office, "Estimated Economic Impacts of a Stimulus Package," February 11, 2009, at http://www.cbo.gov/ftpdocs/99xx/doc9987/Gregg_Year-by-Year_Stimulus.pdf.

[3] See CRS Report RL34730, *The Emergency Economic Stabilization Act and Recent Financial Turmoil: Issues and Analysis*, by Baird Webel and Edward V. Murphy.

[4] See CRS Report R40107, *The Role of Public Works Infrastructure in Economic Stimulus*, coordinated by Claudia Copeland.

[5] See CRS Report R40104, *Economic Stimulus: Issues and Policies*, by Jane G. Gravelle, Thomas L. Hungerford, and Marc Labonte.

[6] Congressional Budget Office, "Estimated Budgetary Impact of H.R. 1 as Passed by the House," January 30, 2009, at http://www.cbo.gov/ftpdocs/99xx/doc9976/hr1aspassed.pdf.

[7] Congressional Budget Office, "Summary of Estimated Cost of H.R. 1 as Passed by the Senate," February 11, 2009, at http://www.cbo.gov/ftpdocs/99xx/doc9984/hr1senatepassed.pdf.

[8] Language in the 2008 farm bill (P.L. 110-246) authorizing broadband loans and loan guarantees excludes rural towns of 20,000 or more and prohibits eligibility to providers serving more than 20% of the market.

[9] House Appropriations Committee, *Report to accompany The American Recovery and Reinvestment Act of 2009*, 111th Cong., January 26, 2009, H.Rept. 111-4.

[10] CRS Report R40149, *Infrastructure Programs: What's Different About Broadband?*, by Charles B. Goldfarb and Lennard G. Kruger; CRS Report RL30719, *Broadband Internet Access and the Digital Divide: Federal Assistance Programs*, by Lennard G. Kruger and Angele A. Gilroy.

[11] The FY2009 Senate-reported agriculture appropriations bill (S. 3289, S.Rept. 110-426) would reduce the biorefinery program's $75 million of mandatory funding to $72 million, and the Rural Energy for America program's $55 million to zero. See also the section "limits on mandatory program spending" in CRS Report R40000, *Agriculture and Related Agencies: FY2009 Appropriations*, coordinated by Jim Monke.

[12] For more information on the mechanics of these programs, see CRS Report RS21212, *Agricultural Disaster Assistance*, by Ralph M. Chite.

[13] FSA also receives over $300 million annually for salaries and expenses to administer the program.

[14] Direct loans are made by the government to the least credit-worthy borrowers who still qualify for loans. The government also guarantees commercial loans made to farmers who otherwise could not get a commercial loan without the government guarantee of repayment. Guaranteed loans are a way of graduating borrowers out of direct loans.

[15] Jason Henderson, "Agricultural Credit Standards Tighten," *The Main Street Economist* (Federal Bank of Kansas City), vol. IV, issue I, February 2009, at http://www.kansascityfed.org/ RegionalAffairs/ MainStreet/MSE_0109.pdf.

[16] For more information on farm income expectations, see CRS Report R40 152, *U.S. Farm Income*, by Randy Schnepf.

[17] Federal Farm Credit Banks Funding Corporation, "Farm Credit System Reports Net Income of $2.916 Billion For 2008," press release, February 19, 2009, at http://www.farmcredit-ffcb.com/farmcredit/serve/public/ pressre/finin/report .pdf?assetId=127528.

[18] For more information on agricultural credit, see CRS Report RS21977, *Agricultural Credit: Institutions and Issues*, by Jim Monke.

[19] Watershed projects are planned and approved under the authority of the Watershed Protection and Flood Prevention Act of 1954 (P.L. 83-566), and the Flood Control Act of 1944 (P.L. 78-534).

[20] Much of the decline was at the request of the Bush Administration.

[21] U.S. Congress, *Conference report to accompany H.R. 1, The American Recovery and Reinvestment Act of 2009*, February 12, 2009, H.Rept. 111-16.

[22] USDA, NRCS, *Watershed Rehabilitation Progress Report—2008*, September 2008, http://www.nrcs.usda.gov/ programs/WSRehab/Nat_Rehab_Report_08.pdf.

[23] The FY2009 Senate-reported agriculture appropriations bill (S. 3289, S.Rept. 110-426) would reduce the $100 million mandatory funding in FY2009 to zero for the Watershed Rehabilitation program. See also the section "limits on mandatory program spending" in CRS Report R40000, *Agriculture and Related Agencies: FY2009 Appropriations*, coordinated by Jim Monke.

[24] USDA Farm Service Agency, "Farm Service Agency Modernization and IT Stabilization Plan: Response to Congressional Directives," August 2008. FSA expects to fund an additional estimated $20 million in annual operations costs for MIDAS from its annual salaries and expenses appropriation.

[25] For more information, see CRS Report R40206, *Trade Adjustment Assistance for Farmers*, by Remy Jurenas.

[26] These regulations are described in more detail in CRS Report RS22819, *Nonambulatory Livestock and the Humane Methods of Slaughter Act*, by Geoffrey S. Becker.

In: American Recovery and Reinvestment Act: History... ISBN: 978-1-61668-355-9
Editor: Paul G. Tellis

Chapter 4

AMERICAN RECOVERY AND REINVESTMENT ACT OF 2009 (ARRA, P.L. 111-5): TITLE V, MEDICAID PROVISION*

Cliff Binder, Evelyne P. Baumrucker, April Grady and Elicia J. Herz
Health Care Financing

SUMMARY

The economy officially was considered in a recession in December 2008, but many forecasters had long recognized the downturn and some believed this economic contraction would be more severe than other post-World War II slowdowns. A combination of factors combined to present policymakers with difficult decisions on how best to stimulate the economy. Troubling instability in the housing and financial services sectors, weak auto manufacturing demand, and high energy costs earlier in 2008 had slowed growth dramatically and forced millions into unemployment. With declining tax revenue and increasing costs to provide unemployment and other benefits to unemployed workers, states were implementing measures to rein in spending, including restricting Medicaid eligibility and services.

Congress considered legislation aimed at stimulating economic activity in selected industrial sectors to save existing and create new jobs, reduce taxes, invest in future technologies, and fund infrastructure improvements. In addition to reducing some taxes and funding infrastructure projects, ARRA provisions were designed to provide: temporary support to families and individuals by increasing unemployment compensation benefits; financial assistance for individuals to maintain their health coverage under provisions in the Consolidated Omnibus Budget Reconciliation Act of 1985 (COBRA); temporary increases in Medicaid matching rates; and increases in disproportionate share hospital allotments.

---

* This is an edited, reformatted and augmented version of a CRS Report for Congress publication dated March 2009.

The House approved the American Recovery and Reinvestment Act of 2009 (H.R. 1) on January 28, 2009. The Senate passed an amendment (S.Amdt. 570) as a replacement for the House- approved version of ARRA on February 10, 2009. ARRA was referred to a joint House and Senate conference committee. The joint Senate and House Conference Committee reached agreement, and ARRA was passed by the House and Senate on February 13, 2009. President Obama signed ARRA (P.L. 111-5) into law on February 17, 2009. This chapter is a summary of ARRA's Medicaid provisions.

For more information on the Medicaid provisions included in House and Senate versions of ARRA, see CRS Report R40 158, *Medicaid Provisions in the House and Senate American Recovery and Reinvestment Act of 2009 (ARRA, H.R. 1, S.Amdt. 570)*, coordinated by Cliff Binder.

BACKGROUND

In December 2008, the National Bureau of Economic Research (NBER) announced that the economy was in a recession and that the recession had begun a year earlier in December 2007.[1] However, some economists and forecasters had been concerned that a combination of factors might make this economic contraction much worse than other post-war slowdowns.[2] At first, economic instability seemed limited to the housing sector as housing values decreased in many markets, forcing some subprime and highly leveraged home owners into foreclosure. The problems that began in housing, quickly spread to banking and financial services and were compounded earlier in 2008 by spikes in energy prices. The solvency of automobile manufacturers rapidly deteriorated, possibly due in part to tight credit policies, rising unemployment, and high fuel costs. National unemployment rose steadily throughout 2008 reaching 7.2% in December.[3]

Due to slower economic activity caused by the recession, many states also faced large tax revenue decreases, forcing them to reduce Medicaid eligibility and spending, just when the demand for additional public sector health care was expanding to fill the gap left when unemployed individuals no longer could afford employer-based health insurance for their families. Although by themselves the problems in housing, financial services, manufacturing, and energy sectors might not have forced the economy into recession, taken together these problems had contributed to the emergence of a recession and, if the underlying fundamentals have changed as some forecasters suspect, perhaps a prolonged, global economic slow down that could have widespread impact on living standards here and abroad.

In response, policymakers quickly moved to prevent the instability in housing and financial services from spilling over into the broader economy. Looking to the future, members of Congress and the Obama Administration sought additional mechanisms to stimulate economic activity. Various approaches were considered to ensure that an economic stimulus package could reach many different segments of the economy, provide a sustained economic boost, and wide spread job growth. Some economic stimulus proposals included infrastructure spending, revenue sharing with states, middle class tax cuts, business tax cuts, unemployment benefits, and food stamps. On January 22, 2009 the House Committee on Energy and Commerce marked-up selected health components and approved a stimulus bill, the American Recovery and Reinvestment Act of 2009 (ARRA, H.R. 1). The full House amended and approved H.R. 1 on January 28, 2009.

Similar legislation to H.R. 1 was introduced in the Senate (ARRA, S. 350) and referred to the Committee on Finance, among others, where provisions were approved on January 27.[4] An amendment in the nature of a substitute (S.Amdt. 570) was offered as a substitute for H.R. 1 and was approved by the full Senate on February 10, 2009. The Senate version of ARRA was referred to a joint Senate and House conference committee. The conference committee reached agreement and referred ARRA to the House and Senate, where it was passed on February 13, 2009. President Obama signed ARRA (P.L. 111-5) on February 17, 2009. This chapter is a summary the Medicaid provisions in P.L. 111-5. For more information on the Medicaid provisions included in House and Senate versions of ARRA, see CRS Report R40158, *Medicaid Provisions in the House and Senate American Recovery and Reinvestment Act of 2009 (ARRA, H.R. 1, S.Amdt. 570)*, coordinated by Cliff Binder.

ARRA, P.L. 111-5: Medicaid Provisions

Table 1 displays a summary of the Medicaid provisions in P.L. 111-5. Although **Table 1** displays 14 Medicaid provisions, ARRA included only eight provisions.

Table 1. Summary: Medicaid Provisions in P.L. 111-5

Medicaid Provision	Senate	House	P.L. 111-5
Temporary FMAP Increase	X	X	X
Coverage of the Unemployed Under Medicaid		X	
Medicaid Regulation Moratoria		X	X
DSH Allotment Increases	X	X	X
Medicare Liability for Special Disability Workload	X		
Medicaid Indian Protections[a]			X
Premiums and Cost Sharing	X	X	X
Eligibility Determinations	X	X	X
Estate Recovery	X	X	X
Medicaid Consultation with Indian Health Programs	X	X	X
Medicaid Managed Care for Indians	X		X
TMA Extension	X	X	X
QI Extension	X		X
OIG Oversight and Implementation Funding[b]	X		X
GAO Study on Recession Effects on Medicaid	X		X
Nursing Home Prompt Pay Requirement[c]	X		X
Selected Medicaid Provisions Sunset	X		

Source: CRS Analysis of ARRA Conference Agreement and Senate and House versions.

a. There were five Indian protection components included in one provision in P.L. 111-5. Some of these components were presented as separate provisions in the Senate or House versions, so they are shown separately on **Table 1**.

b. Funding ($5M) for implementation of the Temporary FMAP Increase was added to the OIG Oversight provision.

c. Nursing home prompt pay requirements were a separate provision in the Senate Bill, but were integrated into the FMAP provision in P.L. 111-5 and expanded to apply to all providers.

Some provisions presented separately in the Senate or House Bills were aggregated under one provision in P.L. 111-5. For instance, there was one provision for Medicaid Indian protections in the Conference Agreement that included five provisions from the earlier House and Senate versions (premiums and cost sharing, eligibility determinations, estate recovery, consultation with Indian health programs, and managed care protections). In addition, the nursing home prompt payment provision from the Senate bill was integrated into the Temporary Federal Medical Assistance Percentage (FMAP) Increase provision in P.L. 111-5, but $5 million in funding to implement the FMAP provision was added to ARRA in the Conference Agreement under the OIG Oversight provision from the Senate Bill. Thus, there are eight Medicaid provisions included in Title V of the Conference Agreement. An additional provision providing funding for Medicaid Health Information Technology (HIT) is in Title IV of P.L. 111-5.

The Congressional Budget Office (CBO) estimated that ARRA's Medicaid provisions (under TITLE V—State Fiscal Relief) would increase federal expenditures by $33.96 billion in FY2009 and $89.74 billion from FY2009 to FY2013, although one provision, a temporary FMAP increase, accounts for $87.2 billion of the five-year increase.

Sec. 5001. Temporary Increase of Medicaid FMAP

The federal medical assistance percentage (FMAP) is the rate at which states are reimbursed for most Medicaid service expenditures. It is based on a formula that provides higher reimbursement to states with lower per capita incomes relative to the national average (and vice versa); it has a statutory minimum of 50% and maximum of 83%. Exceptions to the FMAP formula have been made for certain states and situations. For example, the District of Columbia's Medicaid FMAP is set in statute at 70%, and the territories have FMAPs set at 50% (they are also subject to federal spending caps). Under the Jobs and Growth Tax Relief Reconciliation Act of 2003 (P.L. 108-27), all states received a temporary increase in Medicaid FMAPs for the last two quarters of FY2003 and the first three quarters of FY2004 as part of a fiscal relief package. In addition to Medicaid, the FMAP is used in determining the federal share of certain other programs (e.g., foster care and adoption assistance under Title IV-E of the Social Security Act) and serves as the basis for calculating an enhanced FMAP that applies to the State Children's Health Insurance Program. (For more details, see CRS Report RL32950, *Medicaid: The Federal Medical Assistance Percentage (FMAP)*, by April Grady.)

During a recession adjustment period that begins with the first quarter of FY2009 and runs through the first quarter of FY2011, the provision holds all states harmless from any decline in their regular FMAPs, provides all states with an across-the-board increase of 6.2 percentage points, and provides qualifying states with an additional unemployment-related increase. It allows each territory to choose between an FMAP increase of 6.2 percentage points along with a 15% increase in its spending cap, or its regular FMAP along with a 30% increase in its spending cap.

States are evaluated on a quarterly basis for the unemployment-related FMAP increase, which equals a percentage reduction in the state share. The percentage reduction is applied to the state share after the hold harmless increase and after one-half of the 6.2 percentage point increase (i.e., 3.1 percentage points). For example, after applying the across-the-board increase, a state with a regular FMAP of 50% would have an FMAP of 56.20%. If the state share (after the hold harmless and one-half of the across-the-board increase) were further reduced by 5.5%, the state would receive an additional FMAP increase of 2.58 percentage points (46.9 state share * 0.055 reduction in state share = 2.58). The state's total FMAP increase would be 8.78 points (6.2 + 2.58 = 8.78), providing an FMAP of 58.78%.

The unemployment-related FMAP increase is based on a state's unemployment rate in the most recent 3-month period for which data are available (except for the first two and last two quarters of the recession adjustment period, for which the 3-month period is specified) compared to its lowest unemployment rate in any 3-month period beginning on or after January 1, 2006. The criteria are as follows:

- unemployment rate increase of at least 1.5 but less than 2.5 percentage points = 5.5% reduction in state share;
- unemployment rate increase of at least 2.5 but less than 3.5 percentage points = 8.5% reduction in state share;
- unemployment rate increase of at least 3.5 percentage points = 11.5% reduction in state share.

If a state qualifies for the unemployment-related FMAP increase and later has a *decrease* in its unemployment rate, its percentage reduction in state share could not decrease until the fourth quarter of FY2010 (for most states, this corresponds with the first quarter of SFY2011). If a state qualifies for the unemployment-related FMAP increase and later has an *increase* in its unemployment rate, its percentage reduction in state share could increase.

The full amount of the temporary FMAP increase only applies to Medicaid, excluding disproportionate share hospital payments and expenditures for individuals who are eligible for Medicaid because of an increase in a state's income eligibility standards above what was in effect on July 1, 2008. A portion of the temporary FMAP increase (hold harmless plus across-the-board) applies to Title IV-E foster care and adoption assistance. To receive the increase, states are:[5]

- required to maintain their Medicaid eligibility standards, methodologies, and procedures as in effect on July 1, 2008;[6]
- prohibited from receiving the increase if they are not in compliance with requirements for prompt payment of health care providers under Medicaid, and required to report to the Secretary of HHS on their compliance;[7]
- prohibited from depositing or crediting the additional federal funds paid as a result of the increase to any reserve or rainy day fund;
- required to ensure that local governments do not pay a larger percentage of the state's nonfederal Medicaid expenditures than otherwise would have been required on September 30, 2008; and
- required to submit a report to the Secretary regarding how the additional federal funds paid as a result of the temporary FMAP increase were expended.

CBO estimated that ARRA's FMAP provision would increase federal spending by $87.2 billon over the five-year period from FY2009-2013.

Sec. 5002. Temporary Increase in DSH Allotments during Recession

Medicaid law requires states to make Medicaid payment adjustments for hospitals that serve a disproportionate number of low-income patients with special needs. Payments to these hospitals that serve a large number of low-income individuals, disproportionate share hospital (DSH) payments, are specifically defined in Medicaid law, including, aggregate annual state-specific limits on federal financial participation and hospital-specific limits on DSH payments.

Under those hospital specific limits, a hospital's DSH payments may not exceed the costs incurred by that hospital in furnishing services during the year to Medicaid beneficiaries and the uninsured, less other Medicaid payments made to the hospital, and payments made by uninsured patients ("uncompensated care costs"). States are required to provide an annual report to the Secretary describing the payment adjustments made to each DSH.

This provision increases states' FY2009 annual DSH allotments by 2.5% above the allotment they would have received in FY2009 (in FY2009, DSH allotments increased by 4% over FY2008 allotment levels). In addition, states' DSH allotments in FY2010 would be equal to the FY2009 DSH allotment (with the adjustment) increased by 2.5%. After FY2010, states' annual DSH allotments will return to 100% of the annual DSH allotments as determined under current law. Under this provision, if states' annual DSH allotments grew at a greater rate than what they would have received without the 2.5% adjustment, then states will receive the higher DSH allotments without the recession adjustment. CBO estimated that the temporary increase in DSH allotments would increase federal expenditures by $228 million in FY2009 and $456 million for the period FY2009-FY2013.

Sec. 5003. Extension of Moratoria on Certain Medicaid Final Regulations

In 2007 and 2008, the Centers for Medicare and Medicaid Services (CMS), issued seven Medicaid regulations that generated controversy during the 110th Congress. To address concerns with the impact of the regulations, several laws passed during the 110th Congress imposed moratoriums on six of the Medicaid regulations until April 1, 2009 (excluding a rule on outpatient hospital facility and clinic services). CBO estimated that the extension of the Medicaid moratoria would increase federal expenditures by $105 million in FY2009, but would not have an additional spending increase beyond FY2009. The seven Medicaid regulations issued during the most recent Congress covered the following areas:

Graduate Medical Education

Most states make Medicaid payments to help cover the costs of training new doctors in teaching programs. The proposed rule would eliminate federal reimbursement for graduate medical education and change how Medicaid upper payment limits for hospital services are calculated. For more information on GME, see CRS Report RS22842, *Medicaid and Graduate Medical Education*, by Elicia J. Herz and Sibyl Tilson.

Cost Limit on Public Providers

Intergovernmental transfers (IGTs) are used by some states to finance the non-federal share of Medicaid costs. Certain IGTs are specifically allowed for funding the state share of program costs. Some states have instituted programs where the state shares of Medicaid spending is paid by hospitals or nursing homes that are public providers, but not units of government, or are units of government, but the state share is returned to the provider sometimes through Medicaid payments. Both a proposed and final regulation were issued, however, a federal court held that the rule had been improperly promulgated and remanded the rule back to CMS for further action. This regulation would clarify the types of IGTs allowable for financing a portion of Medicaid costs, impose a limit on Medicaid reimbursement for government-owned hospitals and other institutional providers, and require certain providers to retain all Medicaid reimbursement. For more information on cost limits on public providers, see CRS Report RS22848, *Medicaid Regulation of Governmental Providers*, by Elicia J. Herz.

Rehabilitative Services

Medicaid rehabilitative services include a full range of treatments designed to reduce physical or mental disability or restore eligible beneficiaries to their best possible functional levels. There has been enough misunderstanding about when Medicaid pays for and what constitutes rehabilitative services that both the executive and legislative branches have addressed this benefit repeatedly. The proposed rule defines the scope of the rehabilitation benefit and identifies services that could be claimed under Medicaid. For more information on rehabilitative services, see CRS Report RL34432, *Medicaid Rehabilitation Services*, by Cliff Binder.

Case Management

Case management services assist Medicaid beneficiaries in obtaining needed medical and related services. Targeted case management (TCM) refers to case management for specific beneficiary groups or for individuals residing in state-designated geographic areas. There has been considerable ambiguity about what services are covered and what is legitimately considered TCM. The case management regulation addresses a provision of the Deficit Reduction Act of 2005 (DRA; P.L. 109-171) that clarifies and narrows the case management definition and directs the Secretary of HHS to issue regulations to guide states' claims for federal matching funds for case management. For more information on case management and targeted case management, see CRS Report RL34426, *Medicaid Targeted Case Management (TCM) Benefits*, by Cliff Binder.

School-Based Services

As a condition of accepting funds under the Individuals with Disabilities Education Act (P.L. 108- 446, IDEA), public schools must provide special education and related services necessary for children with disabilities to benefit from public education. States can finance only a portion of these costs with federal IDEA funds. Medicaid may cover IDEA required health-related services for enrolled children as well as related administrative activities. According to federal investigations and congressional hearings, Medicaid payment to schools have sometimes been improper. To address these problems, CMS issued a regulation that would restrict federal Medicaid payments for school-based administrative activities (e.g., outreach, service coordination, referrals performed by school employees or contractors), and certain transportation services (e.g., from home to school and back for certain school-age children). For more information on school-based services under Medicaid, see CRS Report RS22397, *Medicaid and Schools*, by Elicia J. Herz.

Provider Taxes

States use provider-specific taxes to help finance their share of the Medicaid program. Under these funding methods, states collect funds (through taxes or other means) from providers and pay the money back to those providers as Medicaid payments, and claim the federal matching share of those payments. Once the state share has been subtracted, the federal matching funds may be used to raise provider payment rates, to fund other portions of the Medicaid program, or for other non-Medicaid purposes. Provider taxes must be consistent with federal laws and regulations, which may have been ambiguous or changing. CMS issued a provider tax regulation to address these issues. For more information on Medicaid provider taxes, see CRS Report RS22843, *Medicaid Provider Taxes*, by Elicia J. Herz.

Outpatient Hospital Services

Under Medicaid, outpatient hospital (OPH) services are a mandatory benefit for most beneficiaries. OPH services include preventive, diagnostic, therapeutic, rehabilitative, or palliative services provided under the direction of a physician or a dentist in the hospital. States use a number of different reimbursement methods for different types of services provided in OPH departments and clinics. CMS issued a regulation that would limit the definition and scope of Medicaid-covered OPH services. For more information on outpatient hospital services, see CRS Report RS22852, *Medicaid and Outpatient Hospital Services*, by Elicia J. Herz and Sibyl Tilson.

P.L. 111-5 extends the existing moratoria on the final regulations on case management services, provider taxes, and school-based administrative and transportation services beyond April 1, 2009, when these moratoria expire, to July 1, 2009. In addition, this provision prohibits the Secretary of HHS from taking any action until after June 30, 2009 (through regulation, regulatory guidance, use of federal payment audit procedures, or other administrative action, policy, or practice, including Medical Assistance Manual transmittal or state Medicaid director letter) to implement the final regulation on OPH facility services (published November 7, 2008 and effective on December 8, 2008).

Under current law, moratoria on further administrative action until April 1, 2009 for the regulations on cost limits for public providers, graduate medical education, and rehabilitative services. A Sense of the Congress clause in this ARRA provision indicates that the Secretary of HHS should not promulgate final regulations for rehabilitative services, cost limits on public providers, or graduate medical education. For more information on Medicaid regulations, see CRS Report RL34764, *Medicaid Regulatory Issues*, by Elicia J. Herz and Vanessa K. Burrows.

Sec. 5004. Extension of Transitional Medical Assistance (TMA)

States are required to continue Medicaid benefits for certain low-income families who would otherwise lose coverage because of changes in their income. This continuation is called transitional medical assistance (TMA). Federal law permanently requires four months of TMA for families who lose Medicaid eligibility due to increased child or spousal support collections, as well as those who lose eligibility due to an increase in earned income or hours of employment. However, Congress expanded work-related TMA under Section 1925 of the Social Security Act in 1988, requiring states to provide at least six, and up to 12, months of coverage. Since 2001, these work-related TMA requirements have been funded by a series of short-term extensions, most recently through June 30, 2009. (For more details, see CRS Report RL31698, *Transitional Medical Assistance (TMA) Under Medicaid*, by April Grady.)

The provision extends work-related TMA under Section 1925 through December 31, 2010. States can opt to treat any reference to a 6-month period (or 6 months) as a reference to a 12-month period (or 12 months) for purposes of the initial eligibility period for work-related TMA, in which case the additional 6-month extension does not apply. States can opt to waive the requirement that a family have received Medicaid in at least three of the last six months in order to qualify. Under the TMA provision, states are required to collect and submit to the Secretary of Health and Human Services (and make publicly available) information on average monthly enrollment and participation rates for adults and children under work-related TMA, and on the number and percentage of children who become ineligible for work-related TMA and whose eligibility is continued under another Medicaid eligibility category or who are enrolled in the Children's Health Insurance Program (CHIP).

CBO estimated that the TMA provision would increase federal spending by $1.3 billion over the five-year period from FY2009-2013.

Sec. 5005. Extension of the Qualifying Individual (QI) Program

Certain low-income individuals who are aged or have disabilities, as defined under the Supplemental Security Income (SSI) program, and who are eligible for Medicare are also eligible to have their Medicare Part B premiums paid for by Medicaid under the Medicare Savings Program (MSP). Eligible groups include Qualified Medicare Beneficiaries (QMBs), Specified Low-Income Medicare Beneficiaries (SLMBs), and Qualifying Individuals (QI-1s). QMBs have incomes no greater than 100% of the federal poverty level (FPL) and assets no greater than $4,000 for an individual and $6,000 for a couple. SLMBs meet QMB criteria, except that their incomes are greater than 100% of FPL but do not exceed 120% FPL. QI-1 s meet the QMB criteria, except that their income is between 120% and 135% of poverty and they are not otherwise eligible for Medicaid. The QI-1 program is currently slated to terminate December 2009. This provision of P.L. 111-5 extends authorization for the QI-1 program through December 2010.

In general, Medicaid payments are shared between federal and state governments according to a matching formula. Unlike the QMB and SLMB programs, federal spending under the QI-1 program is subject to annual limits. Expenditures under the QI-1 program are paid 100% by the federal government (from the Part B trust fund) up to a state's allocation level. States are required to cover only the number of people which would bring their annual spending on these population groups to their allocation levels. For the period beginning on January 1, 2009, and ending on September 30, 2009, the total allocation amount was $350 million. For the period beginning on October 1, 2009 and ending on December 31, 2009, the total allocation is $150 million. This provision allocates $412.5 million for the period that begins January 1, 2010, and ends September 30, 2010; and allocates $150 million for the period that begins October 1, 2010 and ends on December 31, 2010.

Sec. 5006. Protections for Indians under Medicaid and CHIP

P.L. 111-5 combined a number of provisions presented separately or together as protections for Indians under Medicaid and the Children's Health Insurance Program (CHIP). Five provisions from either the Senate or House Bills were combined in P.L. 111-5, including premiums and cost sharing, eligibility determinations, estate recovery, managed care protections, and consultation with Indian health providers (IHP). CBO estimated that the Indian protections under Medicaid and CHIP would increase federal expenditures by $6 million in FY2009 and by $54 million from FY2009-FY2013.

Premiums and Cost-Sharing

Under Medicaid, premiums and enrollment fees generally are prohibited for most beneficiaries. Nominal amounts specified in federal regulations may be imposed on selected groups (e.g., certain families qualifying for transitional Medicaid, medically needy). Service-related cost- sharing (e.g., coinsurance, copayments) is prohibited for selected groups (e.g., children under 18, pregnant women) and selected benefits (e.g., hospice care, emergency services, family planning services and supplies). For most other groups and services, states may impose nominal cost- sharing amounts specified in federal regulations at state option. Premiums and cost-sharing may exceed nominal amounts for selected groups (e.g., workers with disabilities and individuals covered under Section 1115 waivers). The Deficit Reduction Act of 2005 (DRA; P.L. 109-171) added a Medicaid state option for alternative premiums and cost-sharing for certain subgroups. Applicable maximum amounts vary by income level. Special rules apply to prescription drugs and non-emergency services provided in hospital emergency rooms.

P.L. 111-5 specifies that no premiums, service-related cost-sharing or similar charges can be imposed on Indians who receive Medicaid services directly from the Indian Health Service (IHS), an Indian tribe (IT), a tribal organization (TO), an urban Indian organization (UIO), or through referral under the contract health service. Medicaid payments due to such providers for services rendered to a Medicaid-eligible Indian cannot be reduced by the amount of such cost-sharing that would otherwise apply to such an Indian. The new law also adds Indians receiving services through Indian entities to the list of individuals exempt from paying premiums or cost-sharing under the DRA option. The effective date of this provision is July 1, 2009.

Treatment of Certain Property from Resources for Medicaid and CHIP Eligibility

The federal Medicaid statute identifies more than 50 eligibility pathways. For some pathways, asset tests are required and for other pathways, such tests are optional. When asset tests apply, some pathways give states flexibility to define specific assets to be counted and which can be disregarded. For other pathways, primarily for people qualifying on the basis of a disability or who are elderly, asset tests are required. States generally follow asset guidelines specified in the Supplemental Security Income (SSI) Program. Medicaid also defines the rules for counting certain assets. Under SSI law, several types of assets related to certain Indian-related lands held in trust by the U.S., certain other Indian held lands, and certain distributions (including land or an interest in land) received by certain Alaskan Natives or their descendants are excluded. There is no similar provision in prior CHIP law.

P.L. 111-5 prohibits consideration of four different classes of property from resources in determining Medicaid eligibility of an Indian. These include certain properties held in trust, certain other properties within the boundaries of a prior reservation, certain ownership interests related to natural resources, and certain other ownership interests not otherwise specified that have unique religious, traditional or cultural significance that support subsistence or a traditional lifestyle. The new law also applies this provision to CHIP in the same manner that it applies to Medicaid. The effective date of this provision is July 1, 2009.

Continuation of Protections of Certain Indian Property from Medicaid Estate Recovery

Under Medicaid, all states are required to recover property and assets of deceased Medicaid beneficiaries for outstanding services provided by Medicaid. At a minimum, states must seek recovery for certain services provided, including nursing home care, services provided by an intermediate care facility for the mentally retarded or other similar medical institutions, and Medicaid payments to Medicare for cost-sharing related benefits. States may grant an exemption if the recovery would place an undue hardship on the estate. The Secretary of HHS specifies the standards for a state hardship waiver for Medicaid estate recovery purposes.

P.L. 111-5 stipulates that certain income, resources, and property remain exempt from Medicaid estate recovery, if they were exempted under Section 191 7(b)(3) of the Social Security Act (allowing the Secretary to specify standards for a state hardship waiver of asset criteria) under instructions regarding Indian tribes and Alaskan Native Villages as of April 1, 2003. The new law also allows the Secretary to provide for additional estate recovery exemptions for Indians under Medicaid. The effective date of this provision is July 1, 2009.

Rules Applicable under Medicaid and CHIP to Managed Care Entities with Respect to Indian Enrollees and Indian Health Care Providers and Indian Managed Care Entities

Under Title XIX, Section 1932(a)(2)(C) stipulates the rules regarding Indian enrollment in Medicaid managed care. A state may not require an Indian (as defined in Section 4(c) of the Indian Health Care Improvement Act or IHCIA) to enroll in a managed care entity unless the entity is one of the following (and only if such entity is participating under the plan): (1) the IHS, (2) an IHP operated by an Indian tribe or tribal organization pursuant to a contract, grant, cooperative agreement, or compact with the IHS pursuant to the Indian Self-Determination Act, or (3) an urban IHP operated by a UIO pursuant to a grant or contract with the IHS pursuant to Title V of the IHCIA.

In general under Medicaid, Federally Qualified Health Centers (FQHCs) are paid on a per visit basis, using a prospective payment system that takes into account costs incurred and changes in the scope of services provided. Per visit payment rates are also adjusted annually by the Medicare Economic Index applicable to primary care services. When an FQHC is a participating provider with a Medicaid managed care entity (MCE), the state must make supplemental payments to the center in an amount equal to any difference between the rate paid by the MCE and the per visit amount determined under the prospective payment system.

P.L. 111-5 requires that Indians enrolled in a non-Indian MCE with an IHP or UIO participating as a primary care provider be allowed to choose such an IHP or UIO as their primary care provider when (1) the Indian is otherwise eligible to receive services from such a provider and (2) the IHP or UIO has the capacity to provide primary care services to that Indian. Contracts between the state and such MCEs must include this requirement, and Medicaid payments to these entities would be conditional on meeting this requirement.

Under P.L. 111-5, Medicaid managed care contracts with MCEs and Primary Care Case Management (PCCMs) companies will be required to meet certain conditions to receive Medicaid payments, including:

- MCEs and PCCMs must demonstrate that the number of participating Indian health care providers is sufficient to ensure timely access to covered Medicaid managed care services for eligible Indian enrollees, and
- MCEs and PCCMs must agree to pay both participating and non-participating IHPs for services rendered to Indians at rates equal to the rates negotiated between these organizations and the provider involved, or, if such a rate has not been negotiated, at a rate that is not less than the level and amount of payment which the MCE or PCCM would make for services rendered by a participating non-Indian health care provider.

In addition, P.L. 111-5 specifies that MCEs and PCCMs must agree to make prompt payment, as required under Medicaid rules for all providers, to Indian health care providers, and states would be prohibited from waiving requirements relating to assurance that payments are consistent with efficiency, economy, and quality.

Further, ARRA applies special payment provisions to certain Indian health care providers that are FQHCs. For non-participating Indian FQHCs that provide covered Medicaid managed care services to Indian MCE enrollees, the MCE must pay a rate equal to the payment that would apply to a participating non-Indian FQHC. When payments to such participating and nonparticipating providers by an MCE for services rendered to an Indian enrollee with the MCE are less than the rate under the state plan, the state must pay such providers the difference between the rate and the MCE payment. Likewise, if the amount paid to a non-FQHC Indian provider (whether or not the provider participates with the MCE) is less than the rate that applies under the state plan, the state must pay the difference between the applicable rate and the amount paid by MCEs. Under this provision, Indian Medicaid MCEs are permitted to restrict enrollment to Indians and to members of specific tribes in the same manner as IHPs may restrict the delivery of services to such Indians and tribal members.

Finally, P.L. 111-5 applies specific sections affecting Medicaid to the CHIP program, including (1) Section 1932(a)(2)(C) regarding enrollment of Indians in Medicaid managed care (e.g., states cannot require Indians to enroll in a MCE unless the entity is the IHS, certain IHPs operated by tribes or tribal organizations, or certain urban IHPs operated by Urban

Indian Organizations (UIOs), and (2) the new provisions described above. The effective date of this provision is July 1, 2009.

Consultation on Medicaid, CHIP and Other Health Care Programs Funded under the Social Security Act Involving Indian Health Programs and Urban Indian Organizations

There are no provisions in prior Medicaid or CHIP law regarding a Tribal Technical Advisory Group (TTAG) within CMS, the federal agency that oversees the Medicare, Medicaid and CHIP programs.

P.L. 111-5 requires the Secretary to maintain within CMS a TTAG, previously established in accordance with requirements of a charter dated September 30, 2003. ARRA also requires that the TTAG include a representative of a national urban Indian Health organization and the IHS. The representative of a national urban Indian Health organization will be exempt from the Federal Advisory Committee Act for certain meetings with federal officials. The P.L. 111-5 also requires certain states to establish a process for obtaining advice on a regular, on-going basis from designees of IHPs and UIOs regarding Medicaid law and its direct effects on those entities. Applicable states include those in which one or more IHPs or UIOs provide health care services. This process must include seeking advice prior to submission of state Medicaid plan amendments, waiver requests or proposed demonstrations likely to directly affect Indians, IHPs or UIOs. This process may include appointment of an advisory panel and of a designee of IHPs and UIOs to the Medicaid medical care advisory committee advising the state on its state Medicaid plan. The provision also applies this new language to CHIP in the same manner in which it applies to Medicaid. Finally, the new law prohibits construing these amendments as superseding existing advisory committees, working groups, guidance or other advisory procedures established by the Secretary or any state with respect to the provision of health care to Indians. The effective date of this provision is July 1, 2009.

Sec. 5007. Funding for Oversight and Implementation

Oversight

Under this provision, the Health and Human Services Office of the Inspector General (HHS OIG) will receive $31.25 million to ensure proper expenditure of federal Medicaid funds. These funds will be appropriated from any money in the Treasury not otherwise appropriated and are available throughout the recession period (defined as October 1, 2008-December 31, 2010). Amounts appropriated under this provision are available until September 30, 2012, without further appropriation, and are in addition to any other amounts appropriated or made available to HHS OIG..

Implementation of Increased FMAP

This provision also includes a $5 million appropriation for FY2009 to be used by the Health and Human Services Secretary to implement the temporary increased FMAP provision described in the Conference Agreement under Sec. 5001. The implementation funding is available to the Secretary until the end of FY2011 (September 30, 2011).

CBO estimated that the funding for the HHS Secretary for implementation of the temporary FMAP increase provision would increase federal expenditures by $5 million in FY2009, with no financial impact beyond FY2009. CBO also estimated that federal expenditures would increase by $31 million in FY2009 for the additional funds provided under this provision for the OIG to monitor the increased recession spending. There would be no financial impact beyond FY2009 for the OIG funding.

Sec. 5008. GA0 Study and Report Regarding State Needs during Periods of National Economic Downturn

Under this provision of P.L. 111-5, the Comptroller General of the United States and the Government Accountability Office (GAO), are to study the current (on the date of enactment of the legislation) economic recession as well as previous national economic downturns since 1974. GAO is required to develop recommendations to address states' needs during economic recessions, including the past and projected effects of temporary increases in FMAP during these recessions. By April 1, 2011, GAO is required to submit a report to appropriate congressional committees that is to include the following:

- Recommendations for modifying the national economic downturn assistance formula for temporary Medicaid FMAP adjustments (a "countercyclical FMAP," as described in GAO report number, GAO-07-97), to improve the effectiveness of the countercyclical FMAP for addressing states' needs during national economic downturns. The report should address:
  - what improvements are needed to identify factors to begin and end the application of a countercyclical FMAP;
  - how to adjust the amount of a countercyclical FMAP to account for state and regional variations; and
  - how a countercyclical FMAP could be adjusted to better account for actual Medicaid costs incurred by states during economic recessions.
- Analysis of the impact on states of recessions, including declines in private health insurance benefits coverage; declines in state revenues; and maintenance and growth of caseloads under Medicaid, CHIP, or any other publically funded programs that provide health benefits coverage to state residents.
- Identification of and recommendations for addressing the effects on states of any other specific economic indicators GAO determines appropriate.

End Notes

[1] See CRS Report R40052, *What is a Recession and Who Decided When It Started*?, by Brian W. Cashell, for more information on how business cycles are defined and measured.

[2] For more information see CRS Report R40104, *Economic Stimulus: Issues and Policies*, by Jane G. Gravelle, Thomas L. Hungerford, and Marc Labonte.

[3] U.S. Bureau of Labor Statistics, Press Release dated January 9, 2009. Available on the internet at http://www.bls.gov/ for more information (accessed January 22, 2009).

[4] See the Senate Committee on Finance website for S.Amdt. 98

http://finance %20Recovery%20and%20Reinvestment%20Act.pdf.

[5] For the requirements related to rainy day funds and local governments' share of nonfederal expenditures, the law was written such that states would be denied the across-the-board and unemployment-related FMAP increases (and territories would be denied cap increases) if they are out of compliance; however, they would not be denied the hold harmless FMAP increase. In contrast, for the requirements related to maintenance of eligibility and prompt payment, states would be denied all of the temporary FMAP increases (including hold harmless) if they are out of compliance.

[6] States that have restricted their eligibility standards, procedures, or methodologies can reinstate them in any quarter to begin receiving the temporary FMAP increase. In addition, those that reinstate them prior to July 1, 2009, can receive the increase for the first three quarters of FY2009.

[7] More specifically, the temporary FMAP increase would not be available for any claim received by the state from a health care practitioner subject to prompt pay requirements for such days during any period in which the state has failed to pay claims in accordance with those requirements.

In: American Recovery and Reinvestment Act: History... ISBN: 978-1-61668-355-9
Editor: Paul G. Tellis

Chapter 5

AMERICAN RECOVERY AND REINVESTMENT ACT OF 2009 (P.L. 111-5): SUMMARY AND LEGISLATIVE HISTORY*

Clinton T. Brass, Carol Hardy Vincent, Pamela J. Jackson, Jennifer E. Lake, Karen Spar and Robert Keith
Government Organization and Management, Natural Resources Policy
Domestic Security, Social Policy, American National Government

SUMMARY

President Barack Obama signed H.R. 1, the American Recovery and Reinvestment Act (ARRA) of 2009, into law on February 17, 2009, as P.L. 111-5 (123 Stat. 115-521). The act is seen as one of the most significant legislative responses made thus far to the current economic turmoil. This chapter provides a summary and legislative history of ARRA and identifies other resources that provide additional information regarding its content and implementation.

ARRA is a relatively lengthy and complex act, amounting to just over 400 pages (in slip law form) and melding together hundreds of billions of dollars in discretionary spending, mandatory spending, and revenue provisions encompassing the jurisdiction of several House and Senate committees. The act consists of two major divisions. Division A (Appropriations Provisions) includes supplemental appropriations for FY2009 (and later fiscal years) covering by separate titles all 12 of the regular appropriations acts, as well as four additional titles dealing with health information technology, a state fiscal stabilization fund, accountability and transparency, and general provisions. Division B (Tax, Unemployment, Health, State Fiscal Relief, and Other Provisions) consists of seven separate titles. Division A includes the discretionary spending provisions, but some significant substantive provisions as well; Division B includes the mandatory spending and revenue provisions, with some exceptions.

---

* This is an edited, reformatted and augmented version of a CRS Report for Congress publication dated April 2009.

ARRA provides almost $800 billion through extensive discretionary spending, mandatory spending, and revenue provisions that the Administration estimates will save or create some 3.5 million jobs. Funding is provided for existing and some new programs in the 15 Cabinet-level departments and 11 independent agencies. Some of the funds are distributed to states, localities, other entities, and individuals through a combination of formula and competitive grants and direct assistance. In addition to new spending and tax provisions, new policies are created regarding unemployment compensation, health insurance, health information technology, broadband communications, and energy, among others.

Numerous oversight, accountability, and transparency provisions are contained in the act. They include various reporting requirements and funding for offices of inspector general, the Government Accountability Office, and a newly established Recovery Accountability and Transparency Board.

With regard to its specific impact on the budget, the act is estimated by the Congressional Budget Office to increase the deficit by $787.2 billion over the 11-year period covering FY2009-FY2019. The estimated deficit impact reflects spending increases of $575.3 billion (in outlays) and revenue reductions of $211.8 billion. The total spending increases consist of $311.2 billion in discretionary new budget authority (yielding $308.3 billion in outlays) and $269.5 billion in mandatory new budget authority (yielding $267.0 billion in outlays).

About 21% of total outlays ($120.1 billion) under ARRA are estimated to occur by the end of FY2009. By the end of FY2010, 59% of total outlays ($339.4 billion) are expected to occur, and by the end of FY2011, 81% of total outlays ($465.6 billion) are expected to occur. Revenue reductions occur more quickly, with reductions of $64.8 billion in FY2009 and $180.1 billion in FY2010, offset somewhat in later years by modest revenue increases.

President Barack Obama signed H.R. 1, the American Recovery and Reinvestment Act (ARRA) of 2009, into law on February 17, 2009, as P.L. 111-5 (123 Stat. 115-521). This chapter provides a summary and legislative history of ARRA and identifies other resources that provide additional information regarding its content and implementation.

BACKGROUND

For well over a year, the economy of the United States has been in significant distress. The Business Cycle Dating Committee of the National Bureau of Economic Research, whose determinations regarding the timing of recessions are widely accepted, announced on December 1, 2008, that the economy had entered recession in December 2007.[1] The recession deepened substantially during 2008 and there is considerable uncertainty regarding how long it will last.

The federal government has responded (and continues to respond) to the economic situation by employing many different tools, encompassing both monetary policy, conducted by the Federal Reserve, and budgetary policy, under existing law and new legislation. With respect to new legislative activity, Congress and the President initially responded with the Economic Stimulus Act of 2008, which President George W. Bush signed into law on February 13, 2008 (P.L. 110- 185). The act, which consisted mainly of "recovery rebates" for individuals and investment incentives for businesses, reduced revenues by $152 billion in FY2008 and $16 billion in FY2009.[2]

As the economic crisis worsened, Congress and the President enacted additional legislative responses, including extensions of unemployment compensation and the Emergency Economic Stabilization Act (EESA) of 2008 (Division A of P.L. 110-343), which President Bush signed into law on October 3, 2008.[3] The EESA created the Troubled Assets Relief Program (TARP), which authorized the Treasury Department to buy up to $700 billion in troubled assets from financial institutions.[4]

Toward the end of the 110th Congress, congressional attention turned to action on a supplemental appropriations act as another legislative response to the economic situation. The House passed such a measure, the Job Creation and Unemployment Relief Act of 2008 (H.R. 7110), on September 26, 2008. President Bush threatened to veto the bill, and the Senate did not consider comparable legislation before the session ended.

In 2009, at the beginning of the 111th Congress, President Barack Obama and congressional leaders made action on an economic recovery bill a top priority. The legislative vehicle, it was determined, would be a supplemental appropriations act with substantial mandatory spending and revenue components.

The supplemental appropriations act addressing economic recovery is one of three major appropriations acts for FY2009 considered by Congress thus far (at least one additional appropriations act, providing supplemental appropriations for overseas military operations and other purposes, is expected to be considered during the session). On September 30, 2008, the Consolidated Security, Disaster Assistance, and Continuing Appropriations Act, 2009 (P.L. 110- 329) was signed into law by President George W. Bush. Three of the 12 regular appropriations acts for FY2009 were funded by the act for the full fiscal year, and continuing appropriations were provided through March 6, 2009, for activities covered by the nine remaining appropriations acts.[5] Consideration of an omnibus appropriations measure addressing the status of the nine remaining appropriations acts for the remainder of FY2009 was postponed until action on the supplemental appropriations measure pertaining to economic recovery (ARRA) was completed. Following the enactment of ARRA on February 17, 2009, the House and Senate then finished consideration of the FY2009 regular appropriations acts in the form of a single, omnibus measure; President Obama signed H.R. 1105, the Omnibus Appropriations Act, 2009, into law on March 11, 2009, as P.L. 111-8.[6]

LEGISLATIVE HISTORY

House and Senate action on ARRA occurred relatively quickly in the opening weeks of the 111th Congress, from the introduction of legislation in late January 2009 to its enactment into law several weeks later. The House passed the bill on January 28, the Senate passed it on February 10, and both chambers agreed to the conference report on February 13.

Earlier Action on Stimulus Legislation

The quick action on ARRA in 2009 was aided in part by the development of similar legislation (although much smaller in scope) during the previous session, as the 110th Congress drew to a close.

On September 26, 2008, the House passed an economic stimulus bill, the Job Creation and Unemployment Relief Act of 2008 (H.R. 7110), by a vote of 264-158. On the same day, the Senate rejected a motion to proceed to the consideration of a similar measure, the Economic Recovery Act, 2008 (S. 3604), by a vote of 52-42 (under a unanimous consent agreement, the motion required 60 votes to be successful). These measures, which originated in the Appropriations Committees, entailed appropriations of roughly $60 billion for such matters as infrastructure projects, energy development, unemployment compensation, job training, and Medicaid and food stamps assistance.

During two lame-duck sessions, held between November 17 and December 11, 2008, an expanded economic stimulus proposal, the Economic Recovery Act of 2008 (S. 3689), was introduced by Senate Majority Leader Harry Reid and Senator Robert C. Byrd, the then-chairman of the Appropriations Committee. According to the sponsors, the measure provided $100.3 billion in infrastructure spending and a wide range of other stimulus and recovery activities. The 110th Congress ended without the House or Senate taking any further action on economic stimulus legislation.

Action on ARRA in 2009

The American Recovery and Reinvestment Act of 2009, H.R. 1, was introduced on January 26, 2009, by Representative David Obey, chairman of the House Appropriations Committee. The measure was an amalgamation of separate legislative components approved by several House committees:

- H.R. 598, the American Recovery and Reinvestment Tax Act of 2009, a measure containing revenue and other provisions, was marked up by the House Ways and Means Committee on January 22 and approved by voice vote (H.Rept. 111-8, Part I (January 27, 2009) and Part II (January 28, 2009)). The bill also was referred to the House Energy and Commerce Committee, Education and Labor Committee, Financial Services Committee, and Science and Technology Committee, but they were discharged from further consideration of the measure;
- H.R. 629, the Energy and Commerce Recovery and Reinvestment Act, a measure containing broadband communications, energy, and health-related provisions, was marked up by the House Energy and Commerce Committee on January 22 and approved by unanimous consent (H.Rept. 111-7, Part I; January 26, 2009). The bill also was referred to the House Education and Labor Committee, Science and Technology Committee, and Ways and Means Committee, but they were discharged from further consideration of the measure; and
- H.R. 679, the American Recovery and Reinvestment Act of 2009, a measure containing the appropriations-related provisions, was marked up by the House Appropriations Committee on January 21 and approved by a vote of 35-22 (H.Rept. 111-4; January 26, 2009).

The House began consideration of H.R. 1 on January 27, under the terms of a special rule, H.Res. 88, reported by the House Rules Committee. In initial action, the House agreed to a "question of consideration," by a vote of 224-199; this action was necessitated by a requirement in Clause 1 0(c)(3) of House Rule XXI (the "PAYGO Rule") that the question of consideration be approved before consideration can occur on a measure including a waiver of the PAYGO rule.[7]

On January 28, the House adopted a second special rule, H.Res. 92, which made several changes to the underlying bill automatically under a "self-executing" feature and prohibited the offering of further amendments except for 11 specified ones.[8] According to the Rules Committee, the self- executing amendment changed provisions in the bill dealing with state certification of the intent to request and use funds provided in the act; the COPS program; the renovation and preservation of buildings on Historically Black Colleges and Universities campuses; funding for the National Mall Revitalization Fund; and family planning. The House then accepted eight of the 11 amendments (offered by Representatives Oberstar, Markey, Shuster, Nadler, Waters, Kissell, Platts, and Teague) and rejected the other three (offered by Representatives Neugebauer, Flake, and Camp), as well as a motion to recommit with instructions offered by Representative Jerry Lewis, the ranking member of the Appropriations Committee, by a vote of 159-270.

The House passed H.R. 1 on January 28, as amended, by a vote of 244-188.

Senate consideration of H.R. 1 occurred over eight days, beginning on February 2 and concluding on February 10 (the Senate was not in session on Sunday, February 8). The first amendment offered to the bill, Reid (for Inouye and Baucus) amendment 98, was a substitute amendment incorporating legislative proposals that had been approved previously by the Senate Appropriations Committee and the Senate Finance Committee:

- S. 336, a measure containing the appropriations-related provisions, was marked up by the Senate Appropriations Committee on January 27 and approved by a vote of 21-9 (S.Rept. 111-3; January 27, 2009); and
- S. 350, the American Recovery and Reinvestment Act of 2009, a measure containing the revenue provisions, was marked up by the Senate Finance Committee on January 27 and approved by a vote of 14-9 (no written report).

The Senate considered 42 amendments, adopting 22 and rejecting 13; seven were withdrawn. The final resolution of issues was addressed by Reid (for Collins and Nelson (NE)) amendment 570, which was a substitute for the entire bill. On February 9, cloture was invoked on the amendment, by a vote of 6 1-36. The next day, following a successful waiver of enforcement procedures under the Congressional Budget Act of 1974, by a vote of 6 1-37, Senate amendment 570 was adopted.

The Senate passed H.R. 1 on February 10, as amended, by a vote of 6 1-37.

On February 10, the House and Senate agreed to hold a conference on the bill and appointed conferees (Senators Inouye, Baucus, Reid, Cochran, and Grassley for the Senate, and Representatives Obey, Rangel, Waxman, Lewis (CA), and Camp for the House). The House agreed that day, by a vote of 403-0, to a motion to instruct conferees, offered by Representative Lewis (CA). The motion moved

> to instruct the managers on the part of the House that they shall not record their approval of the final conference agreement (as such term is used in clause 12(a)(4) of rule XXII of the Rules of the House of Representatives) unless the text of such agreement has been available to

> the managers in an electronic, searchable, and downloadable form for at least 48 hours prior to the time described in such clause.[9]

While the House-passed and Senate-passed versions of H.R. 1 were roughly comparable in scope, significant differences in the two versions had to be resolved. According to the Congressional Budget Office, the House-passed version would have increased the deficit by nearly $820 billion over FY2009-FY2019 (reflecting $359 billion in discretionary outlay increases, $279 billion in mandatory outlay increases, and $182 billion in revenue reduction), while the Senate-passed version would have increased the deficit by about $838 billion for the same period (reflecting $287 billion in discretionary outlay increases, $259 billion in mandatory outlay increases, and $292 billion in revenue reduction). Thus, the net increase in the deficit over FY2009-FY2019 was about $19 billion higher in the Senate version compared to the House version:

> The Senate-passed version includes $72 billion less in spending from discretionary appropriations in Division A (mostly the result of less funding for education, including the proposed State Stabilization Fund) and about $20 billion less in direct spending in Division B. Those spending decreases would be more than offset by revenue reductions in Division B totaling about $110 billion (mostly because the Senate-passed version would raise the exemption amount allowed against an individual's income for the alternative minimum tax for tax year 2009).[10]

The conference report on H.R. 1 (H.Rept. 111-16) was filed on February 12. The conferees developed compromise levels between the House and Senate positions on each major component ($308 billion in discretionary outlay increases, $267 billion in mandatory outlay increases, and $211 in revenue reduction) in a way that lessened the overall impact of the bill on the deficit to $787 billion, well below the House and Senate levels (see **Table 1** in the next section).

On February 13, the House took up the conference report after agreeing to the question of consideration required by the PAYGO rule, by a vote of 232-195. Consideration of the conference report occurred pursuant to the terms of a special rule, H.Res. 168. Following the defeat of a motion to recommit with instructions offered by Representative Miller (MI), by a vote of 186- 244, the House agreed to the conference report, by a vote of 246-183.

Later on February 13, the Senate considered the conference report. By identical votes of 60-38, the Senate waived enforcement procedures under the Congressional Budget Act of 1974 and then agreed to the conference report.

President Obama signed H.R. 1 into law on February 17, 2009, as P.L. 111-5.[11]

OVERVIEW OF THE ACT

ARRA is a relatively lengthy and complex act, amounting to just over 400 pages (in slip law form) and melding together hundreds of billions of dollars in discretionary spending, mandatory spending, and revenue provisions encompassing the jurisdiction of several House and Senate committees. Discretionary spending is provided in, and controlled by, annual appropriations acts under the jurisdiction of the House and Senate Appropriations

Committees. Spending in this category typically funds the routine operations of federal agencies and many grant programs. Mandatory spending (sometimes referred to as direct spending) generally is provided in, and controlled by, substantive legislation under the jurisdiction of the various authorizing committees in the House and Senate. Mandatory spending, for the most part, funds entitlement programs such as Social Security, Medicare, and unemployment compensation.[12] Revenue laws are under the jurisdiction of the House Ways and Means Committee and the Senate Finance Committee.

ARRA provides almost $800 billion through extensive discretionary spending, mandatory spending, and revenue provisions that the Administration estimates will save or create some 3.5 million jobs. Funding is provided for existing and some new programs in the 15 Cabinet-level departments and 11 independent agencies. Some of the funds are distributed to states, localities, other entities, and individuals through a combination of formula and competitive grants and direct assistance. In addition to new spending and tax provisions, new policies are created regarding unemployment compensation, health insurance, health information technology, broadband communications, and energy, among others.

With regard to its specific impact on the budget, the act is expected to increase the deficit by $787.2 billion over the 11-year period covering FY2009-FY2019; the cost estimate prepared by the Congressional Budget Office (CBO) is presented in **Table 1**. The estimated deficit impact reflects spending increases of $575.3 billion (in outlays) and revenue reductions of $211.8 billion.[13]

The total spending increases consist of $311.2 billion in discretionary new budget authority (yielding $308.3 billion in outlays) and $269.5 billion in mandatory new budget authority (yielding $267.0 billion in outlays).[14]

Table 2 provides information on the rate at which spending under the act is expected to occur.

Table 1. Summary of the Budgetary Impact of the ARRA of 2009: FY2009-FY2019 (amounts in billions of dollars)

	2009	2010	2011	2012	2013	2014	2015	2016	2017	2018	2019	2009-2019
Discretionary Spending												
(Division A)												
Estimated Budget Authority	288.7	7.1	4.6	3.6	2.5	1.1	1.1	1.1	1.1	0.5	0.0	311.2
Estimated Outlays	34.8	110.7	76.3	38.1	22.9	12.8	7.0	3.1	1.6	0.8	0.1	308.3
Mandatory Spending												
(Division B)												
Estimated Budget Authority	90.3	107.6	49.0	7.6	7.3	15.1	4.7	-4.7	-4.1	-1.9	-1.4	269.5
Estimated Outlays	85.3	108.6	49.9	8.1	7.4	15.1	4.7	-4.7	-4.1	-1.9	-1.4	267.0
Revenues												
(Division B)												
Estimated Revenues	-64.8	-180.1	-8.2	10.0	2.7	5.5	7.1	5.8	5.1	5.0	0.1	-21 1.8
Net Impact on the Deficit												
Net Increase or Decrease (-)	184.9	399.4	134.4	36.1	27.6	22.4	4.7	-7.3	-7.5	-6.1	-1.4	787.2

Sources: Congressional Budget Office, *Letter to the Honorable Nancy Pelosi*, Table 1 (Summary of Estimated Cost of the Conference Agreement for H.R. 1, The American Recovery and Reinvestment Act of 2009, as Posted on the website of the House Committee on Rules), Feb. 13, 2009, available on the CBO website at http://www.cbo.gov/ ftpdocs/99xx/doc9989/hr 1 conference.pdf.

Notes: ARRA refers to the American Recovery and Reinvestment Act of 2009 (P.L. 111-5). The net impact on the deficit reflects estimated outlays and revenues.

Components may not sum to totals because of rounding. The totals for Division A include about $29 billion in mandatory spending increases and $0.1 billion in revenue reductions over FY2009-FY2019.

Table 2. Estimated Cumulative Outlay Impact of the ARRA of 2009: FY2009-FY2019 (amounts in billions of dollars)

	2009	2010	2011	2012	2013	2014	2015	2016	2017	2018	2019
Discretionary Spending (Division A)											
Cumulative Outlay Impact	34.8	145.5	221.8	259.9	282.8	295.6	302.6	305.7	307.3	308.1	308.3
Cumulative Outlay Impact as a Percentage of Total Division A Outlays	11.3%	47.2%	71.9%	84.3%	91.7%	95.9%	98.2%	99.2%	99.7%	99.9%	100.0%
Mandatory Spending (Division B)											
Cumulative Outlay Impact	85.3	193.9	243.8	251.9	259.3	274.4	279.1	274.4	270.3	268.4	267.0
Cumulative Outlay Impact as a Percentage of Total Division B Outlays	31.9%	72.6%	91.3%	94.3%	97.1%	102.8%	104.5%	102.8%	101.2%	100.5%	100.0%
Total Discretionary and Mandatory Spending											
Cumulative Outlay Impact	120.1	339.4	465.6	511.8	542.1	570.0	581.7	580.1	577.6	576.5	575.3
Cumulative Outlay Impact as a Percentage of Total Division A and Division B Outlays	20.9%	59.0%	80.9%	89.0%	94.2%	99.1%	101.1%	100.9%	100.4%	100.2%	100.0%

Sources: Prepared by the Congressional Research Service from data provided in: Congressional Budget Office, *Letter to the Honorable Nancy Pelosi*, Table 1 (Summary of Estimated Cost of the Conference Agreement for H.R. 1, The American Recovery and Reinvestment Act of 2009, as Posted on the website of the House Committee on Rules), Feb. 13, 2009, available on the CBO website at http://www.cbo.gov/ftpdocs/99xx/ doc9989/ hr1conference.pdf.

Notes: ARRA refers to the American Recovery and Reinvestment Act of 2009 (P.L. 1 1 1-5). Components may not sum to totals because of rounding. The totals for Division A include about $29 billion in mandatory spending increases and $0.1 billion in revenue reductions over FY2009-FY2019.

As **Table 2** shows, 20.9% of total outlays ($120.1 billion) are estimated to occur by the end of FY2009. By the end of FY2010, 59.0% of total outlays ($339.4 billion) are expected to occur, and by the end of FY2011, 80.9% of total outlays ($465.6 billion) are expected to occur. The cumulative rate of mandatory spending compared to discretionary spending over the first several fiscal years differs, with mandatory spending occurring more quickly. By the end of FY2011, for example, 91.3% of mandatory outlays ($243.8 billion) are expected to occur, compared to 71.9% of discretionary outlays ($221.8 billion).

Revenue reductions (as shown in **Table 1**) occur more quickly, with reductions of $64.8 billion in FY2009 and $180.1 billion in FY2010. The combined revenue reduction for these two years ($244.9 billion) exceeds the net revenue reduction of $211.8 billion over the 11-year period ending in FY2019; a modest revenue reduction occurs in FY2011, followed by modest revenue increases in all subsequent years.

CBO also prepared a year-by-year assessment of the macroeconomic effects of ARRA.[15]

With regard to its structure, the act consists of several opening sections (e.g., short title) and two major divisions. Division A (Appropriations Provisions) includes supplemental appropriations for FY2009 (and later fiscal years) covering all 12 of the parallel regular appropriations acts. The supplemental appropriations corresponding to each regular appropriations act are presented separately in Titles I-XII of the division. Four additional titles, dealing with health information technology, a state fiscal stabilization fund, accountability and transparency, and general provisions complete the division.

Division B (Tax, Unemployment, Health, State Fiscal Relief, and Other Provisions) consists of seven separate titles.

Division A includes the discretionary spending provisions, but some significant substantive provisions as well. Division B includes the mandatory spending and revenue provisions, with some exceptions. In addition, Division B includes two titles that are not budgetary in nature: Title VI (Broadband Technology Opportunities Program) and Title VII (Limits on Executive Compensation). In the summary sections that follow, related provisions are discussed together, regardless of the division in which they were placed.

Summary of Discretionary Spending Provisions

Division A of ARRA provides $311.20 billion in appropriations for a broad array of agencies, programs, and activities. The funds are provided in twelve titles corresponding with the twelve annual appropriations bills, and also an additional title for the State Fiscal Stabilization Fund. Not every agency typically funded through the annual appropriations bills received funding in ARRA. Moreover, the agencies that were funded received widely varying dollar amounts. In turn, these amounts constitute widely varying percentages of each agency's most recent annual appropriations (FY2009).

Table 3. ARRA of 2009: Contents Listing and Page References

			Conference Report		Congressional Record	
		P.L. 111-5	(H.Rept. 111-16)		(February 12, 2009)	
Section/ Division	**Content**	**(123 Stat. 115-521)**	**Legislative Text**	**Explanatory Statement**	**Legislative Text**	**Explanatory Statement**
Sec. 1	Short Title	123 Stat. 115	1	—	H1307	—
Sec. 2	Table of Contents	123 Stat. 115	1	—	H1307	—
Sec. 3	Purposes and Principles	123 Stat. 115	2	—	H1308	—
Sec. 4	References	123 Stat. 116	2	—	H1308	—
Sec. 5	Emergency Designations	123 Stat. 116	2	413	H1308	H1413
Division A	**Appropriations Provisions**	123 Stat. 116	3	413	H1308	H1413
Title I	Agriculture, Rural Development, FDA	123 Stat. 116	3	413	H1308	H1413
Title II	Commerce, Justice, Science	123 Stat. 127	14	417	H1310	H1414
Title III	Defense	123 Stat. 132	18	422	H1312	H1415
Title IV	Energy and Water Development	123 Stat. 134	20	423	H1312	H1416
Title V	Financial Services and General Government	123 Stat. 148	34	431	H1316	H1418

Table 3. (Continued)

			Conference Report		Congressional Record	
		P.L. 111-5	(H.Rept. 111-16)		(February 12, 2009)	
Section/ Division	**Content**	**(123 Stat. 115-521)**	**Legislative Text**	**Explanatory Statement**	**Legislative Text**	**Explanatory Statement**
Title VI	Homeland Security	123 Stat. 162	48	435	H1319	H1419
Title VII	Interior, Environment	123 Stat. 166	53	438	H1321	H1420
Title VIII	Labor-Health and Human Services-Education	123 Stat. 172	59	447	H1322	H1422
Title IX	Legislative Branch	123 Stat. 191	77	463	H1327	H1426
Title X	Military Construction and Veterans Affairs	123 Stat. 191	78	463	H1327	H1426
Title XI	State, Foreign Operations	123 Stat. 202	89	466	H1330	H1427
Title XII	Transportation, Housing and Urban Development	123 Stat. 203	90	469	H1330	H1428
Title XIII	Health Information Technology	123 Stat. 226	113	473	H1337	H1429
Title XIV	State Fiscal Stabilization Fund	123 Stat. 279	166	505	H1350	H1438
Title XV	Accountability and Transparency	123 Stat. 286	174	509	H1352	H1439
Title XVI	General Provisions—This Act	123 Stat. 302	190	511	H1357	H1439
Division B	**Tax, Unemployment, Health, State Fiscal Relief, and Other Provisions**	123 Stat. 306	193	514	H1357	H1440
Title I	Tax Provisions	123 Stat. 306	193	514	H1357	H1440
Title II	Assistance for Unemployed Workers and Struggling Families	123 Stat. 436	325	695	H1391	H1491
Title III	Premium Assistance for COBRA Benefits	123 Stat. 455	344	710	H1396	H1496
Title IV	Medicare and Medicaid Health Information Technology; Miscellaneous Medicare Provisions	123 Stat. 467	356	735	H1399	H1503
Title V	State Fiscal Relief	123 Stat. 496	386	756	H1406	H1509
Title VI	Broadband Technology Opportunities Program	123 Stat. 512	402	772	H1411	H1513
Title VII	Limits on Executive Compensation	123 Stat. 516	406	776	H1412	H1514

Sources: P.L. 111-5, slip law (Legislative Information System); conference report to accompany H.R. 1, H.Rept. 111-16, Feb. 12, 2009; and *Congressional Record* (daily ed.), vol. 155, no. 29, Feb. 12, 2009, pp. H 1307-H15 16.

Note: ARRA refers to the American Recovery and Reinvestment Act of 2009 (P.L. 111-5).

Table 3 provides a contents listing of ARRA, by opening section and division and title, with page references to the text of the public law. In addition, the table provides page references to the legislative text and explanatory statements in the conference report—as printed as a separate document (H.Rept. 111-16) and as inserted into the *Congressional Record* of February 12, 2009.

For each of the funding titles of Division A, the entries below identify the total funding provided in the title and describe the primary purposes of the funding. The entries also include percentages that indicate the extent to which the funding in ARRA is a supplement to other FY2009 funding.[16] There are 12 entries each corresponding to one title of Division A.

However, the entry for Title VIII, Departments of Labor, Health and Human Services, and Education, and Related Agencies, also discusses the State Fiscal Stabilization Fund (Title XIV) which received appropriations for education programs.

Table 4 indicates the total discretionary budget authority for FY2009-FY2019 provided by title in Division A. **Table 5** and **Table 6**, at the end of this section, provide additional information on appropriations in Division A, including funding by department and agency.

Of the $311.20 billion in total funding, $288.73 billion is identified as for FY2009. The remainder is identified for future fiscal years, specifically $7.08 billion for FY2010 and $15.39 billion for FY2011 through FY2019.[17] The ARRA states that the appropriations are in addition to amounts otherwise appropriated for the fiscal year involved,[18] and that all funding is designated as emergency funding.

Table 4. Total Discretionary Budget Authority for Fiscal Years 2009-2019, by Title (Division A – Appropriations Provisions) (amounts in millions of dollars)

Title	Name	Budget Authority
Title I	Agriculture, Rural Development, Food and Drug Administration and Related Agencies	26,466
Title II	Commerce, Justice, Science, and Related Agencies	15,922
Title III	Department of Defense	4,555
Title IV	Energy and Water Development	50,825
Title V	Financial Services and General Government	6,858
Title VI	Department of Homeland Security	2,755
Title VII	Interior, Environment, and Related Agencies	10,950
Title VIII	Departments of Labor, Health and Human Services, and Education, and Related Agencies	72,564
Title IX	Legislative Branch	25
Title X	Military Construction and Veterans Affairs and Related Agencies	4,281
Title XI	State, Foreign Operations, and Related Programs	602
Title XII	Transportation, Housing and Urban Development, and Related Agencies	61,795
Title XIII	Health Information Technology	0
Title XIV	State Fiscal Stabilization Fund	53,600
Title XV	Accountability and Transparency	0
Title XVI	General Provisions—This Act	0
Total		**311,198**

Source: *Congressional Record*, daily edition, vol. 155 (February 13, 2009), pp. H 1540-H1 553.

Notes: Most of the budget authority ($288.73 billion) was appropriated for FY2009, but some was appropriated for future fiscal years (FY20 10 through FY20 19). Title XIII (State Fiscal Stabilization Fund) in the *Congressional Record* funding table of February 13, 2009, (p. H 1553) is incorrectly labeled. It should read Title XIV (State Fiscal Stabilization Fund).

The monies in the law are available for obligation until September 30, 2010 (the end of FY2010) unless otherwise specified.[19] Most of the accounts funded in Division A of the law do not contain different periods of obligation, although there are a number of exceptions. For instance, funding for the Inspectors General of the agencies typically is provided for a longer period of obligation. By comparison, the 12 regular, annual appropriations laws typically contain varied periods of obligation for funds therein. Some funds are made available until expended, while others are provided for one or multiple fiscal years.

The ARRA contains a variety of provisions requiring agencies receiving the funds to notify Congress on how the money is to be spent. For example, it requires that each agency receiving funding in the Interior, Environment, and Related Agencies title notify the House and Senate Appropriations Committees as to how the monies are to be spent. Specifically, it provides that each such agency is to submit to the House and Senate Committees on Appropriations, within 30 days of enactment, a general plan for the expenditure of the funds. Each agency also is to submit to the committees, within 90 days of enactment, a report "containing detailed project level information associated with the general plan."[20] As another example, several of the appropriations included in the Departments of Labor, Health and Human Services, and Education, and Related Agencies title require the pertinent agency head to submit an operating plan to the Appropriations Committees prior to making any obligations of the funds provided. The timelines and requirements for the plans vary, but they generally focus on detailing activities to be supported and describing the planned allocation of resources, to be followed by subsequent reports on actual obligations and expenditures.

Among the general provisions of ARRA,[21] agencies are to begin spending the funds "as quickly as possible consistent with prudent management."[22] With regard to funds for infrastructure, recipients are to give preference to activities "that can be started and completed expeditiously," with a goal of using at least 50% of the monies for activities that can be started within 120 days of enactment.[23]

The ARRA also requires the establishment of a website with information on how the funds in Division A are allocated. The Administration has established a website to monitor implementation of the AARA—(http://www.recovery. For further information on implementation and oversight provisions of ARRA, see the "Summary of General Oversight Provisions" and "Additional Resources" sections of this chapter.

Agriculture, Rural Development, Food and Drug Administration, and Related Agencies (Division A, Title I)[24]

Agriculture programs—including nutrition assistance, rural development, farmer assistance, and conservation—receive $26.47 billion in ARRA.[25] This is 24% over the $108.09 billion in the Omnibus Appropriations Act, 2009 (P.L. 111-8) for Agriculture, Rural Development, Food and Drug Administration, and Related Agencies.

Of the $26.47 billion, nutrition assistance programs receive the largest share at $20.74 billion. Increased food stamp benefits and expanded eligibility in the newly renamed Supplemental Nutrition Assistance Program (SNAP) represent the largest single increase; monthly food stamp benefits for families rise 20% on average from current levels. Second, rural development receives $4.36 billion (160% of the regular FY2009 amount), focused primarily on broadband infrastructure but also rural water and waste disposal infrastructure, community facilities, and rural housing. In particular, the rural broadband program receives $2.50 billion, allowing outlays through FY20 15 that are 20-3 0 times more than recent annual appropriations. Third, assistance for farmers totals $744.0 million, primarily for crop insurance/disaster programs but also for the farm loan program, which is facing higher demand during the financial crisis. Fourth, conservation programs receive $348.0 million for watershed flood prevention infrastructure. Finally, USDA receives $250.0 million for its own facilities maintenance and computer infrastructure.[26]

Commerce, Justice, Science, and Related Agencies (Division A, Title II)[27]

The ARRA provides $15.92 billion for agencies covered under the Commerce, Justice, Science, and Related Agencies (CJS) appropriations bill. This is a 27% supplement to the $59.93 billion in other FY2009 appropriations.

Commerce

The ARRA includes $7.92 billion for the Department of Commerce (DOC). Of this amount, $5.35 billion (68%) is for the National Telecommunications and Information Administration (NTIA) for activities such as broadband deployment in the United States and the conversion from analog to digital television broadcasts. (Division B, Title VI contains the authorization for the Broadband Technology Opportunities Program (BTOP) at NTIA.[28])

For the 2010 census, the Bureau of the Census receives $1.00 billion to hire and train additional personnel, increase targeted media purchases, and improve risk management. Up to $250.0 million of the $1.00 billion is to be used for partnership and outreach efforts to hard-to-count groups. The National Oceanic and Atmospheric Administration receives $830.0 million, with $600.0 million for facility and fleet construction and maintenance and $230.0 million for research, restoration, navigation, conservation, and management activities. The National Institute of Standards and Technology receives $580.0 million for construction and research activities (plus a $20.0 million transfer). The Economic Development Administration receives $150.0 million for Economic Development Assistance programs, and the Office of Inspector General receives $6.0 million.

Justice

The Department of Justice (DOJ) receives $4.00 billion, with $2.0 million for the Inspector General and the rest for grant programs. Specifically, the Office on Violence Against Women receives $225.0 million for violence against women prevention and prosecution programs, and the Community Oriented Policing Services Office receives $1.00 billion for its hiring program. The Office of Justice Programs receives $2.77 billion, including $2.00 billion for the Edward Byrne Memorial Justice Assistance Grant program, $225.0 million for Byrne Competitive grants, $225.0 million for construction of correctional facilities on tribal lands, $125.0 million for rural law enforcement assistance, $100.0 million for victim compensation grants, $50.0 million for Internet Crimes Against Children taskforces, and $40.0 million for law enforcement assistance along the southern border and in High-intensity Drug Trafficking Areas.

Science

Two science agencies receive a total of $4.00 billion. The National Aeronautics and Space Administration (NASA) receives $1.00 billion, including $400.0 million for science, to accelerate the development of the tier 1 set of Earth science climate research missions and to increase the agency's supercomputing capabilities; $400.0 million for exploration; $150.0 million for aeronautics; $50.0 million for cross-agency support, with the highest priority for restoring NASA-owned facilities damaged by natural disasters during 2008; and $2.0 million for the Inspector General. The National Science Foundation (NSF) receives $3.00 billion, comprised of $2.50 billion for research and related activities (R&RA), $400.0 million for its major research equipment and facilities construction account, $100.0 million for education and human resources (EHR), and $2.0 million for the Inspector General. Language in the joint explanatory statement provides further direction, such as to allocate $300.0 million of the R&RA funds to NSF 's major research instrumentation program and $60.0 million of the EHR funds to the Robert Noyce scholarship program.

Department of Defense (Division A, Title III)[29]

The ARRA provides $4.56 billion to DOD accounts that had been funded by the FY2009 Department of Defense Appropriations Act (Division C, P.L. 110-329). Apart from these stimulus funds and funds appropriated for military construction (which are provided separately), a total of $543.57 billion[30] has been appropriated for DOD in FY2009. The funds in ARRA increase that total by 0.8%.

The additional DOD funds provided by ARRA are aimed largely at programs that serve one of two goals. A total of $4.24 billion is for maintenance of DOD facilities, of which $400.0 million is for medical facilities, $153.5 million is for renovation of barracks, and $3.69 billion is for repair and maintenance of other facilities and for projects that would improve the energy efficiency of DOD facilities. An additional $300.0 million is for research and development projects that would improve DOD's energy efficiency. The law also provides an additional $15.0 million for the office of the DOD Inspector General.

Energy and Water Development (Division A, Title IV)[31]

In total, ARRA contains $50.83 billion for Energy and Water Development programs,[32] a 128% supplement to the $39.56 billion included in regular and supplemental appropriations for FY2009 ($33.80 billion in the omnibus appropriations law, P.L. 111-8, and $5.76 billion in the supplemental appropriations law, P.L. 110-252). The three major programs in the Energy and Water Development bill support the Army Corps of Engineers (Corps) Civil Programs, the Bureau of Reclamation in the Department of the Interior, and the Department of Energy (DOE).

The ARRA appropriates $4.60 billion for construction, operation, maintenance, and planning of Corps navigation, flood control, and ecosystem restoration projects and for other Corps civil works activities. This is a 41% supplement to the $11.16 billion in FY2009 appropriations for these activities—$5.40 billion in regular appropriations (P.L. 111-8) and

$5.76 billion in supplemental appropriations (P.L. 110-252). The ARRA amount, therefore, represents 85% of the regular appropriations for the Corps. The Bureau of Reclamation receives $1.00 billion in ARRA, a 93% addition to the $1.08 billion in regular FY2009 appropriations. Reclamation funds are to be used for elements of projects, programs, or activities that can be completed within the funding amounts provided in ARRA and not create budgetary obligations in future fiscal years, and include specific appropriations for water reuse and recycling, certain restoration, rural water supply, and canal projects in the 17 western states.

The Department of Energy receives $38.73 billion in ARRA, a 144% supplement to the $26.97 billion in other appropriations for FY2009. DOE has many programs, and the distribution of ARRA money varies widely among them. While some programs do not receive any appropriation from ARRA, others are funded many times over their regular budgets. Among the major recipients, Energy Efficiency and Renewable Energy programs receive $16.80 billion, more than eight times the $1.93 billion in the regular FY2009 appropriations law. Electricity Delivery and Energy Reliability, funded at $137.0 million in the FY2009 appropriations, receives $4.50 billion in ARRA, a 32-fold increase. Fossil Fuel Research and Development receives $3.40 billion in ARRA, almost four times as much as the $876.3 million in the FY2009 appropriations law.

Other major DOE programs that receive ARRA money are Defense Environmental Cleanup, which receives $5.13 billion, a 91% addition to the $5.66 billion in the FY2009 appropriations law, and Science programs, which receive $2.00 billion from ARRA, a 42% addition to the $4.77 billion in the regular FY2009 appropriations law.

Financial Services and General Government (Division A, Title V)[33]

The ARRA provides $6.86 billion for Financial Services and General Government agencies. This is a 15% supplement to the $44.58 billion in other appropriations for Financial Services and General Government agencies for FY2009. Of the $6.86 billion, $5.86 billion is provided to the General Services Administration (GSA). The large majority of GSA's appropriation, $5.55 billion, is for construction projects and "green" building initiatives. GSA receives an additional $300.0 million for the purchase of energy–efficient motor vehicles, and $7.0 million for the agency's Office of Inspector General.

Of the $6.86 billion total, the Small Business Administration (SBA) receives $730.0 million.[34] Of that amount, $630.0 million is provided for loan guarantees and loan subsidies, $69.0 million for salaries and expenses, $15.0 million for the Surety Bond Guarantee Revolving Fund, $10.0 million for the Office of Inspector General, and $6.0 million for direct loans.

Another $187.0 million of the total is provided to the Department of the Treasury. Of that amount, $100.0 million is for programs funded through the Community Development Financial Institutions Fund, $80.0 million is for the Internal Revenue Service to implement the TAA[35] Health Coverage Improvement Act of 2009, and $7.0 million is for the Treasury Inspector General for Tax Administration. The remaining $84.0 million of the total Title V funding is for the Recovery Act Accountability and Transparency Board, which was established to coordinate and conduct oversight of funds distributed under ARRA in order to prevent fraud, waste, and abuse.[36]

Department of Homeland Security (Division A, Title VI)[37]

The ARRA includes $2.76 billion for a number of agencies and programs within the Department of Homeland Security (DHS). Funding provided in ARRA represents a 7% supplement to the $41.33 billion in other appropriations for DHS for FY2009. Of the $2.76 billion total, ARRA provides $200.0 million to the Office of the Under Secretary for Management for various activities and costs associated with the consolidation of DHS headquarters. It contains $5.0 million for the Office of Inspector General for the oversight and audit of programs, grants, and projects funded under Title VI. The law includes $680.0 million for Customs and Border Protection, comprised as follows: $100.0 million for non-intrusive inspection technology; $60.0 million for tactical communications equipment and radios; $100.0 million to deploy SBInet technology to the border; and $420.0 million for the construction and modification of ports of entry. Further, ARRA contains $20.0 million for tactical communications equipment and radios for Immigration and Customs Enforcement.

The law includes $1.00 billion for the Transportation Security Administration for checked baggage explosives detection systems and checkpoint explosives detection equipment. It contains $240.0 million for the Coast Guard, of which $142.0 million is dedicated to the Alteration of Bridges program for those bridges that are ready to proceed to construction and $98.0 million is for a variety of acquisition and maintenance activities. Finally, ARRA also provides $610.0 million to the Federal Emergency Management Agency, of which $100.0 million is for the Emergency Food and Shelter program and $510.0 million is for selected DHS assistance programs for states and localities: $150.0 million for the Transit Security Grant Program; $150.0 million for the Port Security Grant Program; and $210.0 million for the Assistance to Firefighters Program.

Interior, Environment, and Related Agencies (Division A, Title VII)[38]

In total, ARRA contains $10.95 billion for Interior, Environment, and Related Agencies. This is a 40% supplement to the $27.59 billion in other appropriations for Interior, Environment, and Related Agencies for FY2009. Of the $10.95 billion, $7.22 billion is provided to the Environmental Protection Agency (EPA). The majority of EPA funding is for clean water ($4.00 billion) and drinking water ($2.00 billion) state revolving fund grants.[39] The remainder of the funds is primarily for cleanup projects, specifically Superfund remediation, grants for cleanup of Brownfields and leaking underground storage tanks, and diesel emission reduction grants. Another portion of the funds is for the Office of Inspector General. EPA funding in ARRA nearly equals the agency's FY2009 regular appropriations of $7.64 billion.

Another $2.50 billion of the $10.95 billion total is provided to the four federal land management agencies: the Bureau of Land Management, Fish and Wildlife Service, National Park Service, and Forest Service. These funds are provided for construction; wildfire management; and maintenance, repair, and rehabilitation of facilities and trails, among other purposes.[40] Still another $1.00 billion of the $10.95 billion is provided to the Bureau of Indian Affairs for activities including repair and restoration of roads, construction and improvement of schools, and maintenance and repair of detention centers ($500.0 million) and to the Indian Health Service for facilities construction, deferred maintenance, sanitation projects, and equipment purchases ($500.0 million), among other activities. The remaining $230.0 million of the $10.95 billion is provided to several other agencies for purposes including deferred maintenance of the U.S. Geological Survey, salaries and expenses of the DOI Inspector General, repair of Smithsonian facilities, and grants for the arts.

Departments of Labor, Health and Human Services, and Education, and Related Agencies (Division A, Title VIII) and State Fiscal Stabilization Fund (Division A, Title XI V)[41]

Two titles of ARRA provide funding for the Departments of Labor, Health and Human Services, and Education, and Related Agencies. Title VIII provides a total of $72.56 billion,[42] including $4.81 billion for the Department of Labor, $21.92 billion for the Department of Health and Human Services, $44.64 billion for the Department of Education, and $1.20 billion for related agencies. Title XIV provides $53.60 billion to the Department of Education for a new State Fiscal Stabilization Fund, bringing ARRA Education total to $98.24 billion. The ARRA total from the two titles is $126.16 billion, a 20% supplement to the $638.47 billion in other appropriations for Labor, Health and Human Services, and Education, and Related Agencies for FY2009. For discretionary programs, however, ARRA total of $124.15 billion is a 78% supplement to the $160.08 billion in regular FY2009 appropriations for the agencies. In contrast, the much smaller ARRA total of $2.01 billion for mandatory programs (provided through Division A) is a 0.4% supplement to the $478.39 billion in regular FY2009 appropriations.

Department of Labor (DOL)

The ARRA includes $4.81 billion for the Department of Labor. The amount is a 31% supplement to the $15.32 billion in other FY2009 appropriations, and a 39% supplement to the $12.41 billion in FY2009 discretionary funding for DOL. Of the $4.81 billion total, $4.20 billion is provided for employment and training programs authorized by the Workforce Investment Act (WIA) and the remaining $606.0 million went to related DOL programs. The amount for WIA programs represents a 79% supplement to the $5.31 billion in the Omnibus Appropriations Act, 2009. Of the $4.20 billion in WIA funding, a total of $3.95 billion is appropriated for Training and Employment Services activities as follows: (1) formula grants to states receive $2.95 billion, including $500.0 million in grants for adult employment and training, $1.20 billion in grants for youth activities, and $1.25 billion in grants for dislocated worker assistance; (2) the Dislocated Workers Assistance National Reserve receives $200.0 million; (3) the YouthBuild program receives $50.0 million; and (4) $750.0 million is provided for a new program of competitive grants for worker training and placement in high-growth and emerging industries. The remaining $250.0 million in WIA funding goes to the Office of Job Corps for construction and renovation of Job Corps Centers. The balance of

ARRA funding for DOL is for the Community Service Employment for Older Americans program ($120.0 million), state unemployment insurance and employment service operations ($400.0 million), departmental management ($80.0 million), and the Office of the Inspector General ($6.0 million).[43]

Department of Health and Human Services (HHS)

The ARRA provides $21.92 billion for the HHS programs funded under this appropriation. This is a 4% supplement to the $501.20 billion in total regular FY2009 appropriations, and a 31% supplement to the $71.38 billion in FY2009 discretionary funding for HHS. Of the $21.92 billion, the National Institutes of Health (NIH) receives the largest share at $10.00 billion (a 33% supplement to regular FY2009 appropriations). The Administration for Children and Families receives $5.15 billion, including $2.00 billion for the Child Care and Development Block Grant (a 94% supplement) and $3.15 billion for Children and Family Services programs (a 34% supplement). The Office of the HHS Secretary receives a total of $3.07 billion for several programs, including $1.00 billion for a new Prevention and Wellness Fund and $2.00 billion to implement activities authorized under the Health Information Technology for Economic and Clinical Health Act (Division A, Title XIII of ARRA).[44] The Health Resources and Services Administration receives $2.50 billion, including $2.00 billion for health centers (a 91% supplement) and $500.0 million for health professions training programs. The Agency for Healthcare Research and Quality (AHRQ) receives a total of $1.10 billion for comparative effectiveness research ($300.0 million for AHRQ programs, $400.0 million for transfer to NIH, and $400.0 million for the Secretary to allocate). Finally, the Administration on Aging receives $100.0 million for senior nutrition programs.[45]

Department of Education (ED)

The ARRA provides $98.24 billion for programs that are or will be administered by the Department of Education. This is a 148% supplement to the $66.51 billion in regular FY2009 appropriations for ED.

Of the $98.24 billion, $42.62 billion is appropriated for existing discretionary ED programs—a 90% supplement to the regular FY2009 appropriations for these programs. Three programs that receive the largest shares of the funding are discussed here; the balance of ARRA funding for existing programs is provided in smaller amounts to numerous other ED programs.[46] Most of ARRA funds for existing elementary education programs are appropriated for programs that provide formula grants directly to states or local educational agencies (LEAs), while most funds at the postsecondary level are appropriated for Pell Grants, which go directly to students. For some programs, these appropriations provide a substantial increase over the amount of funding provided through the regular appropriations process in recent years. The ARRA provides $10.00 billion for Title I-A, Education for the Disadvantaged, Grants to LEAs, a 69% supplement to the $14.49 billion in regular FY2009 appropriations for the program. Similarly, ARRA provides $11.30 billion for the Individuals with Disabilities Education Act (IDEA), Part B Grants to States, a 98% supplement to the $11.51 billion in regular FY2009 appropriations. At the postsecondary level, ARRA provides $15.64 billion in discretionary funding for Pell Grants, a 90% supplement to the $17.29 billion in regular FY2009 appropriations.[47]

The remaining \$53.60 billion in ARRA funding for ED is appropriated for the new State Fiscal Stabilization Fund. After making reservations from the appropriation, including a \$5.00 billion reservation for the Secretary of Education to provide State Incentive Grants and establish an Innovation Fund, \$48.32 billion will be provided to governors through formula grants to each state that chooses to apply for funding through this program. At the state level, the governor must use 81.8% of the funds received to restore state support for public elementary and secondary education[48] and for public institutions of higher education (IHEs)[49] to the greater of the FY2008 or FY2009 level for FY2009, FY2010, and FY2011. The governor is required to use the remaining 18.2% of the state allocation for "public safety and other government services," which may include assistance for elementary and secondary education and public IHEs.

Related Agencies

The ARRA includes \$1.20 billion for related agencies. This is a 2% supplement to the \$55.43 billion in total regular FY2009 appropriations, and a 9% supplement to the \$12.75 billion in FY2009 discretionary funding for these agencies. Of the \$1.20 billion, ARRA provides \$1.00 billion to the Social Security Administration (SSA). Of this amount, \$500.0 million is to replace SSA's National Computer Center and \$500.0 million is for processing disability and retirement claims. SSA's Office of the Inspector General receives \$2.0 million.[50] The ARRA provides \$201.0 million to the Corporation for National and Community Service. This amount includes \$89.0 million for AmeriCorps State and National Grants, \$65.0 million for the AmeriCorps Volunteers in Service to America program, and \$40.0 million for the National Service Trust. Among other activities, the National Service Trust provides educational awards to participants in AmeriCorps, VISTA, and the National Civilian Community Corps.

Legislative Branch (Division A, Title IX)[51]

The ARRA contains \$25.0 million for the legislative branch, all of which is provided for the Government Accountability Office (GAO). This amount is a 0.6% supplement to the \$4.40 billion in other appropriations for Legislative Branch for FY2009. The ARRA requires GAO to conduct bimonthly reviews of selected states and localities on their use funds provided by the act. It also seeks to ensure GAO access to various records related to contracts awarded with funds provided in the act.

Military Construction and Veterans Affairs and Related Agencies (Division A, Title X)[52]

The ARRA includes \$4.28 billion for Military Construction and Veterans Affairs and Related Agencies, a 4% addition to the \$119.61 billion otherwise appropriated for FY2009. Of the \$4.28 billion, \$2.88 billion is devoted to military construction, military family housing construction and operation, and the Department of Defense (DOD) Homeowners Assistance Fund. Army construction (\$180.0 million) is specified for use on child development centers and "warrior transition complexes."[53] Army family housing construction receives an additional $34.5 million and operations another $3.9 million. Navy and Marine Corps construction ($280.0 million) is to be used for troop housing, child development centers, and energy conservation and alternative energy projects. Air Force construction ($180.0 million) is to be devoted to troop housing and child development centers. Air Force family housing construction receives $80.1 million and operations an additional $16.5 million. Defense-wide construction ($1.45 billion) is dedicated to hospitals, with a small portion reserved for the Energy Conservation Investment Program. The Army National Guard construction account is allocated $50.0 million, and the Air National Guard an additional $50.0 million. The Homeowners Assistance Fund, which provides assistance to DOD personnel forced to sell primary homes in depressed housing markets because of relocations due to base closures or downsizing, receives a $555.0 million appropriation, and additional legislative language expands eligibility to new categories of personnel.

Of the $4.28 billion, ARRA provides $1.40 billion to the Department of Veterans Affairs. This amount includes $1.00 billion for the medical facilities account, and $50.0 million for the National Cemetery Administration. The funding for these accounts is for non-recurring maintenance and energy conservation projects in VA medical facilities and monument and memorial repairs in VA national cemeteries. The law does not specify which VA medical facilities or cemeteries would receive funding. The ARRA also provides: $150.0 million for the general operating expenses account to temporarily increase the number of claims processing personnel; $50.0 million for information technology; $1.0 million for the Office of the Inspector General; and $150.0 million for grants for construction of state extended care facilities.

State, Foreign Operations, and Related Programs (Division A, Title XI)[54]

The ARRA contains $602.0 million for programs under the Department of State and the U.S. Agency for International Development (USAID). This is a 1.5% supplement to the other $40.46 billion in other appropriations for State, Foreign Operations, and Related Programs for FY2009. Of the $602.0 million, $382.0 million is provided for State Department activities, including $90.0 million under Diplomatic & Consular Programs to address facilities requirements for passport and training functions, $290.0 million to the Capital Investment Fund (CIF) for security upgrades to the information technology system (of which $38.0 million is to be transferred to USAID's CIF for coordination of State and USAID information technology systems), and $2.0 million to the Office of the Inspector General for oversight requirements. The remaining $220.0 million is provided for the U.S.-Mexico International Boundary and Water Commission for immediate repair and rehabilitation requirements, of which up to $2.0 million may be merged with funds for salaries and expenses.

Transportation, Housing and Urban Development, and Related Agencies (Division A, Title XII)[55]

The ARRA provides $61.80 billion for programs within the Department of Transportation (DOT) and the Department of Housing and Urban Development (HUD).[56] This is a 57% supplement to the $109.06 billion provided in the Transportation, Housing and Urban Development, and Related Agencies Appropriations Act, 2009 (Division I, P.L. 111-8).

DOT

DOT receives a total of $48.12 billion from ARRA, primarily to make capital assistance grants. This additional funding represents a 72% supplement to DOT's regular FY2009 funding ($67.22 billion).

The ARRA funding is allocated among ten grant programs, focusing on different modes of transportation. The largest allocation, $27.50 billion, goes to states and localities for highway projects, though passenger and freight rail and port infrastructure projects also are eligible for this funding in certain circumstances. The next largest allocation, $9.30 billion, is for states and Amtrak for intercity passenger rail projects, including high-speed rail. Transit projects receive $8.40 billion; aviation projects receive $1.30 billion; and small shipyards receive $100.0 million. The law also provides $1.50 billion for competitive grants for surface transportation projects of national and regional significance, whether highways, bridges, transit, rail, or port infrastructure. For most of these programs, the grants provided with funding from ARRA will not require any local match. States will be required to certify that they are using these grants to supplement their planned transportation spending, rather than substituting the additional funding for their planned spending. Further, the DOT Inspector General's Office is given $20.0 million to help audit these expenditures.

HUD

The ARRA provides $13.68 billion for HUD in FY2009.[57] This funding is a 33% supplement to the $41.54 billion provided for HUD in P.L. 111-8.

The $13.68 billion in HUD funding includes $4.00 billion for the repair and modernization of public housing and $2.00 billion for the acquisition, rehabilitation, and sale of abandoned and foreclosed housing through the Neighborhood Stabilization Program. It includes $2.00 billion to fund the full-year renewal of project-based rental assistance contracts between HUD and private property owners and another $2.25 billion is included to provide gap financing for certain tax credit financed affordable housing developments. The HUD funding also includes $1.50 billion for homelessness prevention activities, to be awarded to localities via the Emergency Shelter Grant program formula.

The remaining HUD funding is provided for: supplemental Community Development Block Grant assistance ($1.00 billion); supplemental grants for Native American block grant recipients ($510.0 million); competitive grants for energy efficiency and green retrofits in HUD-assisted multifamily properties ($250.0 million); supplemental funding for the lead paint hazard reduction program ($100.0 million); and supplemental funding for HUD's Office of Inspector General ($15.0 million). Administrative provisions in the law increase the Federal Housing Administration loan limits and the government sponsored enterprises (GSE) conforming loan limits. The GSE changes are estimated to cost $37.0 million in FY2009 and $13.0 million in FY2010.

Table 5. Total Discretionary Budget Authority for Fiscal Years 2009-2019, by Department/Agency and Title (Division A– Appropriations Provisions) (amounts in millions of dollars)

Department/Agency	Budget Authority
Agriculture	**27,616**
Title I: Agriculture, Rural Development, Food and Drug Administration, and Related Agencies	26,466
Title VII: Interior, Environment, and Related Agencies	1,150
Commerce	
Title II: Commerce, Justice, Science, and Related Agencies	7,916
Defense	**12,035**
Title III: Department of Defense	4,555
Title IV: Energy and Water Development	4,600
Title X: Military Construction and Veterans Affairs and Related Agencies	2,880
Education	**98,238**
Title VIII: Departments of Labor, HHS, and Education, and Related Agencies	44,638
Title XIV: State Fiscal Stabilization Fund	53,600
Energy	**45,225**
Title IV: Energy and Water Development	
Health and Human Services	**22,417**
Title VII: Interior, Environment, and Related Agencies	500
Title VIII: Departments of Labor, HHS, and Education, and Related Agencies	21,917
Homeland Security	**2,755**
Title VI: Department of Homeland Security	
Housing and Urban Development	**13,675**
Title XII: Transportation, Housing and Urban Development, and Related Agencies	
Interior	**3,005**
Title IV: Energy and Water Development	1,000
Title VII: Interior, Environment, and Related Agencies	2,005
Justice Title	**4,002**
II: Commerce, Justice, Science, and Related Agencies	
Labor	**4,806**
Title VIII: Departments of Labor, HHS, and Education, and Related Agencies	
State	**602**
Title XI: State, Foreign Operations, and Related Programs	

Table 5. (Continued)

Department/Agency	Budget Authority
Transportation Title XII: Transportation, Housing and Urban Development, and Related Agencies	**48,120**
Treasury Title V: Financial Services and General Government	**187**
Veterans Affairs Title X: Military Construction and Veterans Affairs and Related Agencies	**1,401**
Corporation for National and Community Service Title VIII: Departments of Labor, HHS, and Education, and Related Agencies	**201**
Environmental Protection Agency Title VII: Interior, Environment, and Related Agencies	**7,220**
General Services Administration Title V: Financial Services and General Government	**5,857**
Government Accountability Office Title IX: Legislative Branch	**25**
National Aeronautics and Space Administration Title II: Commerce, Justice, Science, and Related Agencies	**1,002**
National Endowment for the Arts Title VII: Interior, Environment, and Related Agencies	**50**
National Science Foundation Title II: Commerce, Justice, Science, and Related Agencies	**3,002**
Recovery Act Accountability and Transparency Board Title V: Financial Services and General Government	**84**
Small Business Administration Title V: Financial Services and General Government	**730**
Smithsonian Institution Title VII: Interior, Environment, and Related Agencies	**25**
Social Security Administration Title VIII: Departments of Labor, HHS, and Education, and Related Agencies	**1,002**

Source: *Congressional Record*, daily edition, vol. 155 (February 13, 2009), pp. H 1540-H1 553.

Notes: Most of the budget authority ($288.73 billion) is appropriated for FY2009, but some is appropriated for future fiscal years (FY2010 through FY2019). Title XIII (State Fiscal Stabilization Fund) in the *Congressional Record* funding table of February 13, 2009, (p. H 1553) is incorrectly labeled. It should read Title XIV (State Fiscal Stabilization Fund).

SUMMARY OF MANDATORY SPENDING PROVISIONS

Most mandatory spending in ARRA is contained in Division B of the act; however, some $29 billion of estimated outlays contained in Division A are also the result of changes in mandatory programs (for example, the Supplemental Nutrition Assistance Program, formerly known as food stamps). Of total amounts shown in **Table 1** for mandatory spending under

Division B, nearly $69 billion is from refundable tax credits. For purposes of this CRS report, these tax provisions are generally discussed in the "Summary of Tax and Public Finance Provisions," although a few that are directly related to the mandatory provisions discussed below also are mentioned here.

Table 6. Total Discretionary Budget Authority for Fiscal Years 2009-2019, Ranked In Descending Order by Department/Agency (Division A – Appropriations Provisions) (amounts in millions of dollars)

Department/Agency	Budget Authority
Education	**98,238**
Title VIII: Departments of Labor, HHS, and Education, and Related Agencies	44,638
Title XIV: State Fiscal Stabilization Fund	53,600
Transportation	**48,120**
Title XII: Transportation, Housing and Urban Development, and Related Agencies	
Energy	**45,225**
Title IV: Energy and Water Development	
Agriculture	**27,616**
Title I: Agriculture, Rural Development, Food and Drug Administration, and Related Agencies	26,466
Title VII: Interior, Environment, and Related Agencies	1,150
Health and Human Services	**22,417**
Title VII: Interior, Environment, and Related Agencies	500
Title VIII: Departments of Labor, HHS, and Education, and Related Agencies	21,917
Housing and Urban Development	**13,675**
Title XII: Transportation, Housing and Urban Development, and Related Agencies	
Defense	**12,035**
Title III: Department of Defense	4,555
Title IV: Energy and Water Development	4,600
Title X: Military Construction and Veterans Affairs and Related Agencies	2,880
Commerce	**7,916**
Title II: Commerce, Justice, Science, and Related Agencies	
Environmental Protection Agency	**7,220**
Title VII: Interior, Environment, and Related Agencies	
General Services Administration	**5,857**
Title V: Financial Services and General Government	
Labor	**4,806**
Title VIII: Departments of Labor, HHS, and Education, and Related Agencies	
Justice	**4,002**
Title II: Commerce, Justice, Science, and Related Agencies	

Table 6. (Continued)

Department/Agency	Budget Authority
Interior	**3,005**
Title IV: Energy and Water Development	1,000
Title VII: Interior, Environment, and Related Agencies	2,005
National Science Foundation	**3,002**
Title II: Commerce, Justice, Science, and Related Agencies	
Homeland Security	**2,755**
Title VI: Department of Homeland Security	
Veterans Affairs	**1,401**
Title X: Military Construction and Veterans Affairs and Related Agencies	
National Aeronautics and Space Administration	**1,002**
Title II: Commerce, Justice, Science, and Related Agencies	
Social Security Administration	**1,002**
Title VIII: Departments of Labor, HHS, and Education, and Related Agencies	
Small Business Administration	**730**
Title V: Financial Services and General Government	
State	**602**
Title XI: State, Foreign Operations, and Related Programs	
Corporation for National and Community Service	**201**
Title VIII: Departments of Labor, HHS, and Education, and Related Agencies	
Treasury	**187**
Title V: Financial Services and General Government	
Recovery Act Accountability and Transparency Board	**84**
Title V: Financial Services and General Government	
National Endowment for the Arts	**50**
Title VII: Interior, Environment, and Related Agencies	
Government Accountability Office	**25**
Title IX: Legislative Branch	
Smithsonian Institution	**25**
Title VII: Interior, Environment, and Related Agencies	

Source: *Congressional Record*, daily edition, vol. 155 (February 13, 2009), pp. H 1540-H1 553.

Notes: Most of the budget authority ($288.73 billion) is appropriated for FY2009, but some is appropriated for future fiscal years (FY2010 through FY2019). Title XIII (State Fiscal Stabilization Fund) in the *Congressional Record* funding table of February 13, 2009, (p. H 1553) is incorrectly labeled. It should read Title XIV (State Fiscal Stabilization Fund).

Non-tax mandatory spending in Division B totals $198 billion over the 10-year period FY2009- FY2019, according to CBO estimates. The vast majority of this spending will occur in the first two years ($160 billion). Almost all funds will be spent during the five-year period FY2009-FY2013 ($194 billion). The key exception to this pattern, however, is the Medicaid/Medicare health information technology provisions (Title IV of Division B), which do not take effect until FY20 11.

The largest single component of spending results from provisions intended to provide fiscal relief to states under the Medicaid program (Title V of Division B). CBO estimates that Title V provisions will result in $90 billion in outlays over 10 years, with $78 billion in spending during the first two years (FY2009 and FY2010) and nearly the full $90 billion spent during FY2009- FY2013.

The next largest category of mandatory non-tax spending results from changes in unemployment compensation (UC), which CBO estimates will cost $39 billion over 10 years, with more than $37 billion of that total occurring during the first two years. UC provisions are combined in Title II of Division B with provisions that amend the Temporary Assistance for Needy Families (TANF) and Child Support Enforcement (CSE) programs and that provide one-time "economic recovery" payments to certain individuals (e.g., recipients of Social Security and other benefit programs). CBO estimates that the combination of TANF, CSE, and economic recovery payments will cost $18 billion over 10 years, with $17 billion of that spending in the first two years. Most of this spending is for the economic recovery payments.

Subsidies for COBRA health insurance premiums will cost an estimated $25 billion over 10 years, and Medicare/Medicaid health information technology (HIT) provisions will cost an estimated $21 billion. Most of the HIT spending will occur in FY2011 -FY2015, with estimated savings starting in FY2016.

Table 7, toward the end of this chapter, provides summary information on the levels of mandatory spending (and revenue changes) provided in ARRA.

Trade Adjustment Assistance (Division B, Title I, Part I)

ARRA reauthorizes and expands the Trade Adjustment Assistance (TAA) programs (for workers, firms and farmers) through the end of calendar year 2010. It also created a TAA for Communities program. These programs provide various forms of assistance (e.g., income support, training, job search and relocation assistance, technical assistance) for individuals, businesses and communities adversely affected by imports or shifts in production out of the United States. In addition, a refundable Health Coverage Tax Credit (HCTC) is available to offset part of the health insurance premiums of eligible workers.

Regarding TAA for *Workers*, ARRA expands eligibility to additional groups (including service and public sector workers) and extends income support benefits an additional 26 weeks. ARRA increases the amount of a worker's job search and relocation expenses that may be reimbursed by the program and increases the amount of annual training funds available. The law also continues and eases eligibility for a wage insurance program for older workers, and increases the portion of a worker's health insurance premium that will be covered by the HCTC.

ARRA also makes significant changes to TAA for *Firms*. The new law extends eligibility to services firms in addition to manufacturing and agricultural firms, and increases a firm's flexibility in demonstrating it has been negatively affected by trade. The law requires the Secretary of Commerce, upon being informed by the Secretary of Labor that a firm's workers are covered by the TAA for Workers program, to notify the firm of its potential eligibility under the TAA for Firms program.

For TAA for *Farmers*, ARRA makes it easier for any group of commodity producers, including fishermen, to qualify for assistance by lowering a key threshold and broadening the scope of the factors to be examined in determining eligibility. Also, instead of receiving cash payments automatically under a formula as before, a producer that meets specified requirements will become eligible for financial assistance only upon the completion of training intended to help him or her become more competitive in producing the same or another commodity.

The TAA for *Communities* program makes communities that have received one or more certifications under the TAA for Workers, Firms, or Farmers program eligible for strategic planning grants as well as for economic development grants if the communities cannot match grant funds as required by other federal programs.[58]

Unemployment Compensation (Division B, Title II, Subtitle A)

ARRA contains several provisions affecting unemployment benefits. The law increases unemployment benefits by $25 per week for all recipients of regular unemployment compensation (UC), extended benefits (EB), emergency unemployment compensation (EUC08), Trade Adjustment Assistance (TAA) programs, and Disaster Unemployment Assistance (DUA). Supplemental compensation will be available from the time a state enters into an agreement with the Labor Secretary and ending in most cases before January 1, 2010.

The act extends the temporary EUC08 program through December 26, 2009, to be financed by federal general revenues. It also provides for 100% federal financing of the EB program to end before January 1, 2010, to be financed through the Unemployment Trust Fund. ARRA allows states the option of changing temporarily the eligibility requirements for the EB program in order to expand the number of persons eligible for EB benefits, to end before June 1, 2010. The law also adds an additional 13 weeks to the maximum amount of time railroad workers may receive extended unemployment benefits.

ARRA suspends income taxation on the first $2,400 of unemployment benefits received in 2009, for taxable years beginning after December 31, 2008. It provides relief to states from the payment and accrual of interest on federal loans to states for the payment of unemployment benefits, from enactment of the stimulus package on February 17, 2009 through December 31, 2010.

ARRA provides for a special transfer of up to $7 billion in federal monies to state unemployment programs as "incentive payments" for changing certain state UC laws. All incentive payments must be made before October 1, 2011. States do not need to repay these sums to the federal government. Any changes that states make to state unemployment programs as a result of ARRA's modernization provisions would be permanent. Finally, the act transfers a total of $500 million to the states for administering their unemployment programs, within 30 days of enactment of the law. States do not need to repay these sums to the federal government.[59]

TANF and Child Support Enforcement (Division B, Title II, Subtitle B)

Most funding to states under the Temporary Assistance for Needy Families (TANF) program is provided through a block grant that totals $16.5 billion a year. TANF has additional funding streams, however, including a $2 billion contingency fund for states that meet criteria of economic need. ARRA retains the current TANF contingency fund and adds a new, temporary "emergency contingency fund," that provides extra funding to states in FY2009 and FY20 10. States receive extra federal grants to cover 80% of increased recession-related costs in those two years. Recession-related costs are defined as increased basic assistance (for states with increased basic assistance caseloads), non-recurrent short-term benefits, or subsidized employment expenditures. A state's cumulative combined funding from both the TANF contingency fund and the temporary emergency fund is limited to 50% of its annual basic TANF block grant for the two years. The ARRA provides an appropriation of $5 billion for the emergency fund.

ARRA also temporarily modifies the caseload reduction credit that applies toward TANF work participation standards. Under existing TANF law, the credit reduces a state's work participation standard for caseload reduction that has occurred since FY2005 to the fiscal year prior to the current fiscal year. If caseloads rise, the credit diminishes, raising the effective (after credit) work participation standard. ARRA modifies the credit for the FY2009, FY2010, and FY2011 standards, allowing the credit to be based on caseload reduction through FY2007 or FY2008 for those years. Thus, caseload increases occurring in FY2008 through FY2010 will not reduce caseload reduction credits. Finally, under pre-ARRA law, states could reserve unspent TANF grants without fiscal year limit for the purpose of providing cash welfare. ARRA allows states to use unspent TANF grants for any TANF benefit and service.

Under the Child Support Enforcement (CSE) program, the federal government provides matching grants to states to reimburse them for part of the costs of running their programs. The federal government also provides incentive payments to states to encourage them to operate effective programs, and requires states to reinvest these incentive payments back into the CSE program or related activities. ARRA requires HHS to temporarily provide federal matching funds on CSE incentive payments that states reinvest back into the CSE program. (This practice had been prohibited by the Deficit Reduction Act of 2005 (P.L. 109-171).) This means that CSE incentive payments received by states and reinvested in the CSE program can be used to draw down additional federal funds. ARRA provides the federal matching funds for FY2009 and FY2010 (i.e., the period October 1, 2008, through September 30, 2010).[60]

Economic Recovery Payments (Division B, Title II, Subtitle C)

ARRA provides for a one-time economic recovery payment of $250 to certain individuals, to be made by the Secretary of the Treasury within 120 days of enactment (before mid-June). The payments will be made to those eligible persons who in November 2008, December 2008, or January 2009, received benefits under: Social Security; Supplemental Security Income (S SI); Railroad Retirement; and certain programs administered by the

Department of Veterans Affairs (i.e., disability compensation; pension; dependency indemnity compensation; and special payments to disabled children of certain veterans).

To be eligible, Social Security recipients must be over age 18 (19 if in school). However, disabled children receiving SSI also are eligible for the economic recovery payment. Individuals must live in the United States, District of Columbia, Puerto Rico, or one of the U.S. possessions, and will receive only one payment even if they are beneficiaries of more than one eligible program (for example, receiving both Social Security and veterans benefits).

Taxpayers cannot benefit from both the economic recovery payment and the Making Work Pay tax credit (provided by Section 1001 of Division B of the act) in a single tax year. The economic recovery payment will reduce the Making Work Pay Credit to be claimed for the 2009 tax year on the tax return filed in 2010. The one-time payment may be offset for outstanding child support or other federal or state debts, but will not be offset for Social Security or SSI overpayments. The one-time payment is not counted as income for income tax purposes or as a resource for other federal programs.

ARRA also created a $250 refundable credit against income taxes owed for tax year 2009 for individuals who receive a government pension or annuity from work not covered by Social Security, and who are not eligible to receive the one-time economic recovery payment described above. This refundable credit will also reduce any Making Work Pay credit claimed on the tax year 2009 return filed in 2010.[61]

Premium Assistance for COBRA Benefits (Division B, Title III)

ARRA includes provisions to subsidize health insurance coverage provided through the Consolidated Omnibus Budget Reconciliation Act of 1985 (COBRA). ARRA includes COBRA premium subsidies of 65% to help the unemployed afford health insurance coverage from their former employer. The subsidy is available for up to 9 months to those individuals who meet the income test and who are involuntarily terminated on or after September 1, 2008, and before January 1, 2010. There is also a special extended enrollment period for two groups of unemployed who were involuntarily terminated from their employment on or after September 1, 2008: (1) individuals who did not elect COBRA coverage at the time, and (2) individuals who had chosen COBRA coverage after September 1, 2008, but dropped their coverage because they could not afford the premiums. Members of these two groups are to be notified by their former employer within 60 days of enactment and will have an additional 60 days after being notified to elect COBRA and receive the subsidy. ARRA also allows employers to permit eligible individuals the right to elect a different plan offered by their former employer, within 90 days of their notification for the subsidy.

Individuals receiving the subsidy are required to pay no more than 35% of their COBRA premium. The remaining 65% is paid by their former employer, who will be reimbursed through either: (1) a credit against any tax liability for payroll taxes, or (2) if the premium subsidy exceeds their tax liability, a refund. The full subsidy is available for individuals whose modified adjusted gross income (AGI) during the tax year is no more than $125,000 for single filers (or $250,000 for joint filers). The subsidy is phased-out for higher income individuals with a reduced subsidy for individuals with modified AGI less than $145,000 for single filers (and $290,000 for joint filers). If individuals receive the subsidy and their income exceeds the levels specified above, the amount of the subsidy will be recaptured when they file their income taxes. To avoid recapture they may waive their rights to the subsidy and still enroll in COBRA and pay the full premium. However, waiving their right is a permanent decision, and they would not be allowed to take the subsidy in the future.[62]

Health Information Technology (Division B, Title IV) (Division A, Title XIII)

Medicare and Medicaid Payments

Division B of ARRA amends the Medicare and Medicaid statutes to authorize incentive payments for hospitals, physicians and other health care providers that adopt and use electronic health record (EHR) technology. The Congressional Budget Office estimates that Medicare and Medicaid providers will receive a total of $32.7 billion in EHR bonuses over a 10-year period (i.e., 2009-2019). (However, the provision is also estimated to achieve savings, resulting in the lower overall cost cited earlier.) Beginning in 2011, the legislation provides Medicare incentive payments to physicians and hospitals who are meaningful users (as defined in the act) of EHR technology. Physicians are eligible for up to $44,000 in bonus payments; rural providers may receive an additional 10%. Eligible hospitals receive a base amount of $2 million plus an amount based on the number of patient discharges during the year. The hospital payments are adjusted according to the share of Medicare patients and the amount of charity care provided. Both the physician and hospital incentive payments are phased out over time and replaced in 2015 with financial penalties for those who are not using EHR technology.

In addition to the Medicare bonuses, ARRA authorizes a 100% federal match (or FMAP; see discussion in next section) for payments to certain qualifying Medicaid providers—including physicians and other eligible professionals, and acute-care and children's hospitals—for the acquisition and meaningful use of EHR technology. Physician payments cover up to 85% of allowable EHR technology costs. Payments are capped at $63,750 and payable over a period of up to six years. To qualify for Medicaid payments, physicians must pay the remaining 15% of EHR technology costs and waive their right to any Medicare EHR incentives. The Medicaid incentive payment for hospitals, also payable over a period of up to six years, is computed using a modified version of the formula for Medicare hospital EHR payments, adjusted for the facility's Medicaid patient share. Eligible hospitals may qualify for both Medicare and Medicaid EHR incentives.

Office of the National Coordinator, Standards and Privacy

The Medicare/Medicaid health IT provisions included in Division B are a component of new legislation, the Health Information Technology for Economic and Clinical Health (HITECH) Act, which is primarily contained in Title XIII of Division A of ARRA. The HITECH Act is aimed at promoting the widespread adoption of HIT for the electronic sharing of clinical data among hospitals, physicians, and other health care providers. The Act includes three sets of provisions. First, it codifies the Office of the National Coordinator for Health Information Technology (ONCHIT) within HHS. Created by a presidential executive order in

2004, ONCHIT has played an important role in directing HIT activities both inside and outside the federal government. It has focused on developing technical standards necessary to achieve interoperability among varying electronic health record applications; establishing criteria for certifying that HIT products meet those standards; ensuring the privacy and security of electronic health information; and helping facilitate the creation of prototype health information networks. The goal is to develop a national capability to exchange standards-based health care data in a secure computer environment. The HITECH Act requires the HHS Secretary, by December 31, 2009, to issue a comprehensive set of initial HIT standards.

Second, the HITECH Act through a number of mechanisms provides financial incentives for HIT use among health care providers. In addition to the Medicare/Medicaid provisions described above, it establishes several grant programs to provide funding for investing in HIT infrastructure, purchasing certified EHRs, training, and the dissemination of best practices. It also authorizes grants to states for low-interest loans to help providers finance HIT. (See earlier discussion of HHS funding under Division A, Title VIII, for information on appropriations for these grants.) Finally, the HITECH Act includes a series of privacy and security provisions that amend and expand the current federal standards under the Health Insurance Portability and Accountability Act (HIPAA). Among other things, it establishes a breach notification requirement for health information that is not encrypted, strengthens enforcement of the HIPAA standards, and creates transparency by allowing patients to request an audit trail showing all disclosures of their electronic health information.[63]

State Fiscal Relief (Division B, Title V)

The federal medical assistance percentage (FMAP) is the rate at which states are reimbursed for most Medicaid service expenditures. It is based on a formula that provides higher reimbursement to states with lower per capita incomes relative to the national average (and vice versa); it has a statutory minimum of 50% and maximum of 83%. In addition to Medicaid, the FMAP is used in determining the federal share of certain other programs (e.g., foster care and adoption assistance under Title IV-E of the Social Security Act) and serves as the basis for calculating an enhanced FMAP that applies to the State Children's Health Insurance Program (CHIP).

During a recession adjustment period that begins with the first quarter of FY2009 and runs through the first quarter of FY2011, ARRA provisions that are intended to provide fiscal relief to states will hold all states harmless from any decline in their regular FMAPs, provide all states with an across-the-board increase of 6.2 percentage points, and provide qualifying states with an additional unemployment-related increase. The act further allows each territory to choose between an FMAP increase of 6.2 percentage points along with a 15% increase in its spending cap, or its regular FMAP along with a 30% increase in its spending cap. The full amount of the temporary FMAP increase only applies to Medicaid (with some exceptions) and a portion of the temporary FMAP increase (hold harmless plus across-the-board) applies to Title IV-E foster care and adoption assistance. States must meet various requirements to qualify for the FMAP increase.

These FMAP provisions account for almost all (nearly 98%) of the spending under Title V of Division B. Additional Medicaid provisions in the state fiscal relief title of ARRA include temporarily increase Medicaid payment adjustments for hospitals that serve a disproportionate number of low-income patients with special needs (known as DSH payments); extend existing moratoria on implementation of certain Medicaid regulations issued in 2007 and 2008; extend through December 2010 a program known as Transitional Medical Assistance (TMA), which provides continued Medicaid benefits for certain low-income families who would otherwise lose coverage because of changes in their income; extend through December 2010 the QI-1 program that allows Medicaid to pay Medicare Part B premiums for certain low-income individuals who are aged or have disabilities; and provide certain protections for Indians under Medicaid and CHIP.[64]

Other Provisions (Division B, Titles VI and VII)

Division B includes two titles that are not budgetary in nature. Title VI (Broadband Technology Opportunities Program) contains the authorization for the Broadband Technology Opportunities Program at the National Telecommunications and Information Administration (NTIA).[65] The program is funded by discretionary appropriations made to NTIA in the Department of Commerce.

Title VII (Limits on Executive Compensation) sets forth restrictions on the compensation of executives of companies during the period in which any obligation arising from financial assistance provided under the Troubled Assets Relief Program (TARP) remains outstanding. The Secretary of the Treasury is required to develop appropriate standards for executive compensation. A Board Compensation Committee must be set up to review employee compensation plans. Any annual or other meeting of the shareholders of a TARP recipient must permit a separate, nonbinding shareholder vote to approve the compensation of executives.[66]

Summary of Tax and Public Finance Provisions[67]

Division B, Title I of ARRA includes tax provisions targeted to individuals, families, and businesses. Other components of Title I include public finance measures designed to encourage economic development investment, energy conservation and efficiency, and a provision to increase the debt limit, which applies to federal debt held by the public and by the government. **Table 7**, toward the end of this chapter, provides summary information on the level of revenue changes (and mandatory spending) provided in ARRA.

Individual Income Tax Relief (Division B, Title I, Subtitle A)

In addition to the provisions mentioned previously in the economic recovery payments section of this chapter, ARRA provides other temporary changes to certain individual income tax provisions. The incentives target families and individuals, education, and housing.

Families and Individuals

ARRA enacts a temporary refundable tax credit of up to $400 for individuals and $800 for married couples for tax years 2009 and 2010. The Making Work Pay Tax Credit is calculated at a rate of 6.2% of earned income and will phase out for taxpayers with modified adjusted gross income in excess of $75,000, or in the case of married couples filing jointly, $150,000. The credit is estimated to cost $116.2 billion over 10 years. For taxpayers receiving paychecks who also are subject to withholding, the credit will typically be handled by their employers through automated withholding changes that began in early April. These changes are expected to result in an increase in take-home pay. Taxpayers who do not have taxes withheld by an employer during the year can also claim the credit on their 2009 tax return. Private pension recipients are not eligible for the credit unless they have earned income.[68]

At an estimated 10-year cost of $14.8 billion, ARRA increases the eligibility for the refundable child tax credit in 2009 and 2010. The child tax credit allows families with qualifying children under the age of 17 a credit against their federal income tax, and for families with three or more children, the child tax credit is refundable. The refundability of the credit depends on a minimum level of household earnings, which, for 2008, was scheduled to be $12,550. ARRA reduces the threshold to $3,000 permitting more taxpayers to use the additional child tax credit and increasing the amount of the payments they may receive.[69]

The legislation temporarily increases the earned income tax credit for working families with three or more children from 40% to 45%. Under current law, working families with two or more children currently qualify for a tax credit up to the family's first $12,570 of earned income. Generally, this credit is phased-out for working families with adjusted gross income in excess of $16,420 ($19,540 for married couples filing jointly) but the new law increases the beginning point of the phase-out range for all married couples filing a joint return (regardless of the number of children) by $1,880.[70]

In response to lagging sales and financial distress of American automakers, a temporary deduction for state and local sales and excise taxes paid on purchases of new cars, light trucks, recreational vehicles, and motorcycles through 2009 is included in ARRA. The deduction is available regardless of whether a taxpayer itemizes deductions and is limited to the tax on up to $49,500 of the purchase price of an eligible motor vehicle. The deduction is subject to a phase-out for taxpayers with adjusted gross income in excess of $125,000 ($250,000 in the case of a joint return).

ARRA includes, for 2009 only, an increase in the amount of income that can be exempted for taxpayers under the individual alternative minimum tax (AMT). The AMT was originally designed to make sure that everyone paid at least a minimum of taxes while still preserving the economic and social incentives in the tax code. The AMT provides an alternative set of rules for calculating income tax and the original amounts of income exempt from tax were not indexed for inflation. As a result, almost annually, temporary adjustments, referred to as patches, are made to the exemption amounts.[71] For the 2009 tax year these exemption amounts are adjusted upward by ARRA to $46,700 for individuals and $70,950 for joint filers.[72]

Education Tax Incentives

ARRA expands the Hope education tax credit for 2009 and 2010, by increasing its value and making it partially refundable. Under the new, temporary version of the tax credit, called the American Education Opportunity Tax Credit, taxpayers can receive a credit based on 100% of the first $2,000 of tuition and related expenses (including books) paid during the taxable year and 25% of the next $2,000 of tuition and related expenses paid during the taxable year. Thus, the maximum value increases from $1,800 to $2,500. Unlike the Hope credit, 40% of the American Education Opportunity credit is refundable and is subject to a phase-out for taxpayers with adjusted gross income in excess of $80,000 ($160,000 for married couples filing jointly). The modifications are estimated to cost $13 .907 billion over 10 years.[73]

Section 529 Programs, also known as Qualified Education Savings Plans, are tax-advantaged savings plans that cover all qualified education expenses, including tuition, room and board, mandatory fees and books. ARRA expands the eligible qualified education expenses to include computer technology or equipment or Internet access and related services.[74]

Expansion of Home Buyer Tax Credit

ARRA modifies and expands the first-time home buyer credit enacted in the Housing and Economic Recovery Act of 2008 (HERA; P.L. 110-289). The original credit was refundable but taxpayers receiving the credit were required to repay any amount received under this provision back to the government over 15 years in equal installments, or, if earlier, when the home is sold. The HERA credit was equivalent to an interest-free loan equal to 10% of the purchase of a home (up to $7,500) by first-time home buyers and applied to homes purchased on or after April 9, 2008 and before July 1, 2009. ARRA eliminates the repayment obligation for taxpayers that purchase homes after January 1, 2009 and increases the maximum value of the credit to $8,000. The tax credit, which is estimated to cost $6.638 billion over 10 years, extends the availability of the credit for homes purchased before December 1, 2009 and is limited to taxpayers with certain income levels.[75]

Energy Tax Incentives (Division B, Title I, Subtitle B)

More than $20 billion in energy-related tax incentives are included in ARRA with $14.1 billion for renewable energy, $2.3 billion for energy efficiency, $2.2 billion for transportation, $1.6 billion for manufacturing, and $1.4 billion for state and local government energy bonds.[76]

Renewable Energy

The renewable energy provisions include incentives for alternative energy investment and alternative energy production. In particular, ARRA expands an energy production tax credit that has been available for wind facilities and other qualifying facilities such as landfill gas, geothermal, hydropower, and others. The length of time to complete such facilities, to place them into service to begin operation, in order to claim the credit is extended three years by ARRA.

Other rules and modifications to investment tax credits are enacted along with several enhancements to existing tax-advantaged bond programs. Clean Renewable Energy Bonds (CREBs) and Qualified Energy Conservation Bonds (QECBs) are two examples. For nonprofit entities, $1.6 billion of new CREBs are authorized to finance facilities that generate electricity from wind, closed-loop biomass, open-loop biomass, geothermal, small irrigation, hydropower, landfill gas, marine renewable, and municipal waste (trash) combustion facilities. Of the $1.6 billion bond authorization for such projects, one-third is available to state/local/tribal governments, one-third to public power providers, and one-third to electric cooperatives. QECBs, initially authorized by the Emergency Economic Stabilization Act of 2008 (P.L. 110-343), can be used to finance capital expenditures to reduce energy use in publicly owned buildings by at least 20%; implementation of green community programs; rural development involving electricity production from renewables; research facilities and grants for the development of cellulosic ethanol or other nonfossil fuels; technologies to capture and sequester carbon dioxide produced by fossil fuel use; more efficient technologies for producing nonfossil fuels; automobile battery technologies and other technologies to reduce fossil fuel use in transportation, or technologies to reduce energy use in buildings; mass commuting facilities that reduce energy use (including pollution reduction for vehicles used for mass commuting); demonstration projects that promote commercialization of green building technology; conversion of agricultural waste for fuel production; advanced battery manufacturing technologies; technologies to reduce peak electricity demand; technologies that capture and sequester carbon dioxide emitted from fossil-fuel-fired power facilities; and public education campaigns to promote energy efficiency. ARRA authorizes $2.4 billion of QECBs to finance state, municipal and tribal government programs, greenhouse gas reduction initiatives, and loans and grants to implement green community programs.[77]

Energy Efficiency

Incentives for energy efficiency improvements to existing homes and residential efficiency are included in ARRA. Specifically, ARRA expands a 10% investment tax credit for home energy efficiency improvements, with caps of $50 for fans, $150 for furnaces and boilers, and $300 for shell improvements. The investment credit is increased to a rate of 30%, is available for an additional year, through 2010, and certain cap adjustments are made. Another provision of ARRA modifies a 30% investment tax credit for a variety of residential energy efficiency and renewable energy equipment. Prior to ARRA, caps were set on the equipment credit and the credit had to be reduced if the qualifying residence received subsidized financing. ARRA eliminates the caps on residential wind, geothermal, and solar thermal equipment. It also repeals the subsidized financing reduction for residential solar, geothermal, wind, and fuel cells.[78]

Transportation

The Energy Policy Act of 2005 (EPAct2005, P.L. 109-58) established tax credits for the installation of retail and residential alternative fuel refueling systems. Eligible fuels include ethanol, natural gas, liquefied petroleum gas, and hydrogen. The retail credit is valued at 30% of the system, up to $30,000. For residential systems, the credit is capped at $1,000. For calendar years 2009 and 2010, ARRA increases the Alternative Fuel Refueling Infrastructure Tax Credit to 50% for all fuels except hydrogen, and raises the limitations to $50,000 for retail systems and $2,000 for residential systems. For hydrogen, the 30% credit is maintained, but the credit limit is raised to $200,000.

ARRA modifies a tax credit for the purchase of new plug-in vehicles (plug-in hybrids and pure electric vehicles). The credit is based on the battery capacity of the vehicle, and, prior to ARRA, was capped at $7,500 for light-duty vehicles and up to $15,000 for the heaviest vehicles. When total U.S. sales of vehicles eligible for the credit reached 250,000, the credit began to phase out. ARRA modifies the existing tax credit to cap the per-vehicle credit at $7,500 for both light-duty vehicles and heavy-duty vehicles up to 14,000 pounds gross weight. It replaces the 250,000 total vehicle limit for phase-out of the credit with a 200,000 per-manufacturer limit. Further, ARRA eliminates the credit for heavier vehicles (after 2009), and establishes a credit of up to $2,500 for low-speed four-wheeled vehicles, as well as two- and three-wheeled electric vehicles. It establishes a credit of up to $4,000 for the conversion of an existing vehicle to battery power. ARRA also allows taxpayers otherwise subject to the Alternative Minimum Tax (AMT) to claim plug-in credit (as well as other alternative fuel and advanced vehicle credits).

Qualified transportation fringe benefits provided by an employer are excluded from an employee's gross income for income tax purposes and from an employee's wages for payroll tax purposes. The benefits include parking, transit passes, vanpool benefits, and qualified bicycle commuting reimbursements. Prior to ARRA, up to $230 (for 2009) per month of employer- provided parking was excludable from income. Up to $120 (for 2009) per month of employer- provided transit, vanpools, and bicycle commuting benefits was excludable from gross income. ARRA increases the benefit for transit, vanpools, and bicycle commuting to $230 per month, thus equalizing the tax-free benefit employers can provide for transit and parking expenses.[79]

Tax Incentives for Business (Division B, Title I, Subtitle C)

Several existing investment tax incentives are enhanced by ARRA along with the addition of some temporary provisions targeted at capital acquisitions.

Under ARRA, business taxpayers may expense (or deduct as a current expense) up to $250,000 of the total cost of certain depreciable assets placed in service in 2009, within certain limits. One limit is a phaseout threshold, which is set at $800,000 in 2009. The act also allows business taxpayers to claim a so-called bonus depreciation allowance in 2009 that is equal to 50% of the cost of qualified assets placed in service that year. Firms unable to use either option for accelerated depreciation have to write off that cost over a longer period, using current depreciation schedules. The rules governing the use of the allowance confine most of its benefits to relatively small firms.[80]

ARRA expands certain rules applying to net operating losses (NOLs). A net operating loss is incurred when a business taxpayer has negative taxable income and can be used to obtain a refund for taxes paid in the past or to reduce future tax obligations. The process of using an NOL to refund previously paid taxes is known as an NOL carryback, whereas the process of using an NOL to reduce future taxes is known as a carryforward. Under current law, there is a two-year carryback period and a 20-year carryforward period for most business taxpayers. ARRA extends the carryback period for up to five years for NOLs incurred in

2008. To qualify as an eligible small business to claim the ARRA incentive, a taxpayer must have $15,000,000 or less in gross receipts.[81]

Other business incentives enacted by ARRA include the deferment of income arising from discharged business indebtedness; special rules applicable to qualified small business stock for 2009 and 2010; temporary reduction in the recognition period for built-in gains tax; and clarification of regulations related to limitations on certain built-in losses following an ownership change.

Prior to ARRA, a taxpayer generally has income where the taxpayer cancels or repurchases its debt for an amount less than its adjusted issue price and is taxed on that income, which is known as cancellation of debt income (CODI). CODI is the excess of the old debt's adjusted issue price over the repurchase price. ARRA allows certain businesses to recognize CODI over 10 years, which essentially defers tax on CODI for the first four or five years and recognizes this income ratably over the following five taxable years. The provision applies for specified types of business debt repurchased by the business after December 31, 2008 and before January 1, 2011.

Section 1202 of the Internal Revenue Code provides a 50% exclusion for the gain from the sale of certain small business stock held for more than five years. The amount of gain eligible for the exclusion is limited to the greater of 10 times the taxpayer's basis in the stock, or $10 million gain from stock in that small business corporation. This provision is limited to individual investments and not the investments of a corporation. The non-excluded portion of section 1202 gain is taxed at the lesser of ordinary income rates or 28%, instead of the lower capital gains rates for individuals. ARRA increases the rate of exclusion to 75% for individuals on the gain from the sale of certain small business stock held for more than five years. This change is for stock issued after the date of enactment and before January 1, 2011.

Manufacturing Recovery Provisions (Division B, Title I, Subtitle D)

Two provisions are included in ARRA with the focus on enhancing manufacturing. Current rules for the industrial development bond are expanded to more broadly define eligibility for manufacturing facilities to include any facility used in the manufacturing, creation, or production of tangible or intangible property. The second provision enacts a new advanced energy investment credit of 30% in value for facilities engaged in the manufacture of advanced energy property.

Certain manufacturing facilities are eligible for tax exempt bond financing. The Internal Revenue Code Section 144(a)(12)(C), however, limits the definition of a manufacturing facility for the purposes of such financing to facilities that are used in the manufacturing or production of tangible personal property. ARRA amends the definition of manufacturing facility to any facility used in the manufacturing, creation, or production of tangible or intangible property described in section 197(d)(1)(C)(iii). Intangible property is any patent, copyright, formula, process, design, pattern, knowhow, format, or other similar item. The new law also clarifies which physical components of a manufacturing facility qualify as "ancillary" and therefore are subjected to a 25% limitation in the amount of bond issuance used to build or re-construct those components.

ARRA establishes a new 30% investment tax credit for facilities engaged in the manufacture of advanced energy property. Advanced energy property includes technology for the production of renewable energy, energy storage, energy conservation, efficient transmission and distribution of electricity, and carbon capture and sequestration. Credits are available only for projects certified by the Secretary of the Treasury, in consultation with the Secretary of Energy, through a competitive bidding process and the Secretary of the Treasury must establish a certification program no later than 180 days after date of enactment in order to allocate the credits. The maximum amount to be allocated is $2.3 billion.

Economic Recovery Tools (Division B, Title I, Subtitle E)

Economic recovery tools include investment and bond finance measures that are expanded by ARRA. Authorization for the new markets tax credit is increased by $1.5 billion a year for 2008 and 2009 to yield an annual available amount of $5 billion each year.[82] Existing bonds for tribal economic development and high speed rail are expanded as certain rules are temporarily relaxed for the purpose of expanding the availability of financing.

ARRA creates a new category of tax credit bonds for investment in economic recovery zones by authorizing $10 billion in recovery zone economic development bonds and $15 billion in recovery zone facility bonds. These bonds can be issued during 2009 and 2010. Each state would receive a share of the national allocation based on that state's job losses in 2008 as a percentage of national job losses in 2008 (each state will receive a minimum allocation of these bonds). These allocations are sub-allocated to local municipalities. Municipalities receiving an allocation of these bonds are permitted to use these bonds to invest in infrastructure, job training, education, and economic development in areas within the boundaries of the state, city or county that has significant poverty, unemployment or home foreclosures.

Under the Internal Revenue Code, Projects funded by bonds issued by tribal governments must satisfy an "essential governmental function" requirement, which limits tribal governments' abilities to issue tax-exempt bonds to finance economic development. ARRA temporarily allows tribal governments to issue $2 billion in tax-exempt bonds for projects without this restriction in order to spur economic development on tribal lands, and requires the Secretary of the Treasury to study whether this restriction should be repealed on a permanent basis.

States are allowed to issue private activity bonds for high-speed rail facilities, which are defined as a facility for the transportation of passengers between metropolitan areas using vehicles that are reasonably expected to operate at speeds in excess of 150 miles per hour between scheduled stops. ARRA modifies the definition of vehicles to include those trains that are capable of attaining speeds in excess of 150 miles per hour.

Infrastructure Financing Tools (Division B, Title I, Subtitle F)

Infrastructure financing tools primarily include bond programs and certain rules and changes are made to many programs in an effort to broaden finance options. Waivers of certain rules for financial institutions to deduct interest expense on the investment in tax-exempt municipal bonds issued during 2009 and 2010 are enacted by ARRA along with modification to a small issuer exception to tax-exempt interest expense allocation rules for financial institutions. New categories of certain tax credit bonds also are added, as well as increases in authorization amounts. These bonds include qualified school construction bonds and Build America Bonds.

Financial Institutions' Deduction of Interest Expense on Tax-Exempt Bonds

Financial institutions have not been allowed to take a deduction for the portion of their interest expense that is allocable to such institution's investments in tax-exempt municipal bonds. In determining the portion of interest expense that is allocable to investments in tax-exempt municipal bonds, ARRA excludes investments in tax-exempt municipal bonds issued during 2009 and 2010 to the extent that these investments constitute less than 2% of the average adjusted bases of all the assets of the financial institution. For purposes of the interest disallowance rule mentioned previously, bonds that have been issued by a "qualified small issuer" are not taken into account as investments in tax-exempt municipal bonds. Under current law, a "qualified small issuer" is defined as any issuer that reasonably anticipates that the amount of its tax-exempt obligations (other than certain private activity bonds) will not exceed $10,000,000. ARRA increases this dollar threshold to $30,000,000 when determining whether a tax-exempt obligation issued in 2009 and 2010 qualifies for this small issuer exception. The small issuer exception also applies to an issue if all of the ultimate borrowers in such issue separately qualify for the exception. For these purposes, the issuer of a qualified 501(c)(3) bond shall be deemed to be the ultimate borrower on whose behalf a bond was issued.

Delay Application of Withholding Requirement on Certain Governmental Payments for Goods and Services

For payments to contractors made after December 31, 2010, the Internal Revenue Code requires withholding at a 3% rate on certain payments made by federal, state, and local governments to persons providing property or services. The withholding is required regardless of whether the government entity making the payment is the recipient of the property or services. Government entities with less than $100 million in annual expenditures for property or services are exempt. Numerous government entities and small businesses have raised concerns about the application of this provision, expressing concern about the administrative burden of implementation. ARRA delays for one year, through December 31, 2011, the application of the 3% withholding requirement on government payments for goods and services in order to provide time for the Treasury Department to study the impact of this provision on government entities and other taxpayers.

Tax-Exempt Bonds and Tax Credit Bonds

The federal government subsidizes the cost of most state and local debt by excluding the interest income from federal income taxation. This tax exemption of interest income is granted because it is believed that state and local capital facilities will be under provided if state and local taxpayers have to pay the full cost.[83] Both tax credit bonds and tax-exempt bonds provide a subsidy to municipalities by reducing the cash interest payments that a state or local government must make on its debt.

Interest on private activity bonds issued by state and local governments typically is not deductible under the alternative minimum tax (AMT), though that interest is deductible under the regular income tax system. This tax treatment can increase the costs of issuing tax-exempt private activity bonds imposed on state and local governments by limiting the marketability of these bonds and, therefore, forces state and local governments to issue these bonds at higher interest rates. ARRA temporarily waives the interest exclusion for the AMT for bonds issued in 2009 or 2010 in order to maximize investment in such bonds, which are typically issued by state and local governments. ARRA also allows AMT relief for current refunding of private activity bonds issued after 2003 and refunded during 2009 and 2010.[84]

ARRA creates a new category of tax credit bonds for the construction, rehabilitation, or repair of public school facilities or for the acquisition of land on which a public school facility will be constructed. There are national limitations imposed by ARRA on the amount of qualified school construction bonds that may be issued. State and local governments have a limit of $22 billion ($11 billion allocated initially in 2009 and the remainder allocated in 2010) and Indian tribal governments have a limit of $400 million ($200 million allocated initially in 2009 and the remainder allocated in 2010).

ARRA also allows an additional $1.4 billion of Qualified Zone Academy Bond (QZAB) issuing authority to state and local governments in 2009 and 2010, which can be used to finance renovations, purchase equipment, develop course material, and train teachers and personnel at a qualified zone academy. In general, a qualified zone academy is any public school (or academic program within a public school) below college level that is located in an empowerment zone or enterprise community and is designed to cooperate with businesses to enhance the academic curriculum and increase graduation and employment rates. QZABs are a form of tax credit bonds which offer the holder a federal tax credit instead of interest.

ARRA created a tax credit bond option for state and local governments (Build America Bonds). For 2009 and 2010, the bill provides state and local governments with the option of issuing a tax credit bond instead of a tax-exempt governmental obligation bond. Because the market for tax credits is currently small given current economic conditions, the bill would allow the state or local government to elect to receive a direct payment from the federal government equal to the subsidy that would have otherwise been delivered through the federal tax credit for bonds.

Other Provisions (Division B, Title I, Subtitle G)

ARRA includes an increase in the debt limit, which applies to federal debt held by the public (that is, debt held outside the federal government itself) and to federal debt held by the government's own accounts.

The 2008 economic slowdown, which reduced federal tax revenues and increased federal outlays, caused federal deficit spending to rise, thus bringing forward the projected date when the federal debt will reach its current limit. In July 2008, the Housing and Economic Recovery Act of 2008 (P.L. 110-289) included a debt limit increase to $10,615 billion. Subsequently, the Emergency Economic Stabilization Act of 2008 (Division A of P.L. 110-

343) raised the debt limit, for the second time in 2008, to $11,315 billion. The debt limit was raised for the third time in less than a year as a result of passage of ARRA, which raises the debt limit to $12,104 billion.[85]

Grants in lieu of tax credits were enacted and the authorization for those credits was assigned to the Treasury Department. Several provisions—electricity production tax credits, investment tax credits for certain renewable property, and low income housing tax credits—have existed in the tax code with the intent of attracting private capital investment in targeted projects. Concern about insufficient demand led to the enactment in ARRA of an option for certain entities to temporarily request grants instead of the tax credits.

Table 7. Total Revenue and Mandatory Spending Changes for Fiscal Years 2009-2019, by Division and Title (amounts in millions of dollars)

Category	Revenue/Outlays
Revenues	
Division A	
Title XII – Transportation and Housing and Urban Development	-143
HOME, Low-Income Housing Tax Credit Program	
Subtotal, Division A	**-143**
Division B	
Title 1 – Tax Provisions	-214,576
Title II – Assistance for Unemployed Workers and Struggling	-879
Families	
Title III – Health Insurance Assistance	392
Title IV – Health Insurance Technology	3,260
Subtotal, Division B	**-211,803**
Mandatory Spending	
Division B	
Title I – Tax Provisions	73,763
Refundable Tax Credits	68,955
Other Provisions	4,808
Title II – Assistance for Unemployed Workers and Struggling Families	57,264
Unemployment Compensation	39,231
Economic Recovery Payments, TANF, and Child Support	18,033
Title III – Health Insurance Assistance	25,069
Title IV – Health Information Technology	20,819
Title V – State Fiscal Relief	90,042
Total	**266,958**

Source: Congressional Budget Office. Letter to the Honorable Nancy Pelosi, Table 2 (Estimated Cost of the Conference Agreement for H.R. 1, The American Recovery and Reinvestment Act of 2009, as Posted on the Website of the House Committee on Rules), February 13, 2009, available on the CBO website at http://www.cbo.gov/ftpdocs/99xx/doc9989/ hr1conference.pdf.

Notes: Positive amounts are increases in revenues or outlays; the minus sign (-) denotes reductions in revenues. Components may not sum to totals because of rounding. About $29 billion in mandatory spending increases in Division A are excluded from this table.

SUMMARY OF GENERAL OVERSIGHT PROVISIONS

Divisions A and B of ARRA contain numerous oversight, accountability, and transparency provisions. Many provisions are specific to individual programs, agencies, and appropriations accounts. Other provisions are more general in nature, applying to multiple programs, agencies, or appropriations. This section concerns the latter type.[86] Most of the general oversight provisions appear to cover activities and provisions associated with Division A rather than the entire law.

The general oversight provisions might be further categorized into two groups:

- appropriations to oversight entities including offices of inspector general (IG), the Government Accountability Office (GAO), and a newly established Recovery Accountability and Transparency Board (RATB); and
- a number of substantive provisions, including establishment of RATB and enumeration of numerous reporting requirements.

Appropriations to IGs, GAO, and RATB are included predominately in Division A. The provisions are distributed among 12 titles in Division A and one title in Division B.[87] In total, 23 IGs receive $254.75 million in 25 separate appropriations.[88] IGs in all 15 executive departments receive appropriations, ranging from the Department of Veterans Affairs on the low side ($1 million in a single appropriation) to the Department of Health and Human Services on the high side ($48.25 million in two appropriations). ARRA provides funding to be available to IGs with widely varying periods of availability. For the IG at the Department of State, for example, funds are available until the end of FY2010. Other IGs variously have funds available until the end of FY2011, FY2012, FY2013, or "until expended" (i.e., "no-year" funds). GAO receives $25 million, available through the end of FY2010, and RATB receives $84 million, available through the end of FY20 11. Some appropriations specify that funds are to be used specifically for oversight of ARRA-related activities, but others essentially are supplemental appropriations that do not restrict use of funds to ARRA-related purposes. It should be noted that RATB has authority to transfer up to 100% of its funds to any office of inspector general, the Office of Management and Budget, the General Services Administration, and an advisory panel for RATB that ARRA establishes (Division A, Title XV, Section 1524(f)). In total, the appropriations provided to these oversight-oriented entities sum to $363.75 million.

The second group of general oversight provisions is included only in Division A—chiefly in Titles XV and XVI—albeit in considerable variety. Among other things, these substantive provisions establish new oversight-oriented entities like RATB, enumerate diverse reporting requirements for federal agencies and nonfederal recipients of funds, and task RATB, IGs, and GAO with several duties. Under ARRA's requirements, for example, RATB's purpose is "to coordinate and conduct oversight of covered funds to prevent fraud, waste, and abuse." RATB's membership is to be comprised of at least 10 IGs, in addition to or including a chairperson, who may be designated or appointed by the President according to certain criteria. RATB has several enumerated functions, including to review whether reporting for contracts and grants "meets applicable standards" and "specifies the purpose of the contract or grant and measures of performance." In addition, RATB is required to establish a website.

The Obama Administration established a rudimentary Recovery.gov web site in anticipation of enactment of stimulus legislation.[89] As agencies implement ARRA, the website is to contain, among many other things, considerable information about how funds are allocated and used. IGs and GAO also are required to conduct certain reviews. State and local governments that receive funds also will have certain certification and reporting requirements, which may be funded, at least in part, by flexibility granted to federal agencies to adjust applicable limits on administrative expenditures for federal awards.

Further requirements and guidance concerning ARRA implementation was forthcoming from the Office of Management and Budget (OMB), some of which went beyond ARRA's statutory requirements. On February 18, 2009, OMB issued "initial implementing guidance" regarding ARRA, including numerous reporting requirements, to agencies in a 62-page document.[90] Some of the required information will be posted on Recovery.gov and agency-specific ARRA-related websites. On March 20, 2009, President Obama issued a five-page presidential memorandum entitled "Ensuring Responsible Spending of Recovery Act Funds."[91] The memorandum directed agencies in how to use "available discretion" when allocating and spending certain ARRA-related funding. On April 3, 2009, OMB issued "updated implementing guidance" to agencies in a 175- page document.[92] Further guidance is expected.

Additional Resources

Many additional resources pertaining to the American Recovery and Reinvestment Act of 2009 are available online. An overview of online resources, particularly with respect to federal, state, and local entities, is provided in CRS Report R40244, *Authoritative Resources on the American Recovery and Reinvestment Act (ARRA)*, by Kim Walker Klarman and Julie Jennings.

Key Congressional Research Service reports on various funding and policy areas affected by ARRA are grouped together under the Current Legislative Issues term "Economy, Recession, and Financial Sector" on the CRS homepage: http://apps.crs.gov/cli/cli.aspx?PRDS_CLI_ITEM_ID=3405&from=3&fromId=4.

In addition, reports on the individual annual appropriations bills are listed under the Current Legislative Issues term "Appropriations and Budget" at http://apps.crs.gov/cli/level_2.aspx?PRDS_CLI_ITEM_ID=73.

"Recovery.gov" is the centerpiece of the Administration's online effort to monitor implementation of the act: http://www.recovery.gov/. The Administration's website is intended to be a repository for information related to implementation and oversight of the stimulus, with information about available funding, distribution of funds, and major recipients. Under the umbrella of "Recovery.gov," separate websites established by federal agencies and states may be accessed:

- Federal agency recovery sites: http://www.recovery.gov/?q=content/agencies; and
- State recovery sites: http://www.recovery.gov/?q=content/state-recovery-page.

Finally, the Office of Management and Budget (OMB) has established a "Recovery Act Guidance" page on its website, including OMB memoranda and other documentation providing guidance to federal agencies: http://www.whitehouse.gov/omb/recovery

ACKNOWLEDGMENTS

Carol Hardy Vincent and Jennifer E. Lake coordinated the preparation of the "Summary of Discretionary Spending Provisions" section.

Karen Spar coordinated the preparation of the "Summary of Mandatory Spending Provisions" section.

Pamela J. Jackson coordinated the preparation of the "Summary of Tax and Public Finance Provisions" section.

Clinton T. Brass prepared the "Summary of General Oversight Provisions" section.

Mary Frances Bley prepared the "Additional Resources" section and several tables.

Robert Keith prepared the remaining sections and several tables.

End Notes

[1] National Bureau of Economic Research, *Determination of the December 2007 Peak in Economic Activity*, Dec. 1, 2008 (revised Dec. 11, 2008 version available at http://www.nber.org/cycles

[2] Joint Committee on Taxation, *Estimated Budget Effects Of The "Economic Stimulus Act Of 2008, " As Passed By The House Of Representatives And The Senate On February 7, 2008*, JCX-17-08, Feb. 8, 2008.

[3] The act consisted of three components: Division A, the Emergency Economic Stabilization Act of 2008; Division B, the Energy Improvement and Extension Act of 2008; and Division C, the Tax Extenders and Alternative Minimum Tax Relief Act of 2008. For an extensive discussion of legislative action relating to economic stimulus issues, see CRS Report R40 104, *Economic Stimulus: Issues and Policies*, by Jane G. Gravelle, Thomas L. Hungerford, and Marc Labonte.

[4] For additional information on the TARP program, see CRS Report RL34730, *Troubled Asset Relief Program: Legislation and Treasury Implementation*, by Baird Webel and Edward V. Murphy.

[5] For additional information on the act, see CRS Report RL3471 1, *Consolidated Appropriations Act for FY2009 (P.L. 110-329): An Overview*, by Robert Keith.

[6] Further continuing appropriations were provided from March 6 through March 11, 2009, by P.L. 111-6.

[7] For more information on PAYGO requirements, see CRS Report RL34300, *Pay-As-You-Go Procedures for Budget Enforcement*, by Robert Keith.

[8] In the report on H.Res. 92 (H.Rept. 111-9; Jan. 27, 2009), the self-executing amendment was presented in Part A and the other 11 amendments were presented in Part B.

[9] See the *Congressional Record* (daily ed.), Feb. 10, 2009, p. H1096.

[10] Congressional Budget Office, *Letter to the Honorable Harry Reid* (transmitting a cost estimate for the bill as passed by the Senate on February 10, 2009), Feb. 11, 2009, p. 1, available on the CBO website at http://www.cbo.gov/ftpdocs/99xx/doc9984/hr1senatepassed.pdf.

[11] See "Remarks by the President and Vice President at Signing of the American Recovery and Reinvestment Act," Feb. 17, 2009, available on the White House website at http://www.whitehouse.gov/the_press_office/Remarks-by-thePresident-and-Vice-President-at-Signing-of-the-American-Recovery-and-Reinvestment-Act/.

[12] Some mandatory programs, such as Medicaid and veterans' compensation, do not have their own funding mechanisms and rely on annual appropriations; the level of spending for such programs effectively is determined by the substantive law.

[13] The Joint Committee on Taxation prepared an estimate of the revenue impact of the act, *Estimated Budget Effects of the Revenue Provisions Contained in the Conference Agreement for H.R. 1, the "American Recovery and Reinvestment Tax Act of 2009, "* JCX-19-09, Feb. 12, 2009. As indicated in footnote 3 of the estimate, the "net change" is considerably greater than the revenue changes shown in the CBO cost estimate because the net

change incorporates more than $100 billion in related outlay increases (e.g., increases from expanded refundable tax credits).

[14] According to the CBO cost estimate, the discretionary spending totals (under Division A of the act) include about $29 billion in mandatory spending increases and $0.1 billion in revenue reductions over FY2009-FY2019.

[15] Congressional Budget Office, *Letter to the Honorable Charles E. Grassley*, Mar. 2, 2009, available at http://www.cbo.gov/ftpdocs/100xx/doc10008/03-02-Macro_Effects_of_ARRA.pdf.

[16] The totals for the other FY2009 funding reflect all FY2009 appropriations to date, regular and supplemental, other than those included in ARRA. They generally are derived from the tables in the conference reports on the FY2009 appropriations bills.

[17] See the table summarizing funding levels in Division A, *Congressional Record* (daily ed.), Feb. 13, 2009, p. H1553.

[18] Sec. 1601, Division A.

[19] Sec. 1603, Division A.

[20] Sec. 701, Division A.

[21] The law contains other provisions on the allocation of appropriations that are beyond the scope of this discussion.

[22] Sec. 3, "Purposes and Principles."

[23] Sec. 1602, Division A.

[24] This section was prepared by Jim Monke.

[25] Of the $26.47 billion total, $11.33 billion was FY2009 funding and the remainder was for other fiscal years.

[26] For more information on funding in Title I of ARRA, see CRS Report R40160, *Agriculture, Nutrition, and Rural Provisions in the American Recovery and Reinvestment Act (ARRA) of 2009*, coordinated by Jim Monke.

[27] This section was prepared by Nathan James, Jennifer D. Williams, Oscar R. Gonzales, and John F. Sargent, Jr.

[28] For additional information on the BTOP authorization in ARRA, see CRS Report R40436, *Broadband Infrastructure Programs in the American Recovery and Reinvestment Act*, by Lennard G. Kruger.

[29] This section was prepared by Pat Towell.

[30] This total does not reflect a $10.35 billion Tricare accrual from contributions to DOD's retiree health care fund. Including this amount, the DOD total would be $553.91 billion.

[31] This section was prepared by Carl E. Behrens and Nicole T. Carter.

[32] Of the $50.83 billion total, $44.34 billion is FY2009 funding and the remainder is for other fiscal years.

[33] This section was prepared by Garrett Hatch.

[34] For more information on funds provided to the Small Business Administration in the economic stimulus law, see CRS Report R40241, *Small Business Provisions in the American Recovery and Reinvestment Act of 2009*, by N. Eric Weiss and Oscar R. Gonzales.

[35] TAA is the acronym for Trade Adjustment Assistance.

[36] For more information on the role of the Board and the oversight provisions of ARRA, see the "Summary of General Oversight Provisions" section of this chapter. Division A, Title XV establishes the board as the "Recovery Accountability and Transparency Board," omitting the word "Act." This chapter uses both versions of the board's name, depending on whether the board's funding is being discussed (Division A, Title V) or the board's establishment is being discussed (Division A, Title XV).

[37] This section was prepared by Jennifer E. Lake and Chad C. Haddal.

[38] This section was prepared by Carol Hardy Vincent.

[39] For information on these grants and other water infrastructure funding in ARRA, see CRS Report R40216, *Water Infrastructure Funding in the American Recovery and Reinvestment Act of 2009*, by Claudia Copeland and Nicole T. Carter.

[40] For more information on funds for these agencies in the economic stimulus law, see CRS Report R40217, *Federal Lands Provisions of Economic Stimulus Legislation (H.R. 1)*, by Carol Hardy Vincent.

[41] This section was prepared by Pamela W. Smith, Rebecca R. Skinner, and Gerald Mayer.

[42] Of the $72.56 billion total, $71.73 billion is FY2009 funding and the remaining $83 1.0 million is FY20 10 funding (mandatory funding for Pell Grants in the Department of Education appropriation).

[43] For more information on ARRA funds for DOL, see CRS Report R401 82, *Funding for Workforce Development in the American Recovery and Reinvestment Act (ARRA) of 2009*, by David H. Bradley and Ann Lordeman.

[44] For more information, see CRS Report R40161, *The Health Information Technology for Economic and Clinical Health (HITECH) Act*, by C. Stephen Redhead. See also the discussion of related health information technology provisions in Division B of the act, in the "Summary of Mandatory Spending Provisions" section later in this chapter.

[45] For more information on HHS programs in ARRA, see CRS Report R401 81, *Selected Health Funding in the American Recovery and Reinvestment Act of 2009*, coordinated by C. Stephen Redhead; CRS Report R4021 1, *Human Services Provisions of the American Recovery and Reinvestment Act*, by Gene Falk et al.; and CRS Report RL33880, *Older Americans Act (OAA) Funding*, by Angela Napili.

[46] For more information on ED programs in ARRA, see CRS Report R4015 1, *Funding for Education in the American Recovery and Reinvestment Act of 2009 (P.L. 111-5)*, by Rebecca R. Skinner et al..

[47] Pell Grants also received mandatory appropriations in ARRA to increase the maximum Pell Grant award. The total provided was $1.47 billion, of which $643.0 million was for FY2009 and $831.0 million was for FY2010.

[48] This may also include, if applicable, funding state formula increases to support elementary and secondary education for FY2010 and FY2011 and the phasing in of state equity and adequacy adjustments if these increases were enacted in state law prior to October 1, 2008.

[49] State support for public institutions of higher education excludes tuition and fees paid by students.

[50] For more information on ARRA funds for SSA, see CRS Report R40188, *Social Security Provisions in the American Recovery and Reinvestment Act of 2009*, by Scott Szymendera.

[51] This section was prepared by Ida A. Brudnick.

[52] This section was prepared by Daniel H. Else.

[53] Warrior transition complexes often contain barracks, family support facilities, and administration spaces near military medical facilities where injured soldiers and their families can reside during convalescence.

[54] This section was prepared by Marian Leonardo Lawson, Susan B. Epstein, and Kennon H. Nakamura.

[55] This section was prepared by David Randall Peterman and Maggie McCarty.

[56] Of the $61.80 billion total, $61.78 billion is FY2009 funding and the remaining $13.0 million is FY2010 funding.

[57] Of the $13.68 billion total, $13.66 billion is FY2009 funding and the remaining $13.0 million is FY2010 funding.

[58] For detailed information, see the following CRS reports: CRS Report RS22718, *Trade Adjustment Assistance for Workers (TAA) and Reemployment Trade Adjustment Assistance (RTAA)*, by John J. Topoleski; CRS Report RS20210, *Trade Adjustment Assistance for Firms: Economic, Program, and Policy Issues*, by J. F. Hornbeck; and CRS Report R40206, *Trade Adjustment Assistance for Farmers*, by Remy Jurenas.

[59] For detailed information, see CRS Report R40368, *Unemployment Insurance Provisions in the American Recovery and Reinvestment Act of 2009*, by Alison M. Shelton, Kathleen Romig, and Julie M. Whittaker.

[60] For detailed information, see CRS Report R40211, *Human Services Provisions of the American Recovery and Reinvestment Act*, by Gene Falk et al..

[61] For detailed information, see CRS Report R40188, *Social Security Provisions in the American Recovery and Reinvestment Act of 2009*, by Scott Szymendera.

[62] For detailed information, see CRS Report R40420, *Health Insurance Premium Assistance for the Unemployed: The American Recovery and Reinvestment Act of 2009*, coordinated by Janemarie Mulvey.

[63] For detailed information, see CRS Report R40161, *The Health Information Technology for Economic and Clinical Health (HITECH) Act*, by C. Stephen Redhead.

[64] For detailed information, see CRS Report R40223, *American Recovery and Reinvestment Act of 2009 (ARRA, P.L. 111-5): Title V, Medicaid Provisions*, coordinated by Cliff Binder.

[65] For additional information on the BTOP authorization in ARRA, see CRS Report R40436, *Broadband Infrastructure Programs in the American Recovery and Reinvestment Act*, by Lennard G. Kruger.

[66] Title VII is discussed in CRS Report RS22583, *Executive Compensation: SEC Regulations and Congressional Proposals*, by Michael V. Seitzinger.

[67] This section was prepared by Pamela J. Jackson, Steve Maguire, Mindy Levit, Mark Keightley, and Maxim Shvedov.

[68] As mentioned earlier in the report, taxpayers cannot receive full benefits from both the economic recovery payment and the Making Work Pay tax credit in a single tax year. The amount of the Making Work Pay Credit claimed must be reduced by the amount, if any, of the economic recovery payment.

[69] For detailed information see CRS Report RL34715, *The Child Tax Credit*, by Maxim Shvedov.

[70] For detailed information see CRS Report RS2 1352, *The Earned Income Tax Credit (EITC): Changes for 2008 and 2009*, by Christine Scott.

[71] Under current law, to calculate AMT tax liability an individual first calculates regular taxable income and then adds back various tax items (called adjustments and preferences). The three major preference items added back to the AMT tax base are state and local tax deductions, personal exemptions, and miscellaneous itemized deductions. This grossed up income becomes the tax base for the AMT. Then the exemption is subtracted to obtain AMT taxable income.

[72] For detailed information see CRS Report RL30149, *The Alternative Minimum Tax for Individuals*, by Steven Maguire.

[73] For detailed information see CRS Report RL32507, *Higher Education Tax Credits: An Economic Analysis*, by Christian Gonzalez and Mark P. Keightley.

[74] For detailed information see CRS Report RL31214, *Saving for College Through Qualified Tuition (Section 529) Programs*, by Linda Levine.

[75] For detailed information see CRS Report R40 153, *The First-Time Homebuyer Tax Credit: An Economic Analysis*, by Mark P. Keightley and CRS Report RL34664, *The First-Time Homebuyer Tax Credit*, by Carol A. Pettit.

[76] For more detailed information see CRS Report R40412, *Energy Provisions in the American Recovery and Reinvestment Act of 2009 (P.L. 111-5)*, coordinated by Fred Sissine.

[77] CRS Report R40412, *Energy Provisions in the American Recovery and Reinvestment Act of 2009 (P.L. 111-5)*, coordinated by Fred Sissine.

[78] Ibid.

[79] Ibid.

[80] For detailed information see CRS Report RL3 1852, *Small Business Expensing Allowance: Current Status, Legislative Proposals, and Economic Effects*, by Gary Guenther.

[81] For more detailed information see CRS Report RL34535, *Net Operating Losses: Proposed Extension of Carryback Period*, by Mark P. Keightley.

[82] For more detailed information see CRS Report RL34402, *New Markets Tax Credit: An Introduction*, by Donald J. Marples.

[83] For more detailed information see CRS Report RL30638, *Tax-Exempt Bonds: A Description of State and Local Government Debt*, by Steven Maguire.

[84] For more detailed information see CRS Report RL30 149, *The Alternative Minimum Tax for Individuals*, by Steven Maguire and CRS Report RL3 1457, *Private Activity Bonds: An Introduction*, by Steven Maguire.

[85] For detailed information see CRS Report RL31967, *The Debt Limit: History and Recent Increases*, by D. Andrew Austin and Mindy R. Levit.

[86] Oversight issues and provisions that are specific to certain programs, agencies, and appropriations may be discussed in other CRS reports. It should be noted that the notion of what constitutes a "general" oversight provision may be in the eye of the beholder. Therefore, some observers might categorize ARRA's oversight provisions in other ways.

[87] A single appropriation to the Office of Inspector General of the Department of Health and Human Services was included in Title V of Division B.

[88] For more information about statutory IGs, see CRS Report 98-3 79, *Statutory Offices of Inspector General: Past and Present*, by Frederick M. Kaiser.

[89] See http://www.recovery

[90] U.S. Executive Office of the President, Office of Management and Budget, "Initial Implementing Guidance for the American Recovery and Reinvestment Act of 2009," memorandum for heads of departments and agencies from Peter R. Orszag, Director, M-09-10, February 18, 2009, http://www.whitehouse.gov/omb/assets 10.pdf.

[91] U.S. President (Obama), "Ensuring Responsible Spending of Recovery Act Funds," memorandum for heads of departments and agencies (contained in press release), March 20, 2009, http://www.whitehouse.gov/the_press_office/Memorandum-for-the-Heads-of-Executive-Departments-and-Agencies-3- 20-09/.

[92] U.S. Executive Office of the President, Office of Management and Budget, "Updated Implementing Guidance for the American Recovery and Reinvestment Act of 2009," memorandum for heads of departments and agencies from Peter R. Orszag, Director, M-09-15, April 3, 2009, http://www.whitehouse.gov/omb/assets

In: American Recovery and Reinvestment Act: History... ISBN: 978-1-61668-355-9
Editor: Paul G. Tellis

Chapter 6

GENERAL OVERSIGHT PROVISION IN THE AMERICAN RECOVERY AND REINVESTMENT ACT OF 2009 (ARRA): REQUIREMENTS AND RELATED ISSUES*

Clinton T. Brass
Government Organization and Management

SUMMARY

In the wake of a rapidly deteriorating economic picture and year-long recession that the Congressional Budget Office has called the most severe since World War II, Congress passed the American Recovery and Reinvestment Act of 2009 (ARRA; P.L. 111-5). This chapter discusses ARRA's "general oversight provisions" and several related issues for Congress. For purposes of this chapter, the term "general oversight provision" means an oversight-related provision that addresses multiple programs, agencies, or appropriations accounts. Provisions that are specific to a single program or appropriation (e.g., appropriations set-asides and reporting requirements) are excluded from the report's scope.

The report includes tabular presentations of ARRA's general oversight provisions. The provisions provide for, among other things, establishment of a Recovery Accountability and Transparency Board, numerous reporting and evaluation requirements, and increased resources for agency Inspectors General (IGs) and the Government Accountability Office (GAO).

Even before considering experience with implementation, several broad issues related to ARRA oversight may be of interest to Congress. These include assessments of ARRA's role in achieving economic objectives. Typical objectives of a fiscal stimulus policy relate to increasing economic activity in the short term, compared to what would have happened without a stimulus. In addition, some stakeholders have emphasized that stimulating the economy in the short term alone is not a sufficient definition of "success." From this

* This is an edited, reformatted and augmented version of a CRS Report for Congress publication dated May 2009.

perspective, the manner in which spending, tax, and other public policies are implemented, and also the impacts of these policies, may be important.

All of these perspectives appear to have been included among the law's explicit purposes and "general principles concerning use of funds." Given ARRA's direction to "commenc[e] expenditures and activities as quickly as possible consistent with prudent management," difficult trade-offs among goals may be inevitable. Over time, Congress may consider whether existing management and oversight mechanisms, in combination with ARRA's additional provisions, adequately support effective management and oversight of ARRA implementation. The experience with ARRA also may offer lessons learned for the "normal," non-ARRA systems of oversight.

Beyond the immediate situation, additional oversight issues for Congress may relate to longer-term questions. These include how to build and monitor capacity within agencies to respond effectively to crises. Questions also may arise regarding how to build and monitor capacity in agencies and government overall to anticipate crises, mitigate their risks, and avoid preventable crises. This chapter analyzes these and other issues after reviewing how the oversight provisions were developed and providing an overview of the enacted provisions themselves, including related appropriations and reporting requirements.

The topic of subsequent implementation of the oversight provisions, including actions by executive agencies and the Office of Management and Budget (OMB), is not included in the scope of this chapter.

In the wake of a rapidly deteriorating economic picture and year-long recession that the Congressional Budget Office (CBO) has called the most severe since World War II, Congress passed the American Recovery and Reinvestment Act of 2009 (ARRA).[1] This chapter discusses ARRA's "general oversight provisions" and several related issues for Congress. For purposes of this chapter, the term "general oversight provision" means an oversight-related provision that addresses multiple programs, agencies, or appropriations accounts. Provisions that are specific to a single program or appropriation (e.g., appropriations set-asides and reporting requirements) are excluded from the report's scope. The provisions provide for, among other things, establishment of a Recovery Accountability and Transparency Board, numerous reporting and evaluation requirements, and increased resources for agency Inspectors General (IGs).

The topic of subsequent implementation of the oversight provisions, including actions by executive agencies and the Office of Management and Budget (OMB), is not included in the scope of this chapter. Nevertheless, even before considering experience with implementation, several broad issues related to ARRA oversight may be of interest to Congress.[2] These include assessments of ARRA's role in achieving economic objectives. Typical objectives of a fiscal stimulus policy relate to increasing economic activity in the short term, compared to what would have happened without a stimulus. In addition, some stakeholders have emphasized that stimulating the economy in the short term alone is not a sufficient definition of "success." From this perspective, the manner in which spending, tax, and other public policies are implemented, and also the impacts of these policies, may be important. All of these perspectives appear to have been included among the law's explicit purposes and "general principles."

Given ARRA's direction to "commenc[e] expenditures and activities as quickly as possible consistent with prudent management" (P.L. 111-5, Section 3), difficult trade-offs among goals may be inevitable. Over time, Congress may consider whether existing management and oversight mechanisms, in combination with ARRA's additional provisions, adequately support effective management and oversight of ARRA implementation. The experience with ARRA also may offer lessons learned for the "normal" systems of oversight that correspond to non-ARRArelated funding and operations. Beyond the immediate situation, additional oversight issues for Congress may relate to longer-term questions. These include how to build capacity within agencies to respond effectively to crises. Questions also may arise regarding how to build capacity in agencies and government overall to anticipate crises, mitigate their risks, and avoid preventable crises. This chapter analyzes these and other issues after reviewing how the oversight provisions were developed and providing an overview of the enacted provisions themselves, including related appropriations and reporting requirements.

DEVELOPMENT OF ARRA'S OVERSIGHT PROVISIONS

Examination of how ARRA and its general oversight provisions were developed may provide perspectives on congressional objectives associated with the legislation. In addition, reflection on the development of the provisions may suggest opportunities to make enhancements in ARRA's existing oversight provisions or to address any perceived gaps in the provisions' coverage of significant matters.

Obama Transition Planning for Fiscal Stimulus and Oversight

On November 7, 2008, then President-elect Barack Obama held his first news conference since the presidential election. In view of continued monthly job losses, he called for a "fiscal stimulus plan that will jump-start economic growth."[3] In response to a question about the prospect that "a stimulus package may be in trouble" during the remainder of the 110th Congress, the President-elect said "[i]f it does not get done in the lame-duck session, it will be the first thing I get done as President of the United States." Later that month, he announced he had directed his transition "economic team to come up with an Economic Recovery Plan."[4] On December 23, 2008, Vice President-elect Joe Biden said "there will be no earmarks in this economic recovery plan."[5] After the holidays, President-elect Obama referred to the plan as an "American Recovery and Reinvestment Plan."[6] He reiterated on January 6, 2009, that under the economic recovery plan, "[w]e are going to ban all earmarks." [7] He also said that the plan "will set a new higher standard of accountability, transparency, and oversight."

Legislative Action in the 111th Congress on Stimulus and Oversight

Planning for Stimulus Legislation and Related Oversight Provisions

In the wake of a rapidly deteriorating economic picture, CBO released an economic forecast on January 7, 2009. CBO issued the forecast "several weeks earlier than usual to aid the new [111th] Congress in its deliberations."[8] The Senate Budget Committee held a hearing on the forecast the next day.[9] In the forecast, CBO said that a "downturn in housing markets across the country, which undermined the solvency of major financial institutions and severely disrupted the functioning of financial markets, has led the United States into a recession that will probably be the longest and the deepest since World War II."[10]

To help establish a basis for Congress to consider alternative courses of action, the forecast was done under an assumption that current laws and policies regarding federal spending and taxation would remain the same. CBO noted, for example, that the forecast did not include "the effects of a possible fiscal stimulus package."[11] CBO anticipated that the recession, which began in December 2007, would last until the second half of 2009. Economic output over the next two years, CBO estimated, would average "6.8 percent below its potential—that is, the level of output that would be produced if the economy's resources were fully employed."[12] CBO explained that this gap in gross domestic product (GDP)—a "GDP gap"—is "the difference between real (inflation-adjusted) gross domestic product and its estimated potential level (which corresponds to a high level of resource—labor and capital—use)."[13] In accompanying testimony, CBO's acting director said that "[m]any economists believe that a stimulative fiscal policy (that is, an increase in spending or reduction in taxes designed to foster faster economic growth in the short run) is desirable under the current economic conditions."[14]

Congress soon considered legislation intended to diminish this GDP gap and, in the process of doing so, to bolster employment and address perceptions of other economic and policy problems. An early version of the legislation reportedly was drafted by then President-elect Barack Obama's transition team working with Members of the House Committee on Appropriations.[15]

On January 14, 2009, then OMB Director-designate Peter Orszag appeared before the Senate Committee on Homeland Security and Governmental Affairs for a confirmation hearing.[16] Among other things, he was asked about his plans for oversight of the economic stimulus package that was anticipated to be considered at the beginning of the 111th Congress. Director-designate Orszag said the incoming Administration would favor creating a special oversight board. The board would be composed of relevant IGs and chaired by a newly established White House position of Chief Performance Officer (CPO). The board "would review problems and ... would conduct regular meetings to examine specific problems that might be identified." Director- designate Orszag also said the Administration planned "to create a website that will contain information about the contracts and include PDFs [of] contracts themselves."[17]

Soon after President Obama was inaugurated, the Obama Administration established a website called Recovery.gov in anticipation of enactment of stimulus legislation. The home page explained the Administration's future intentions for the website: "Check back after the passage of the American Recovery and Reinvestment Act to see how and where your tax dollars are spent. An oversight board will routinely update this site as part of an unprecedented effort to root out waste, inefficiency, and unnecessary spending in our government."[18]

Action on Legislation and Oversight Provisions

Numerous oversight provisions subsequently were included in economic stimulus legislation considered by the House and Senate.[19] On January 21, 2009, after mark-up of a draft bill by the House Committee on Appropriations, the committee issued a press release that characterized the stimulus as providing "unprecedented accountability" (see **Box 1**).[20]

Box 1. Excerpt from House Appropriations Committee Press Release

Unprecedented Accountability: A historic level of transparency, oversight and accountability will help guarantee taxpayer dollars are spent wisely and Americans can see results for their investment.

- In many instances funds are distributed through existing formulas to programs with proven track records and accountability measures already in place.
- How funds are spent, all announcements of contract and grant competitions and awards, and formula grant allocations must be posted on a special website created by the President. Program managers will also be listed so the public knows who to hold accountable.
- Public notification of funding must include a description of the investment funded, the purpose, the total cost and why the activity should be funded with recovery dollars. Governors, mayors or others making funding decisions must personally certify that the investment has been fully vetted and is an appropriate use of taxpayer dollars. This will also be placed on the recovery website.
- A Recovery Act Accountability and Transparency Board will be created to review management of recovery dollars and provide early warning of problems. The seven member board includes Inspectors General and Deputy Cabinet secretaries.
- The Government Accountability Office and the Inspectors General are provided additional funding and access for special review of recovery funding.
- State and local whistleblowers who report fraud and abuse are protected.
- There are no earmarks in this package.

On January 26, 2009, the American Recovery and Reinvestment Act of 2009 (H.R. 1, 111th Congress) was introduced in the House.[21] Shortly before introduction, the White House reportedly had released a document describing several goals of the legislation, both in terms of economic stimulus and achievement of various public policy objectives relating to energy, health care, education, infrastructure, tax policy, income maintenance, and accountability.[22] On January 28, the House passed an amended version of the measure by 244-188. Senate versions of components of ARRA were introduced and reported on January 27 (S. 336, with written report) and January 29 (S. 350).

At the same time, general concerns had been expressed about the capacity of agencies and "a depleted contracting workforce" to spend funds rapidly "while also improving competition and oversight."[23] In addition, the question had been raised whether IGs and the Government Accountability Office (GAO) have sufficient resources to conduct oversight of the stimulus legislation.[24] Situated in the context of these concerns, however, many observers felt quick action on the stimulus legislation was critical. According to one press report, "[w]hile economists remain divided on the role of government generally, an overwhelming number from both parties are saying that a government stimulus package—even a flawed one—is urgently needed to help prevent a steeper slide in the economy."[25]

The Senate amended the House version and passed an amendment in the nature of a substitute on February 10, 2009, by a vote of 61-37.[26] A conference report, which included a joint explanatory statement, was filed on February 12, 2009, stating that it contained no congressional earmarks, limited tax benefits, or limited tariff benefits.[27] The conference report was agreed to in the House on February 13, 2009, by a vote of 246-183, with one Member voting present. On the same day, the Senate agreed to the conference report by a vote of 60-38, clearing the measure for presentment to the President. President Obama signed the measure into law on February 17, 2009.[28]

General Oversight Provisions in ARRA

Context in Which Oversight Provisions Will Operate

Several aspects of ARRA establish the context in which the legislation's general oversight provisions will operate. These include the structure of the legislation, the legislation's explicit purposes and "general principles," and the scale of the oversight task at hand.

Structure of Legislation

ARRA was enacted in two divisions. Division A, titled "Appropriations Provisions," included many discretionary appropriations provisions in 16 titles. Some of the appropriations were provided for IGs and other oversight-related institutions. Division A also included substantive legislative provisions in some titles. These included provisions to, among other things, promote health information technology (Title XIII), establish a State Fiscal Stabilization Fund (Title XIV), and create a variety of mechanisms and entities focused on oversight (Title XV). A title containing general provisions for Division A focused on oversight (Title XVI). Division B, titled "Tax, Unemployment, Health, State Fiscal Relief, and Other Provisions," included seven titles. Titles in Division B appeared to contain very few general oversight provisions, as discussed later.

References to "the Act" within ARRA generally refer to either Division A or Division B, not to the entire law.[29] Therefore, most of ARRA's substantive general oversight provisions that are located in Titles XV and XVI of Division A appear to cover activities and provisions associated with Division A rather than the entire law. Many, but not all, oversight-related appropriations also focused on oversight of funding provided by Division A, as opposed to the entire law.[30]

ARRA's Purposes and "General Principles"

A conventional approach for oversight is to assess a program, agency, or law in terms of its purposes and related objectives. ARRA identified several explicit purposes and "general principles concerning use of funds," which are excerpted in **Box 2**.

As discussed later in this chapter, the purposes and principles might be thought of as falling roughly into three categories:

- macroeconomic objectives related to recovery from the recession;

- discrete programmatic, microeconomic, and other policy objectives; and
- process objectives, which include balancing speed (to address macroeconomic objectives) with "prudent management" (e.g., to minimize waste and fraud).

Box 2. ARRA's "Purposes and Principles" (P.L. 111-5; Section 3)

(a) Statement of Purposes.—The purposes of this Act include the following:

(1) To preserve and create jobs and promote economic recovery.

(2) To assist those most impacted by the recession.

(3) To provide investments needed to increase economic efficiency by spurring technological advances in science and health.

(4) To invest in transportation, environmental protection, and other infrastructure that will provide long-term economic benefits.

(5) To stabilize State and local government budgets, in order to minimize and avoid reductions in essential services and counterproductive state and local tax increases.

(b) General Principles Concerning Use of Funds.—The President and the heads of Federal departments and agencies shall manage and expend the funds made available in this Act so as to achieve the purposes specified in subsection (a), including commencing expenditures and activities as quickly as possible consistent with prudent management.

Many of ARRA's specific appropriations and nonfunding provisions, which concern myriad policy areas, might be viewed as falling roughly into these categories, as well.

In some cases, there may be ambiguity around, or disagreement about, the specific purposes and objectives of a law and how to define "success" in its implementation.[31] To the extent these phenomena may be evident, stakeholders may believe other criteria are important to consider when overseeing or evaluating a program, agency, or law. Unintended consequences also may be of interest or concern.

Scale of Oversight Task: CBO Estimates of ARRA Impacts

In response to a congressional request, CBO prepared a year-by-year estimate of the short-term economic impacts of ARRA.[32] In addition, CBO included tables that showed estimated economic "multipliers" corresponding to many provisions,[33] and, in addition, the agency's cost estimate for the conference agreement on H.R. 1.[34] In the letter, CBO estimated that ARRA would increase the federal government's budget deficit by an overall total of $787.2 billion over 11 years.[35] CBO also broke down the legislation's estimated fiscal impacts on spending and revenues.

With regard to spending, CBO estimated that Division A of the legislation would increase discretionary spending by $308.3 billion over the 11-year period from FY2009 through FY2019.[36] Nearly half of the total amount would be spent by the end of FY20 10 (September 30, 2010), and nearly 72% would be spent by the end of FY20 11 (September 30, 2011). CBO estimated that Division B would increase direct spending by $267.0 billion over the same 11-year period. Nearly 73% of this total would be spent by the end of FY2010, and over 91%

would be spent by the end of FY2011. Overall, spending from the perspective of the federal government's unified budget was estimated to total $575.3 billion from FY2009 through FY2019.

CBO estimated that Division A would decrease revenues by $0.1 billion over 11 years. Division B would decrease *net* revenues by $211.8 billion over 11 years, with $244.9 billion in revenue reductions occurring by the end of FY20 10. The tax provisions of Division B's Title I accounted for the vast majority of these estimated decreases. The total revenue decrease would be $211.9 billion over 11 years.

Two Categories of General Oversight Provisions

ARRA's general oversight provisions might be grouped into two categories:

- *nonfunding* provisions, which established federal agencies, required agencies to undertake certain tasks, established procedures that must be followed, etc.;[37] and
- *funding* provisions, which provided appropriations to oversight-related entities including IGs, GAO, and the newly established Recovery Accountability and Transparency Board.

General oversight provisions that fall within each category are discussed in the sections below.

Nonfunding General Oversight Provisions

Nonfunding general oversight provisions appeared to be included only in Division A, chiefly in Titles XV and XVI. Nevertheless, they were included in considerable variety. Among other things, these substantive provisions established new oversight-oriented entities like the Recovery Accountability and Transparency Board (RATB), enumerated diverse reporting requirements for federal agencies and nonfederal recipients of funds, and tasked RATB, IGs, and GAO with numerous duties. Some highlights of these statutory provisions and related reporting requirements are summarized in bulleted form, below. A more comprehensive tabular presentation of provisions, their ARRA citations, and related reporting requirements, including when ARRA requires specific information to be posted on the Recovery.gov website, is provided in **Table B-1**, in **Appendix B**.

IG and GAO Reviews and Reports

- IGs are required to review "any concerns raised by the public about specific investments using funds made available in [Division A]" and relay findings to agency heads. (Title XV, Sections 1514 and 1515).
- The Comptroller General is required to conduct bimonthly reviews on the use of funds made available in Division A by selected states and localities. (Title IX, Sections 901 and 902).

Reports on Use of Funds

- Recipients of funds are required to report certain information within 180 days of ARRA's enactment, where *recipient* is defined as a state or any entity "other than an individual" that receives funds directly from the federal government from appropriations in Division A. (Title XV, Section 1512(c)).
- Federal agencies are required to publicly report information submitted by funding recipients to the agency. (Title XV, Section 1512(d)).
- State and local governments' reporting and recordkeeping may be funded, at least in part, by flexibility granted to federal agencies to adjust applicable limits on administrative expenditures for federal awards. (Title XV, Section 1552).

State and Local Certification

- Chief executives of state and local governments are required to certify that infrastructure investments have "received the full review and vetting required by law and that the chief executive accepts responsibility that the infrastructure investment is an appropriate use of taxpayer dollars." (Title XV, Section 1511).

Establishment and Functions of RATB

- RATB is established "to coordinate and conduct oversight of covered funds to prevent fraud, waste, and abuse." RATB's membership is to consist of at least 10 IGs, including, or in addition to, a chairperson, who may be designated or appointed by the President according to certain criteria (Title XV, Sections 1521 and 1522).
- RATB has several enumerated functions, including to review whether reporting for contracts and grants "meets applicable standards" and "specifies the purpose of the contract or grant and measures of performance." The board also is required to coordinate oversight activities with the Comptroller General and state auditors. RATB is tasked with four categories of reporting requirements. (Title XV, Sections 1523 and 1528).
- RATB is required to make recommendations to agencies "on measures to prevent fraud, waste, and abuse relating to covered funds." An agency that receives a RATB recommendation is required to submit a "responsive report" to the President, the congressional committees of jurisdiction, and RATB within 30 days of receipt. (Title XV, Section 1523).
- RATB is required to conduct audits and reviews, and in doing so, may issue subpoenas to compel testimony from nonfederal officers and employees. RATB is authorized to hold public hearings and may enter into certain contracts. RATB has authority to transfer up to 100% of its appropriated funds to any office of inspector general, OMB, the General Services Administration, and an independent advisory panel established by Section 1541 of Title XV. (Title XV, Section 1524).
- RATB is required to establish a website. (The website was established by the Obama Administration as Recovery.gov in anticipation of enactment of ARRA.) As agencies

implement ARRA, the website is to contain, among many other things, considerable information about how funds are allocated and used. Fifteen specific requirements for the website are identified in one provision of Title XV, and other provisions in Division A describe additional information that is required to be posted on, or linked to, the RATB website. (Title XV, Section 1526).

- IGs are instructed that nothing in the provisions related to RATB shall affect the independent authority of an IG "to determine whether to conduct an audit or investigation of covered funds." An IG's decision "shall be final." (Title XV, Section 1527).

Additional Oversight Provisions

- Contracts funded under Division A are required to be awarded as fixed-price contracts through the use of competitive procedures "to the maximum extent possible," and exceptions are required to be posted on RATB's website. (Title XV, Section 1554).
- The Council of Economic Advisers, an entity in the Executive Office of the President, is required to submit quarterly reports to the House and Senate Appropriations Committees that "detail the impact of programs funded through covered funds on employment, estimated economic growth, and other key economic indicators." (Title XV, Section 1513).
- Employees of nonfederal employers receiving funds are granted certain whistleblower protections when disclosing certain information to RATB, an IG, the Comptroller General, a Member of Congress, or other specified entities and persons. (Title XV, Section 1553).

Funding Provisions with Appropriations for IGs, GAO, and RATB

Appropriations to IGs, GAO, and RATB were included predominately in Division A.[38] In total, the appropriations provided to these oversight-oriented entities summed to $363.75 million. Highlights of these appropriations are discussed here. A more comprehensive listing of the various oversight entities for which ARRA provided funds is presented in **Table C-1**, located in **Appendix C**.[39]

Twenty-three IGs received $254.75 million in 25 separate appropriations.[40] Sixteen IGs in all 15 executive departments received appropriations, ranging from a single appropriation of $1 million for the Department of Veterans Affairs to two appropriations totaling $48.25 million for the Department of Health and Human Services. IGs in an additional seven independent agencies also received appropriations.

ARRA provided the funding with widely varying periods of availability. For the IG at the Department of State, for example, funds are available until the end of FY2010. Other IGs variously have funds available until the end of FY2011, FY2012, FY2013, or "until expended" (i.e., "no-year" funds). GAO received $25 million, available through the end of FY2010, and RATB received $84 million, available through the end of FY2011.

Some of the appropriations were designated for specific purposes, chief among them oversight of programs, grants, and projects funded by ARRA. Other appropriations were essentially supplemental increases without a restrictive specification of purpose.[41] RATB has authority to transfer up to 100% of its funds to any office of inspector general, OMB, the General Services Administration, and an advisory panel for RATB that ARRA established.[42]

POTENTIAL ISSUES FOR CONGRESS

With enactment of ARRA, a flurry of activity commenced in executive agencies and the Executive Office of the President. Further requirements and guidance concerning ARRA implementation were forthcoming from the White House and OMB. These documents focused especially on issues related to oversight, accountability, and transparency. Some of the requirements also went beyond ARRA's statutory requirements.

On February 18, 2009, OMB issued to agencies "initial implementing guidance" regarding ARRA, including numerous reporting requirements, in a 62-page document.[43] Some of the required information is to be posted on Recovery.gov and agency-specific ARRA-related websites. A month later, President Obama issued a presidential memorandum entitled "Ensuring Responsible Spending of Recovery Act Funds."[44] The memorandum directed agencies in how to use "available discretion" when allocating and spending certain ARRA-related funding. The memorandum also directed agencies to disclose certain communications with federally registered lobbyists. On April 3, 2009, OMB issued "updated implementing guidance" to agencies in a 175- page document.[45] Further guidance from OMB and RATB is expected.

In addition, the White House announced the designation of RATB's chairperson (Department of the Interior IG Earl E. Devaney) and the board's full membership in February and March 2009, respectively.[46] The Obama Administration also identified a number of leadership roles for purposes of ARRA implementation (e.g., the appointment of Mr. Edward DeSeve to a White House coordination role for ARRA implementation). Several congressional committees have incorporated ARRA into their oversight agendas and convened hearings.

Based on experience with ARRA implementation and other emerging developments, Congress may revisit the structure and contents of ARRA's general oversight provisions. Even before considering experience with implementation, however, several broad issues related to ARRA oversight may be of interest to Congress.

Oversight and Crises: Short- and Long-Term Perspectives

In the event of a crisis to which Congress, the President, and federal agencies feel compelled to respond, several challenges may present themselves. Some challenges might be characterized as relatively short term. Others may involve a longer-term orientation.

Among the short-term challenges, in the present context, is the question of how to balance speed (to address macroeconomic objectives) with "prudent management" (e.g., to minimize waste and fraud). Other challenges in formulating a response to a crisis occur when allocating funding during budget execution. When allocating resources to specific projects and priorities, how should the federal government reconcile values of accountability, efficiency, effectiveness, transparency, public participation, fairness, and equity? Oftentimes in such circumstances, values "trade off" against each other. In making these judgments, agencies and policy makers typically have little time for planning or reflection.

For purposes of oversight, prioritization likely will be necessary. The need to prioritize raises a number of difficult questions. Which policy areas (e.g., transportation, health care information technology) or processes (e.g., contracting, grant management) should receive initial attention? Which should receive the most attention? Also, what types of oversight activity will be most effective at preventing future problems, catching current problems when changes still may be made, or identifying problems after the fact?[47] Some of these shorter-term issues are explored in greater detail under subsequent headings.

Some longer-term issues include questions of how to build the capacity of federal agencies, Congress, and the President to better prepare for and respond to crises. For example, concerns have been expressed by some observers for years about the adequacy of agency capabilities and workforces in areas such as contract management and program evaluation.[48] To address longer-term issues like these, Congress might explore advantages and disadvantages of options for assessing (or grading) the adequacy of agency management capabilities, both under "normal" circumstances and for contingencies.[49] If Congress wished to consider related options, Congress might explore how systematic, periodic, and transparent such assessments could be.

In addition, and arguably no less significant, questions arise of how to anticipate, avoid, and mitigate preventable crises. For example, the National Commission on Terrorist Attacks Upon the United States, generally known as the 9-11 Commission, described an aspect of this capability as "institutionalizing imagination."[50] Organizational, procedural, and system-related options might be explored to address any of these questions.[51]

Overseeing Extent to Which ARRA Meets Objectives

A typical purpose of oversight is to assess the extent to which an agency, program, or law is meeting its objectives.[52] Through a variety of tools and approaches, Congress may learn what seems to be working well or not well, where more study may be necessary, and about consequences that may not have been intended. Furthermore, both oversight activity and the prospect of scrutiny may prompt behavior changes by agencies and nonfederal actors to address areas of concern.

Potential Frameworks for Evaluation

As noted earlier, ARRA specified several explicit purposes and "general principles concerning use of funds" (see **Box 2**, earlier in this chapter).[53] These purposes and principles might be thought of as falling into three general categories:

- macroeconomic objectives (e.g., creating or saving jobs; other indicators of economic activity affected by a reduction of the GDP gap, compared to situation without stimulus);[54]
- programmatic, microeconomic, and other discrete policy objectives (e.g., impact on public policy outcomes in myriad policy areas addressed by ARRA);[55] and

- process objectives (e.g., quick action; transparency; prudent management; low levels of waste, fraud, error, and abuse).[56]

ARRA also could be examined through the lens of additional or different criteria, which may be based on corresponding views about the proper goals of public policy. For example, alternative criteria could be used if an observer perceived the law's specified purposes as not being sufficiently comprehensive.[57] Certain non-governmental and non-ARRA activities, such as scams perpetrated on the public by impersonators of federal agencies and personnel, also may be of concern for oversight purposes.[58]

For objectives related to the first two general categories, many quantitative and qualitative data may be informative, including data from metrics, studies, and program evaluations. For example, in testimony before the Senate Budget Committee, CBO identified three criteria for judging the effectiveness of a fiscal stimulus policy: timeliness (i.e., the increase in aggregate demand caused by a stimulus should match the period when there is a GDP gap); cost-effectiveness (i.e., for a given budgetary cost, the increase in aggregate demand should be maximized, in order to bring real GDP as close as possible to potential GDP and thereby diminish the GDP gap); and consistency with long-term budget objectives (i.e., a short-term stimulus should not significantly exacerbate the nation's long-run fiscal imbalance).[59]

For the third general category, relating to process objectives, a typical inference is that effective implementation (e.g., balancing speed with prudent management) increases the probability of achieving objectives associated with the first two categories. Nevertheless, some aspects of speed or prudent management may prove to be more important than others, or to trade off against each other (see related discussion further below). Experience with implementation may yield corresponding "lessons learned."

Likely Considerations

In assessing the extent to which ARRA meets its objectives, several related considerations likely will be significant. For example, a frequent challenge with metrics and evaluations is estimating the impact of a policy. That is, did a policy intervention such as ARRA (or one of its constituent parts) change the state of affairs for the better, compared to what would have happened without the policy intervention?[60] The task of validly estimating an answer to this question may require grappling with another, related question: to what extent are observed outcomes due to the policy intervention, as opposed to other factors? In order to estimate ARRA's impact, it therefore may be necessary to make comparisons between observed data, on one hand, and estimates of what would have happened in the absence of ARRA, on the other.[61]

From a macroeconomic perspective, for example, what impact is ARRA having on GDP, employment, and other indicators of economic activity, compared to what would have happened without a fiscal stimulus? What often makes this evaluation difficult is that experience without a fiscal stimulus, under identical conditions, is not observed. In addition, other factors unrelated to the stimulus may affect macroeconomic results or modify the stimulus' potential impact. For example, CBO cited the importance of an assumption in its March 2009 economic forecast, which included the estimated impact of ARRA. Specifically, the forecast assumed "that financial markets will begin to function more normally and that the housing market will stabilize by early next year. The possibility that financial markets might not stabilize represents a major source of downside risk to the forecast."[62] Because a number of such factors may influence overall economic results, some level of uncertainty arguably is unavoidable in making any estimates of ARRA's impact.[63]

Another potential consideration relates to trade-offs among ARRA's multiple objectives. A frequent complication of multidimensional goals (e.g., speed, effectiveness, efficiency, transparency, fairness, and accountability) is that some goals may trade off against each other. For example, the use of speed in the obligation of funds has been seen as essential for economic recovery. Greater speed may promote economic stimulus, but at a cost of some efficiency in the use of tax dollars to achieve public policy outcomes in discrete areas. Speed also may increase the risk of waste or fraud, particularly when agency capacities to handle a sudden infusion of funding may be in question. On the other hand, greater scrutiny and accountability may diminish speed and therefore economic stimulus. They also may increase or decrease efficiency and effectiveness, depending on whether the nature and level of scrutiny are adequately calibrated. When governmental decision makers evaluate policy options and make choices, they implicitly make trade-offs.[64] Decision making regarding ARRA most likely will be no exception. The reconciliation of trade-offs in decision making may be informed by policy analysis and management of risks. Ultimately, however, judgments about trade-offs arguably always are informed by an observer's priorities, beliefs, values, and ethics.

A third consideration relates to assessing what is realistically achievable in the short to medium term for each of the three general categories of objectives that were outlined above (i.e., macroeconomic, policy-specific, and process). With respect to process objectives, for example, a subject of considerable attention has been how to build the capability of the Recovery.gov website to provide full transparency for federal funds. Data availability, however, hinges on a number of complex factors, including legacy information technology systems, disparate state and federal systems and data definitions, uneven data quality, and a need for effective project management across a variety of jurisdictions. In that light, it is unclear how much capability may be realistically achievable by the end of FY2010, at which point CBO estimated nearly half of ARRA's discretionary spending will have been spent. In building the capacity of Recovery.gov, the experience of implementing the USASpending.gov website may in some ways be instructive with regard to data availability and quality.[65]

Assessing Oversight Systems, Coverage, and Objectives

Potential Questions Regarding ARRA Oversight

An Obama Administration official has called ARRA "the largest peacetime economic expansion program in the country's history."[66] The Administration and Congress negotiated numerous general oversight provisions for inclusion in the legislation. ARRA's oversight provisions—a collection of new institutions, processes, systems, and resources—supplement the federal government's existing systems of oversight in numerous respects. Some of ARRA's provisions cover all government operations funded by Division A (e.g., many provisions in Title XV). Others operate in specific policy areas (e.g., specific appropriations set-asides). Over time, Congress may consider whether existing management and oversight mechanisms, in combination with ARRA's additional provisions, adequately support effective management and oversight of ARRA implementation. In so doing, several topics and questions that are specific to ARRA might be examined.

- Does the combination of existing and new oversight mechanisms adequately address ARRA's objectives and risks?
- Are there some potential oversight topics that are not explicitly addressed in ARRA? Does the combination of new and existing oversight systems leave gaps?
- Is there a point at which oversight efforts and scrutiny become counterproductive? If so, in what sense(s)? How are competing imperatives (transparency, accountability, flexibility, cost, etc.) to be reconciled?
- Are some approaches to oversight more helpful than others? Do some approaches produce unintended consequences?
- Does the experience with ARRA offer lessons learned for the "normal" systems of oversight? If so, are some changes in the "normal" system of oversight advisable?
- What approaches to oversight work well in a separation of powers system, in which federal government branches compete for control over public policy, and in a federal system,[67] in which the federal government and states have potentially overlapping lines of authority?

If Congress wishes to assess the overall oversight framework for ARRA, several overarching considerations about federal oversight may be relevant to assessing questions like the foregoing. A number of these considerations are analyzed below.

Federal Oversight Systems and Objectives

As a threshold matter, the federal government might be viewed as embodying a system of "nested" oversight. That is, multiple entities engage in simultaneous and multi-tiered oversight activities.[68] For example, Congress oversees the President, EOP (including OMB), agencies, and nonfederal entities. Furthermore, Congress has established, structured, and funded executive agencies to allow for oversight of agency actions. Congress also has passed a variety of "general management laws" for executive agencies to establish procedures that may be overseen.[69] At the same time, IGs and congressional support agencies such as GAO provide assistance to Congress, agencies, and the President with oversight. Within the executive branch, OMB has a statutory responsibility to provide management leadership for many agencies, including monitoring and oversight of their activities.[70] Agencies oversee their own activities, the activities of regulated entities, and the activities of recipients of federal funds. Agencies undertake these tasks through a variety of organizational and procedural arrangements, often as Congress has mandated via statute. When state governments receive federal dollars, they may oversee the activities of local governments. All of the foregoing entities also oversee in many respects the activities of industries, firms, and other nongovernmental actors.

Viewed together, for example, GAO may attempt to oversee OMB's oversight of an agency's oversight of a state agency, which in turn attempts to oversee the use of funds it made available via contract or grant to a firm, local government, or nonprofit organization. Throughout, tools such as monitoring, analysis, and evaluation may be utilized.

In assessing and potentially considering how to modify an oversight framework, there also are multiple perspectives on the potential objectives of oversight. These include the following:

- compliance with applicable laws and regulations (e.g., adherence to legal requirements and avoidance of fraud);
- implementation that is faithful with congressional intent, when an agency or the President exercises discretion;
- avoidance of mismanagement (e.g., adherence to sound management practices);
- avoidance of undesired bias in funding allocations and policy execution (e.g., fair allocation of resources and fair implementation of policy, with intended equity);
- effectiveness of funded activities (e.g., achievement of programmatic missions and purposes); and
- efficiency of funded activities (e.g., minimization of avoidable "waste" and unnecessary redundancy).

The ways in which RATB, IGs, GAO, OMB, implementing agencies, and nonfederal recipients of funds (e.g., state governments) approach these perspectives on oversight, in the context of ARRA, may reveal lessons learned and patterns over time.

Topics Not Explicitly Addressed by General Oversight Provisions in ARRA

Assessments of ARRA's implementation and oversight framework likely will be informed by an observer's values, short- versus long-term orientation, and perspectives on the proper structure and objectives of oversight. Nonetheless, as a point of departure, some initial observations still might be made regarding topics that do not appear to be explicitly addressed by general oversight provisions in ARRA.

Coverage of Division B

Almost all of ARRA's general oversight provisions apply to provisions included in Division A of the legislation. Very few appear to apply explicitly to Division B (e.g., regarding tax expenditures).[71] At the same time, however, some provisions in Division B are subject to study or oversight in specific cases.[72] In addition, although some appropriations to IGs in Division A specified that funds were to be used for oversight of activities related to Division A (thereby restricting their use to that purpose), other appropriations to IGs and GAO did not contain a specification of purpose related only to Division A.[73] Therefore, some appropriations presumably could be used for oversight of activities and funding associated with Division B.

Consideration of the extent to which ARRA's general oversight provisions cover Division B may raise questions. For implementation purposes, will Division B receive the same level of oversight as Division A? Will existing oversight mechanisms provide adequate oversight for all of ARRA's provisions, notwithstanding the focus of ARRA's general oversight provisions on Division A?[74]

Funding for, and Capacity of, State and Local Oversight Entities

State and local governments will receive a surge of many billions of dollars under ARRA, raising the potential issue of whether these governments will have capacity to effectively manage the influx of funds. ARRA authorized agencies that receive funds under Division A to "reasonably adjust applicable limits on administrative expenditures for Federal awards to help award recipients defray the costs of data collection requirements initiated pursuant to [Division A]" (Division A, Title XV, Section 1552). However, it is not clear if state and local oversight entities (e.g., state-level auditors general) will have access to increased resources, if they are needed in order to accommodate a surge in activities funded by ARRA. To what extent might this be an issue that state and local governments confront?

Transparency Regarding Agency and OMB Decision Making

In addition, many of the general oversight provisions in Division A focus on transparency regarding final allocations of funds and the outcomes of expenditures. However, not as much attention in ARRA appears to focus on the process within executive agencies for deciding how to allocate funds in the first place. When early versions of ARRA were being developed, then President-elect Obama and Vice President-elect Biden indicated an Obama Administration position that ARRA should contain no congressionally originated earmarks. The President later made a policy statement on the general subject of congressionally originated earmarks, outside the context of ARRA. He said that "on occasion, ... [p]rojects have been inserted [in legislation and report language] at the 11th hour, without review, and sometimes without merit, in order to satisfy the political and personal agendas of a given legislator, rather than the public interest."[75]

Some of the same concerns, however, might be raised in the context of OMB and agency decision making during budget execution under ARRA. Agencies frequently are granted considerable discretion during budget execution. Given this discretion, to what extent might political appointees within agencies cause certain projects to be funded, without substantial review or merit? Similar concerns about "presidential earmarking" and "executive earmarking" sometimes have been raised.[76] At the same time, the Obama Administration has issued presidential memoranda regarding agency use of discretion under ARRA and in contracting.[77] Experience with ARRA's implementation may indicate what level of transparency regarding executive agency and OMB decision making ultimately will be forthcoming.

APPENDIX A. CBO JANUARY 2009 ESTIMATE OF GDP GAP, WITHOUT ENACTMENT OF ARRA

Graphical displays may assist with visualizing the concept of a GDP gap.[78] CBO's January 2009 testimony before the Senate Budget Committee included such a graphic, showing an estimate of the GDP gap without enactment of a stimulus law. Based on CBO 's economic forecast, which assumed no changes in policy, CBO projected "that the economy will produce about $1 trillion less output per year than its estimated potential in each of 2009 and 2010 and significantly less than its potential in 2011 and 2012 as well."[79] See **Figure A-1**.

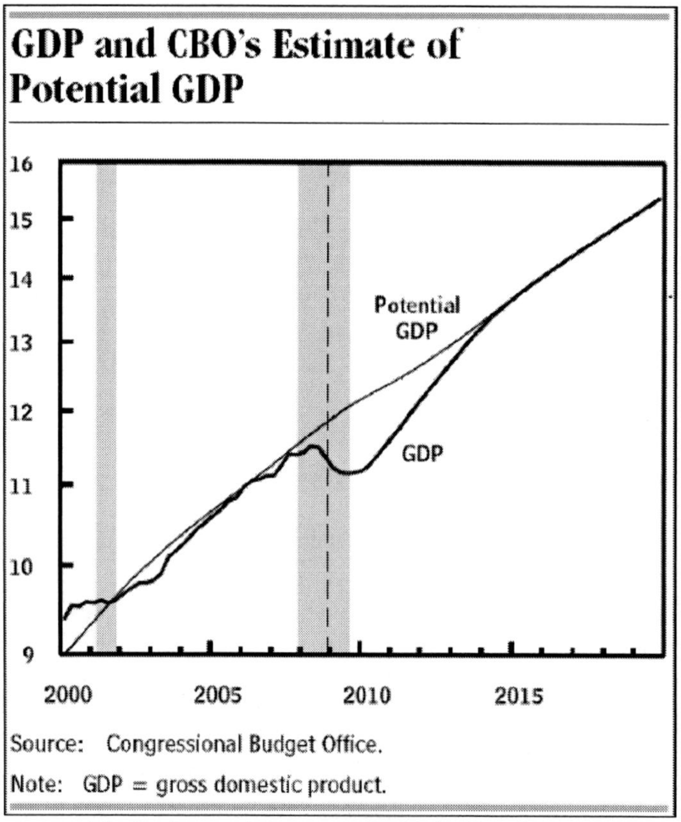

Source: CBO, *Testimony, The Budget and Economic Outlook: Fiscal Years 2009 to 2019*, January 8, 2009, Figure 12, p. 31.

Notes: Numbers on the vertical axis show trillions of dollars, adjusted for inflation. The gray areas indicate actual or estimated time periods of recessions. The dashed vertical line indicates when CBO produced its forecast. After the projected end of the recession that began in late 2007 (i.e., end of the second gray area), CBO forecasted actual output (i.e., GDP) to grow temporarily at a rate faster than potential GDP, until GDP equals potential GDP and resumes its estimated long-term rate of growth.

Figure A.1. CBO's January 2009 Forecast of GDP Gap, Assuming No Changes in Policy

APPENDIX B. TABLE OF SELECTED ARRA GENERAL OVERSIGHT PROVISIONS

Table B.1. Selected Substantive General Oversight Provisions in ARRA, Including Reporting Requirements

Subject	ARRA Citation	Overview of Provision (*see also next column*)	Reporting Requirement(s)
IG and GAO Reviews and Reports			
IG reviews, and access to information and employees	Division A, Title XV, Sections 1514 and 1515	Any IG of a federal department or executive agency shall review, as appropriate, "any concerns raised by the public about specific investments using funds made available in [Division A]." With respect to each contract or grant awarded using covered funds, the statute authorizes any representative of an "appropriate" IG who is appointed under Sections 3 or 8G of the Inspector General Act of 1978 (5 U.S.C. App.) (i.e., appointed by the President or by the head of a designated federal entity, respectively) to examine certain records and interview certain officers and employees. Section 1501 defines "covered funds" as any funds expended or obligated under from appropriations made under Division A. The specified records include "any records of the contractor or grantee, any of its subcontractors or subgrantees, or any state or local agency administering such contract, that pertain to, and involve transactions relating to, the contract, subcontract, grant, or subgrant." The authority to interview officers or employees provides that "any officer or employee of the contractor, grantee,	Findings from a review that are not related to an ongoing criminal proceeding are required to be "relayed immediately" to the head of the department and agency concerned. The findings of such reviews, along with any audits conducted by an IG of funds made available in Division A, are required to be posted on the IG's website and linked to the website established by RATB under Division A, Title XV, Section 1526. A portion of a report may be redacted to the extent it would disclose information that is "protected" from public disclosure under the Freedom of Information Act (FOIA; 5 U.S.C. § 552) and the Privacy Act (5 U.S.C. § 552a). (On January 21, 2009, President Obama issued a memorandum to the heads of executive departments and agencies outlining Administration policy on FOIA and directing the Attorney General to issue new guidelines to agencies.[a])

Table B.1. (Continued)

Subject	ARRA Citation	Overview of Provision (*see also next column*)	Reporting Requirement(s)
		subgrantee, or agency" may be interviewed regarding the transactions noted above.	
GAO reviews and reports, and access to information and employees	Division A, Title IX, Sections 901 and 902	Requires the Comptroller General (CG) to conduct bimonthly reviews on the use of funds made available in Division A by selected states and localities. The CG is required to prepare reports on these reviews. The CG is authorized to examine "any records related to obligations and use by any Federal, State, or local government agency of funds made available in [Division A]." Requires that each contract awarded using funds made available in Division A shall provide that the CG and his representatives are authorized to examine any records of the contractor or any of its subcontractors, or any state of local agency administering such a contract, "that directly pertain to, and involve transactions relating to, the contract or subcontract." Requires that each contract also provide that the CG and his representatives are authorized to interview any officer or employee of the contractor or any of its subcontractors, or of any state or local government agency administering the contract, regarding such transactions.	The CG is required to prepare reports on the subject of the bimonthly reviews. The reports are required to be posted on the Internet, along with any audits of funds made available by Division A. The reports and audits are required to be linked to the website established by RATB under Division A, Title XV, Section 1526. A portion of a report or audit may be redacted when made publicly available, if the portion would disclose information that is not subject to disclosure under FOIA (GAO is not covered as an "agency" under FOIA, 5 U.S.C. § 552(f).)
Recipient reports	Division A, Title XV, Section 1512(c)	Requires certain reporting by a "recipient" of "recovery funds" within 180 days of enactment, as a condition of receipt of funds. Defines recipient as a state or any entity "other than an individual" that	Not later than 10 days after the end of each calendar quarter, each recipient receiving funds from a federal agency is required to submit a report to the agency. The report is required to

Table B.1. (Continued)

Subject	ARRA Citation	Overview of Provision (*see also next column*)	Reporting Requirement(s)
		receives funds made available from appropriations in Division A (including funds received through grant, loan, or contract) "directly from the Federal Government." Defines these funds as "recovery funds." Requires some information in recipient reports to include data elements required to comply with the Federal Funding Accountability and Transparency Act of 2006 (FFATA; P.L. 109-282). (For more information about FFATA, see CRS Report RL347 18, *The Federal Funding Accountability and Transparency Act: Implementation and Proposed Amendments*, by Garrett Hatch.)	contain (1) the total amount of recovery funds received from that agency; (2) the amount of received funds that were expended or obligated to projects or activities; (3) a "detailed list" of all projects or activities for which recovery funds were expended or obligated; and (4) "detailed information on any subcontracts or subgrants awarded by the recipient." Each item on the "detailed list" (i.e., the list required by (3)) is required to include the name of the project or activity, a corresponding description, an evaluation of its "completion status," and "an estimate of the number of jobs created and the number of jobs retained by the project or activity." For infrastructure investments made by state and local governments, an item on the "detailed list also is required to include "the purpose, total cost, and rationale of the agency for funding the infrastructure investment with funds made available under [Division A]," and the name of an agency contact person "if there are concerns with the infrastructure investment." The "detailed information" on subcontracts and subgrants (i.e., the information required by (4)) is required to include "the data elements required to comply with [FFATA], allowing aggregate reporting on awards below $25,000 or to individuals, as prescribed by the Director of [OMB]."

Table B.1. (Continued)

Subject	ARRA Citation	Overview of Provision (*see also next column*)	Reporting Requirement(s)
Agency reports	Division A, Title XV, Section 1512(d)	Requires certain reporting by each agency that made recovery funds available to any recipient. In Title XV, the term "agency" has the meaning given under 5 U.S.C. § 551 (Administrative Procedure Act).	Not later than 30 days after the end of each calendar quarter, each agency that made recovery funds available to any recipient is required to make the information submitted in recipient reports (i.e., the reports required by Section 1512(c)) publicly available by posting the information on "a website."
Other reports	Division A, Title XV, Section 1512(e)	Requires CBO and GAO to "comment" on recipients' reports of jobs created and retained.	Within 45 days of the submission of recipient reports (i.e., the reports required by Section 1512(c)), CBO and GAO are required to "comment on the information" relating to "an estimate of the number of jobs created and the number of jobs retained by the project or activity." This is to be done "for any reports submitted" under Section 1512(c). (ARRA does not specify the audience to whom the comments are due to be submitted or the means by which comments are to be submitted.)
Compliance, guidance, and registration	Division A, TitleXV, Section 1512(f), 15 12(g), and 1512(h)	Within 180 days of enactment, as a condition for receipt of funds under Division A, federal agencies shall require recipients to provide information required to be included in recipient reports. In coordination with the director of OMB, agencies are required to "provide for user- friendly means" for recipients to meet requirements. Funding recipients that are required to report FFATA-compliant information are required to register with the Central Contractor Registration database or	N/A (not applicable)

Table B.1. (Continued)

Subject	ARRA Citation	Overview of Provision (*see also next column*)	Reporting Requirement(s)
		complete other registration requirements as determined by the director of OMB.	
Set-aside for state and local government reporting and recordkeeping	Division A, Title XV, Section 1552	After following notice and comment rulemaking requirements under the Administrative Procedure Act (5 U.S.C. § 553), federal agencies receiving funds under Division A may "reasonably adjust applicable limits on administrative expenditures for Federal awards to help award recipients defray the costs of data collection requirements initiated pursuant to [Division A]." (ARRA cites 5 U.S.C. § 500 instead of § 553.)	None, but any adjustments presumably would be published in the *Federal Register*.
State and Local Certification			
State and local certification requirements for infrastructure investments	Division A, TitleXV, Section 1511	With respect to "covered funds" made available to state or local governments for infrastructure investments, the governor, mayor, or other chief executive, as appropriate, is required to certify that "the infrastructure investment has received the full review and vetting required by law and that the chief executive accepts responsibility that the infrastructure investment is an appropriate use of taxpayer dollars." Section 1501 defines "covered funds" as any funds expended or obligated under from appropriations made under Division A. A state or local agency may not receive infrastructure investment funding from funds made available by Division A "unless this certification is made and posted."	The certification is required to include a description of the investment, the estimated total cost, and the amount of covered funds to be used. The certification is required to be posted "on a website" and linked to the website established by RATB under Division A, Title XV, Section 1526.

Table B.1. (Continued)

Subject	ARRA Citation	Overview of Provision (*see also next column*)	Reporting Requirement(s)
Certification by governor or acceptance by state legislature	Division A, TitleXVI, Section 1607	Not later than 45 days after enactment, a governor must certify that (1) the state will request and use funds provided by Division A, and (2) the funds will be used to create jobs and promote economic growth. If funds are not accepted by the governor, acceptance by the state legislature by means of the adoption of a concurrent resolution "shall be sufficient to provide funding to such state."	A certification-related document may be issued. For analysis of this provision, see CRS Report R40467, *Authority of State Legislatures to Accept Funds Under the American Recovery and Reinvestment Act of 2009*, by Kenneth R. Thomas.
Establishment and Functions of RATB and Advisory Panel			
Establishment of RATB, termination	Division A, Title XV, Sections 1521 and 1530	Establishes the Recovery Accountability and Transparency Board "to coordinate and conduct oversight of covered funds to prevent fraud, waste, and abuse." RATB terminates at the end of FY2013.	N/A
Chairperson of the board	Division A, Title XV, Section 1522	Requires the President to designate or appoint a chairperson, using any of three options: (a) designate the OMB deputy director for management; (b) designate another Senate-confirmed presidential appointee; or (c) appoint an individual, subject to Senate confirmation. If (c), the individual is required to be compensated at the rate of basic pay for level IV of the Executive Schedule.	N/A
Board membership in addition to chair, and term length of members	Division A, Title XV, Section 1522	Ten IGs are specified as being members of RATB. These include IGs from USDA, DOC, ED, DOE, HHS, DHS, DOJ, DOT; Treasury, and the Treasury IG for Tax Administration. In addition, the President may designate as a member any other IG from "any agency that expends or obligates covered funds."	N/A

Table B.1. (Continued)

Subject	ARRA Citation	Overview of Provision (*see also next column*)	Reporting Requirement(s)
Functions of the board; reporting requirements	Division A, Title XV, Sections 1523 and 1528	The board is required to, in general, "coordinate and conduct oversight of covered funds in order to prevent fraud, waste, and abuse." In addition, RATB has six enumerated functions: (A) reviewing whether reporting for contracts and grants "meets applicable standards" and "specifies the purpose of the contract or grant and measures of performance"; (B) reviewing whether competition requirements for contracts and grants have been "satisfied"; (C) auditing or reviewing covered funds to determine whether "wasteful spending, poor contract or grant management, or other abuses are occurring," and referring matters it considers appropriate for investigation to the IG for the agency that disbursed the covered funds; (D) reviewing whether there are "sufficient qualified acquisition and grant personnel overseeing covered funds"; and (E) reviewing whether acquisition and grant personnel receive "adequate training"; and (F) reviewing whether there are "appropriate mechanisms for interagency collaboration," including coordinating and collaborating "to the extent practicable" with the Inspector Generals Council on Integrity and Efficiency. The board also is required to coordinate oversight activities with the Comptroller General and state auditors. Because the	RATB's functions suggest issues that may receive attention in RATB's reports and for which agencies may be held accountable. RATB is tasked with four categories of reporting requirements: "flash" reports, "other" reports, quarterly reports, and annual reports. Requires the board to submit to the President and Congress, including the Committees on Appropriations of the Senate and House of Representatives, "flash reports" on "potential management and funding problems that require immediate attention." RATB also is required to submit to Congress "such other reports as the Board considers appropriate on the use and benefits of funds made available in [Division A]." Quarterly reports are required to be submitted to the President and Congress, including the appropriations committees of both chambers. These reports are to summarize "the findings of the Board and the findings of inspectors general of agencies." The board is authorized also to submit "additional reports as appropriate." RATB is required to submit annual reports to the President and Congress (including the appropriations committees of both chambers), which are to consolidate "applicable quarterly

Table B.1. (Continued)

Subject	ARRA Citation	Overview of Provision (*see also next column*)	Reporting Requirement(s)
		term "covered funds" is defined in Title XV as "any funds that are expended or obligated from appropriations made under [Division A]," activities undertaken by agencies in compliance with Division B would appear to not be within scope of RATB's charge, unless the activities were funded by Division A or specific ARRA provisions directed otherwise.	reports." All reports submitted under these provisions are required to be made publicly available and posted on the website established by RATB under Division A, Title XV, Section 1526. Any portion of a report may be redacted when made publicly available, if the portion would disclose information that is not subject to disclosure under FOIA and the Privacy Act.
RATB recommendations and agency responses	Division A, Title)(V, Section 1523	RATB is required to make recommendations to agencies "on measures to prevent fraud, waste, and abuse relating to covered funds."	An agency that receives a recommendation from RATB is required to submit a "responsive report" to the President, the congressional committees of jurisdiction (including the appropriations committees of both chambers), and RATB not later than 30 days after receipt of the recommendation. A responsive report is required to indicate "whether the agency agrees or disagrees with the recommendations," and "any actions the agency will take to implement the recommendations." (Beyond the 30-day requirement for agencies to submit a report responding to board recommendations, an agency is not required to report on subsequent implementation.)
Powers of the board	Division A, Title XV, Section 1524	RATB is required to conduct audits and reviews of spending of covered funds. These activities are required to be coordinated with the IGs of relevant agencies to avoid duplication and overlap of work. The board is authorized to conduct its own	No provision appears to specifically require RATB to report on the use of its appropriations transfer authority. However, because RATB would appear to be an "agency" for purposes of

Table B.1. (Continued)

Subject	ARRA Citation	Overview of Provision (*see also next column*)	Reporting Requirement(s)
		independent audits and reviews and also to collaborate on audits with any IG of an agency. In conducting audits and reviews, RATB has authorities provided under Section 6 of the Inspector General Act of 1978 (i.e., various IG authorities), may issue subpoenas to compel testimony from nonfederal officers and employees, and may enforce the subpoenas in the same manner as IG subpoenas under Section 6 of the Inspector General Act of 1978. RATB is required to carry out its powers in accordance with standards prescribed in Section 4(b)(1) of the Inspector General Act of 1978. The board is authorized to hold public hearings, to which the head of each agency is required to make all officers and employees available. RATB is authorized to enter into certain contracts. RATB has authority to transfer up to 100% of its appropriated funds to "any office of inspector general, the Office of Management and Budget, the General Services Administration, and the [Recovery Independent Advisory Panel established by Section 1541]." Section 1524(f) authorizes the board to make these transfers for "expenses to support administrative support services and audits, reviews, or other activities related to oversight by the Board of covered funds." Further insight into congressional intent may be gleaned from the joint explanatory statement, which says "[t]he conferees note that	Title)(V, it appears that RATB would be required to comply with requirements for an agency to post a "plan ... for using funds made available in [Division A]" on the board's website (Section 1526(c)(1 1)). The same requirement would seem to apply to OMB, GSA, IGs, and the Recovery Independent Advisory Panel, if any received transferred funds from RATB. For more information about requirements for the board's website, see below in this table (Title XV, Section 1526).

Table B.1. (Continued)

Subject	ARRA Citation	Overview of Provision (*see also next column*)	Reporting Requirement(s)
		funding appropriated to the Board will support activities related to accountability, transparency, and oversight of spending under the Act. Funds may be transferred to support the operations of the Recovery Independent Advisory Panel established under section 1541 of the Act and for technical and administrative services and support provided by the General Services Administration. Funds may also be transferred to the Office of Management and Budget for coordinating and overseeing the implementation of the reporting requirements established under section 1526 of the Act" (H.Rept. 111-16, p. 510).	
RATB staffing, administrative support, and information access	Division A, Title XV, Section 1525	The board may exercise most provisions of 5 U.S.C. § 3161 (relating to employment and compensation of employees in a temporary organization established by law or executive order), subject to time periods of appointment that may not exceed the board's termination date at the end of FY20 13. (Pay provisions of 5 U.S.C. § 3161 allow the rate of basic pay for an executive director to be up to the maximum rate of pay for the Senior Executive Service (SES) under 5 U.S.C. § 5382, which under some conditions may be level II of the Executive Schedule.) Upon RATB's request, the head of "any agency or other entity of the Federal Government" is required, "insofar as is practicable and not in contravention of any existing law," to furnish information or assistance to RATB or an authorized	If information or assistance requested by RATB is "unreasonably refused or not provided" in the board's judgment, RATB is required to report the circumstances "without delay" to congressional committees of jurisdiction, including the House and Senate Appropriations Committees.

Table B.1. (Continued)

Subject	ARRA Citation	Overview of Provision (*see also next column*)	Reporting Requirement(s)
		designee. GSA is required to provide the board with administrative support services, including office space.	
Establishment of RATB website	Division A, Title XV, Section 1526	Requires the board to establish and maintain a "user-friendly, public- facing website to foster greater accountability and transparency in the use of covered funds," no later than 30 days after enactment. (This website was established in anticipation of ARRA's enactment as Recovery.gov.) The website's purpose is to "be a portal or gateway to key information relating to [Division A] and provide connections to other Government websites with related information." The board is tasked with ensuring the website meets 15 requirements concerning content and function. Many of the 15 requirements are essentially reporting requirements. These include providing: (1) materials about what Division A means for citizens; (2) accountability information, including audit findings from IGs and GAO; (3) data on relevant economic, financial, grant, and contract information; (4) detailed data on contracts awarded, including, among other things, "information about the competitiveness of the contracting process"; (5) printable reports of funds obligated by month to each state and congressional district; (6) a means for the public to give feedback on the performance of contracts; (7) detailed information on federal contracts and grants, to include certain data elements required by FFATA; (8) a link to estimates of jobs	In addition to the requirements of Section 1526 in the previous column, several other provisions in ARRA's Division A require the posting of certain information on RATB's website. See references elsewhere in this column, including for Title IX, Section 901 (links to GAO reports and audits); Title XV, Sections 1511 (relating to state and local certifications), 1514 (IG reviews), 1523 (RATB reports), and 1554 (non-fixed-price and non-competitively awarded contracts); and Title XVI, Section 1612 (use of general 1% transfer authority). Some reports required by Division A (e.g., Title XV, Section 1513 (Council of Economic Advisers reports)) and information about some activities authorized by Division A (e.g., Title XV, Section 1524 (RATB's 100% transfer authority)) are not explicitly required to be posted on the RATB website. RATB is authorized to exclude posting contractual or other information on a "case-by-case basis when necessary to protect national security or protect information that is not subject to disclosure under [FOIA and the Privacy Act]." It is not clear the extent to which information will be included on the website about activities and funding associated with Division B of ARRA.

Table B.1. (Continued)

Subject	ARRA Citation	Overview of Provision (*see also next column*)	Reporting Requirement(s)
		"sustained or created" by Division A; (9) a link to information about announcements of grant competitions and solicitations for contracts to be awarded; (10) links to other government websites with information about covered funds, including federal agency and state websites; (1 1) a plan from "each Federal agency for using funds made available in [Division A] to the agency; (12) information on "Federal allocations of formula grants and awards of competitive grants using covered funds"; (13) information on "Federal allocations of mandatory and other entitlement programs by State, county, or other appropriate geographical unit; (14) to the extent practical, links to and information about how to access certain job opportunities, "in order to direct job seekers to job opportunities created by [Division A]"; and (15) necessary enhancements and updates.	
Independence of IGs	Division A, Title XV, Section 1527	Nothing in Title XV, Subtitle B (Sections 152 1-1530, establishing RATB) shall affect the independent authority of an IG "to determine whether to conduct an audit or investigation of covered funds." An IG's decision "shall be final."	If RATB requests that an IG conduct or refrain from conducting an audit or investigation and the IG rejects the request in whole or in part, the IG is required to not later than 30 days after rejecting the request submit a "report" to RATB, the head of the applicable agency, and the congressional committees of jurisdiction, including the appropriations committees of both chambers. The report is required to state the reason that the IG has rejected the request.

Table B.1. (Continued)

Subject	ARRA Citation	Overview of Provision (*see also next column*)	Reporting Requirement(s)
Establishment of Recovery Independent Advisory Panel (RIAP)	Division A, TitleXV, Sections 1541-1546	Establishes a panel of five presidentially appointed members to advise RATB on how it could prevent fraud, waste, and abuse relating to covered funds. Provisions address hearings, securing information from federal agencies, using the U.S. mails, gifts, compensation and travel expenses for members, appointment of staff, detail of federal employees, procurement of services, and administrative support. RIAP terminates at the end of FY2013.	N/A
Oversight Provisions Relating to Additional Budgetary, Contractual, Economic, Environmental, and Whistleblower Matters			
Separate Treasury accounts for Division A appropriations	Division A, Title)(V, Section 1551	Requires the Secretary of the Treasury to "ensure that all funds appropriated in [Division A] shall be established in separate Treasury accounts," unless waived by the director of OMB, in order to "facilitate tracking these funds through Treasury and agency accounting systems."	For reporting purposes, separate accounts will allow separation of supplemental Division A-provided funding from previous appropriations that correspond to the same programs, projects, and activities.
General transfer authority, and oversight thereof	Division A, Title)(VI, Section 1612	Provides that "[d]uring the current fiscal year, not to exceed 1 percent of any appropriation made available by [Division A] may be transferred by an agency head between such appropriations funded in [Division A] of that department or agency," subject to several provisos and reporting requirements.	Requires that an agency head notify the Committees on Appropriations of the Senate and House of Representatives of the transfer 1 5 days in advance. Also requires that notice of any transfer made pursuant to this authority be posted "15 days following such transfer" to the website established by RATB.
Limit on funds	Division A, Title XVI, Section 1604	Prohibits use of funds made available by Division A from being used by a state or local government or a private entity "for any casino or other gambling establishment, aquarium, zoo, golf course, or swimming pool."	N/A

Table B.1. (Continued)

Subject	ARRA Citation	Overview of Provision (*see also next column*)	Reporting Requirement(s)
Non-fixed-price or non-competitively awarded contracts	Division A, Title XV, Section 1554	Requires that contracts funded under Division A be awarded as fixed- price contracts through the use of competitive procedures "to the maximum extent possible."	Requires that "a summary" of any contract awarded "that is not fixed-price and not awarded using competitive procedures" shall be posted in "a special section" of the RATB website required to be established by Title XV, Section 1526. (On March 4, 2009, President Obama issued a memorandum to the heads of executive departments and agencies outlining Administration policy on government contracting, directing the director of OMB and other officials to issue new guidelines to agencies regarding "noncompetitive" contracts.[b])
Employment and economic impacts of stimulus legislation	Division A, Title XV, Section 1513	Requires chairperson of Council of Economic Advisers (CEA), an entity located in the EOP, to submit reports that "detail the impact of programs funded through covered funds on employment, estimated economic growth, and other key economic indicators." The reporting is required to be done in consultation with the director of OMB and the Secretary of the Treasury.	Reports are required to be sent quarterly to the Committees on Appropriations of the Senate and House of Representatives. Because Section 150 1 defines "covered funds" as any funds expended or obligated under from appropriations made under Division A, the provision does not apply to provisions in Division B (e.g., Title I tax changes).
Compliance with National Environmental Policy Act (N EPA)	Division A, TitleXVI, Section 1609	Premised on several "findings," provision says "[a]dequate resources within this bill must be devoted to ensuring that applicable environmental reviews under [NEPA] are completed on an expeditious basis and that the shortest existing applicable process under [NEPA] shall be utilized." For more information on N EPA, see CRS Report RL33 152, *The National Environmental Policy Act*	Requires the President to report to the Senate Environment and Public Works Committee and the House Natural Resources Committee every 90 days following the date of enactment until the end of FY20 11 on the status and progress of projects and activities funded by Division A with respect to compliance with NEPA "requirements and

Table B.1. (Continued)

Subject	ARRA Citation	Overview of Provision (*see also next column*)	Reporting Requirement(s)
		(NEPA): Background and Implementation, by Linda Luther.	documentation." The provision makes no reference to posting reports on the Internet.
Protections for state and local government and contractor whistleblowers	Division A, Title XV, Section 1553	Employees of nonfederal employers receiving funds may not be discharged, demoted, or otherwise subject to a reprisal for disclosing to RATB, an IG, the CG, a Member of Congress, a state or federal regulatory or law enforcement agency, a person with supervisory authority over the employee (or such other person working for the employer who has the authority to investigate, discover, or terminate misconduct), a court or grand jury, the head of a federal agency, or their representatives, several kinds of information relating to covered funds, including about mismanagement, waste, a substantial and specific danger to public health or safety, an abuse of authority, or a violation of law, rule, or regulation related to an agency contract or grant. Provides for investigation of complaints by IGs, remedy and enforcement authority, nonenforceability of certain waivers of rights and remedies, and requirement for any employer receiving covered funds to post notice of certain rights and remedies. An IG has discretion not to investigate complaints, in which case the complainant shall assume the right to a civil remedy.	Upon completion of an investigation, the investigating IG is required to submit a report of the findings to the person making the complaint, the person's employer, the head of the appropriate agency, and RATB. An IG is required to include in semi-annual reports to Congress a list of the investigations the IG decided not to conduct.

Source: CRS

a. See U.S. President (Obama), "Freedom of Information Act," memorandum for the heads of executive departments and agencies, January 21, 2009, http://www.whitehouse. gov/the_press_office/Freedom_of_Information_Act/.

b. U.S. President (Obama), "Government Contracting," memorandum for the heads of executive departments and agencies, March 4, 2009, http://www.whitehouse.gov/ the_press_office/economy_in _government_ contracting/.

APPENDIX C. DETAIL OF ARRA APPROPRIATIONS TO IGS, GAO, AND RATB

IGs are listed in alphabetical order of their parent departments, followed by IGs located within independent agencies. GAO and RATB are listed at the table's end. The table indicates the division and title of ARRA in which the appropriation was included, the funding amount, the period of availability for the funds, and, in the last column, whether appropriations language specified that resources be used only for the purpose of overseeing ARRA-provided funds.

Table C.1 . Appropriations for IGs, GAO, and RATB in ARRA (P.L. 1 1 1 -5).

Entity	Div. / Title	Budget Authority ($ millions)	Available Until	ARRA Oversight Purpose Specified?
Inspectors General				
Dept. of Agriculture (USDA)	A / I	$22.5	end of FY2013	yes[a]
Dept. of Commerce (DOC)	A / II	10.0	expended	yes
	A / II	6.0	end of FY2013	no
Dept. of Defense (DOD)	A / III	15.0	end of FY2011	no
Dept. of Education (ED)	A / VIII	14.0	end of FY2012	yes
Dept. of Energy (DOE)	A / IV	15.0	end of FY2012	no
Dept. of Health and Human Services (HHS)	A / VIII	17.0	end of FY2012	no
	B / V	31.25	end of FY2011	yes
Dept. of Homeland Security (DHS)	A / VI	5.0	end of FY2012	yes
Dept. of Housing and Urban Development (HUD)	A / XII	15.0	end of FY2013	no[b]
Dept. of the Interior (DOI)	A / VII	15.0	end of FY2012	no
Dept. of Justice (DOJ)	A / II	2.0	end of FY2013	no
Dept. of Labor (DOL)	A / VIII	6.0	end of FY2012	yes
Dept. of State (DOS)	A / XI	2.0	end of FY2010[c]	no[d]
Dept. of Transportation (DOT)	A / XII	20.0	end of FY2013	yes
Dept. of the Treasury, Treasury IG for Tax Administration (TIGTA)	A / V	7.0	end of FY2013	yes
Dept. of the Treasury (Treasury)	A / V	7.0	end of FY2013	yes
Dept. of Veterans Affairs (VA)	A / X	1.0	end of FY2011	yes
Corporation for National and Community Service	A / VIII	1.0	end of FY2012	no
Environmental Protection Agency (EPA)	A / VII	20.0	end of FY2012	no
General Services Administration	A / V	7.0	end of FY2013	yes
National Aeronautics and Space Administration (NASA)	A / II	2.0	end of FY2013	no

(Continued)

Entity	Div. / Title	Budget Authority ($ millions)	Available Until	ARRA Oversight Purpose Specified?
National Science Foundation (NSF)	A / II	2.0	end of FY2013	no
Small Business Administration (SBA)	A / V	10.0	end of FY2013	yes
Social Security Administration (SSA)	A / VIII	2.0	end of FY2012	yes
Total, Appropriations for IGs		**254.75**		
Non-IG Entities				
Government Accountability Office (GAO)	A / IX	25.0	end of FY2010	no
Recovery Accountability and Transparency Board (RATB)[e]	A / V	84.0	end of FY2011	yes[f]
Grand Total, Appropriations for IGs, GAO, and RATB		**363.75**		

Source: CRS; P.L. 111-5 and H.Rept. 111-16.

a. Report language in the joint explanatory statement indicated that $7.5 million is for oversight of the U.S. Forest Service (H.Rept. 111-16, p. 413).

b. Report language in the joint explanatory statement said the "funding will assist the IG in monitoring the use of these funds to ensure that funding provided in this bill is used in an effective and efficient manner" (H.Rept. 111-16, p. 473).

c. The Department of State IG's appropriation language was silent on its period of availability, therefore making the funding available until the end of FY2010 under a general provision in Division A, Title XVI (Section 1603).

d. Report language in the joint explanatory statement indicated the funds are for "oversight of the funds made available to the Department of State by [Division A]" (H.Rept. 111-16, p. 468).

e. Division A, Title V ("Financial Services and General Government") provided funds for the "Recovery Act Accountability and Transparency Board" to carry out provisions in Title XV of Division A ("Accountability and Transparency"). Section 1521 of Title XV established the slightly differently named "Recovery Accountability and Transparency Board."

f. Many of RATB's functions and duties refer to "covered funds," which Title XV defined as funds provided by Division A (Title XV, Section 1501). RATB has authority under Division A, Title XV, Section 1524(f) to transfer up to 100% of its funds to "any office of inspector general, the Office of Management and Budget, the General Services Administration, and the [Recovery Independent Advisory Panel established by Section 1541]." Section 1 524(f) authorized the board to make these transfers for "expenses to support administrative support services and audits, reviews, or other activities related to oversight by the Board of covered funds." Section 1501 defined "covered funds" as "any funds that are expended or obligated from appropriations made under [Division A]." See this chapter's next table for more information about the 1 00% transfer authority.

APPENDIX D. EARLY CBO ESTIMATES OF GDP GAP , INCLUDING IMPACT OF ARRA

Congress required in ARRA's Division A that the law's impact on economic indicators be evaluated (Title XV, Section 1513). Congress may conduct oversight over the federal government's attempts to diminish the recession's GDP gap and ARRA's contribution to the effort. Graphical displays may assist with visualizing the concept.[80] After ARRA was enacted, CBO prepared a year-by-year estimate of the short-term economic impacts of the law. CBO noted that "[t]he macroeconomic impacts of any economic stimulus program are very uncertain," and that "[e]conomic theories differ in their predictions about the effectiveness of stimulus."[81] Nonetheless, CBO developed a range of estimates of the impacts of ARRA "that encompasses a majority of economists' views." CBO's letter included a graphic that showed the estimated impact of ARRA on actual GDP.

Figure 1. Difference Between Potential GDP in CBO's Baseline and Actual GDP Without and With the Impact of the American Recovery and Reinvestment Act of 2009

(Percentage difference in the fourth quarter of each year)

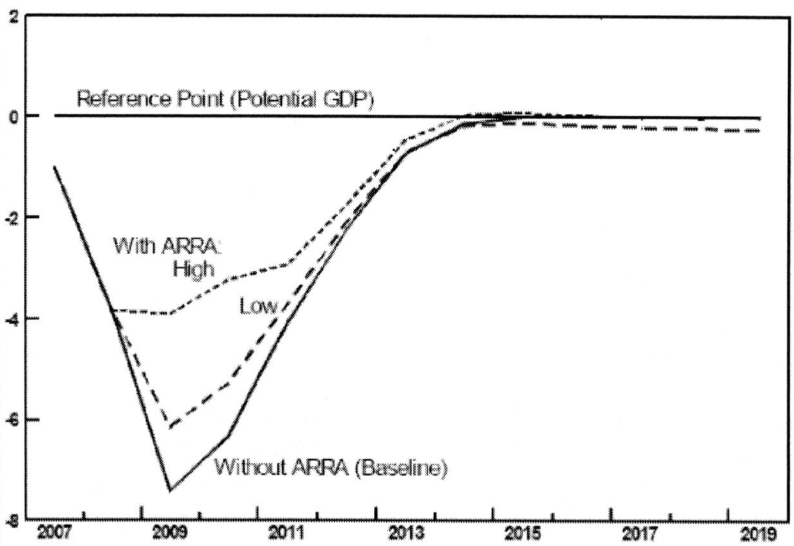

Source: Congressional Budget Office.

Notes: CBO's January 2009 baseline projection of potential gross domestic product (GDP) is set as a reference point. The projection of actual GDP without the effects of the American Recovery and Reinvestment Act of 2009 (ARRA) is CBO's January 2009 estimate, as presented in *The Budget and Economic Outlook: Fiscal Years 2009-2019*. The projections of actual GDP with the effects of ARRA incorporated (the high and low estimates) reflect a range of assumptions.

Source: Letter from Douglas W. Elmendorf, Director, to Senator Charles E. Grassley, Ranking Member, Senate Committee on Finance, March 2, 2009, Figure 1 (unnumbered p. 13 of PDF file).

Figure D-1. CBO's March 2009 "High" and "Low" Estimates of ARRA's Impact on Previously Forecasted GDP Gap (January 2009 Forecast)

CBO explained that the previous figure "shows three different projections of the economy's actual output: CBO's January baseline projection of GDP (which does not include the effects of ARRA), GDP using CBO 's high estimate of the effects of the legislation; and GDP using CBO's low estimate of the effects of the legislation."

CBO subsequently updated its economic forecast of the GDP gap in its analysis of the Obama Administration's preliminary budget proposals for FY2010.[82] In two graphics, CBO showed "the middle of the range of the agency's [March 2009] estimates of ARRA's impact on GDP and employment. "[83]

In brief, CBO estimated ARRA likely would contribute to helping end the recession, in concert with actions by the Federal Reserve and Department of the Treasury.

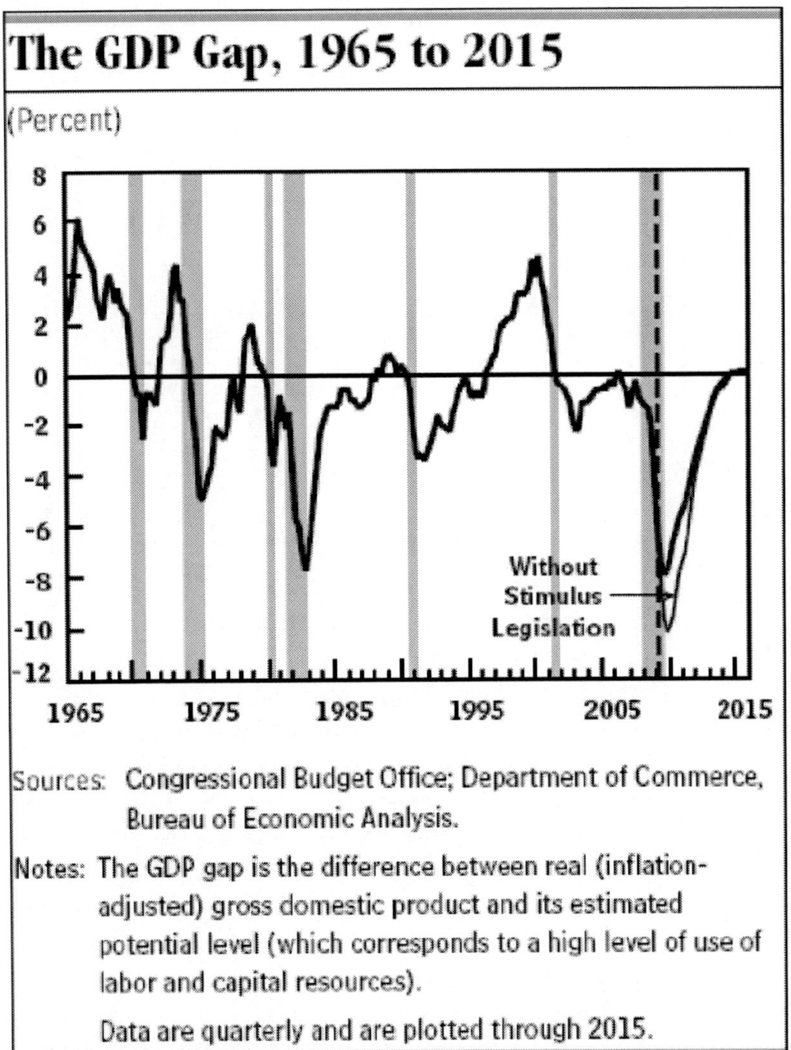

Source: CBO, *A Preliminary Analysis of the President's Budget and an Update of CBO's Budget and Economic Outlook*, March 2009, Figure 2-1, p. 21.

Figure D-2. CBO's Updated March 2009 Forecast of GDP Gap, Showing March 2009 "Middle" Estimated Impact of ARRA

The current recession, which began in December 2007, took a sudden and severe turn for the worse late last year. Of the 4.4 million jobs lost since the recession began, more than half have been lost in just the past four months. According to the Congressional Budget Office's economic projections, the economy will continue to deteriorate for some time, although the adoption of the American Recovery and Reinvestment Act and very aggressive actions by the Federal Reserve and the Treasury will help end the recession this fall.[84]

CBO performed similar analysis regarding the unemployment rate. See **Figure D-3**, below.

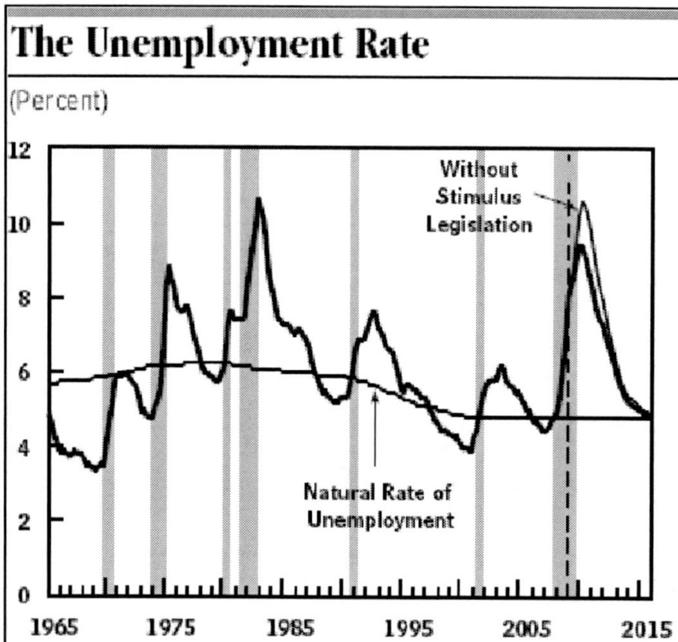

Sources: Congressional Budget Office; Department of Labor, Bureau of Labor Statistics.

Notes: CBO's estimate of the natural rate of unemployment is the rate of unemployment that is not due to the business cycle but to underlying characteristics of the labor market, such as normal rates of job turnover and the degree to which the job seekers' skills and locations match available openings.

Although the rate of unemployment is projected to peak at a lower level than in 1982, the peak unemployment gap (the difference between the unemployment rate and the estimate of the natural rate of unemployment) is projected to be about the same as in 1982.

Data are quarterly and are plotted through 2015.

Source: CBO, *A Preliminary Analysis of the President's Budget and an Update of CBO's Budget and Economic Outlook*, March 2009, Figure 2-2, p. 21.

Figure D-3. CBO's Updated March 2009 Forecast of Unemployment, Showing March 2009 "Middle" Estimated Impact of ARRA

CBO noted, however, that the range of estimates of ARRA's impact "is quite large,"[85] and that CBO's "current [economic] forecast, particularly for the near term, is subject to a greater than normal degree of uncertainty."[86]

Key Policy Staff

Area of Expertise	Name	Phone	E-mail
General Oversight Provisions in ARRA and Related Implementation	Clinton T. Brass	7-4536	cbrass@
Economic Analysis of ARRA	Jane G. Gravelle	7-7829	jgravelle@crs.loc.gov
	Thomas L. Hungerford	7-6422	thungerford@crs.loc.gov
	Marc Labonte	7-0640	mlabonte@crs.loc.gov
Budget Execution Processes	Clinton T. Brass	7-4536	cbrass@crs.loc.gov
Government Procurement	L. Elaine Halchin	7-0646	ehalchin@crs.loc.gov
Grant and Cooperative Agreement Processes	Garrett Hatch	7-7822	ghatch@crs.loc.gov
FFATA and USASpending.gov	Garrett Hatch	7-7822	ghatch@crs.loc.gov
Inspectors General	Frederick M. Kaiser	7-8682	fkaiser@crs.loc.gov
	Vanessa K. Burrows	7-083 1	vburrows@crs.loc.gov
Oversight Issues for Specific Agencies or Policy Areas	Relevant CRS Experts	7-5700	n/a

End Notes

1 P.L. 111-5, February 17, 2009; 123 Stat. 115. For CBO's statements, see U.S. Congressional Budget Office (hereafter CBO), *A Preliminary Analysis of the President's Budget and an Update of CBO 's Budget and Economic Outlook*, March 2009, pp. 19, 33. For more on the economic situation and ARRA, see CRS reports at "American Recovery and Reinvestment Act," http://apps.crs.gov/cli/cli.aspx?PRDS_CLI_ITEM_ID=3405&from=3&fromId=4.

2 The potential purposes of oversight are numerous; see CRS Report RL30240, *Congressional Oversight Manual*, by Frederick M. Kaiser et al.

3 "President-elect Obama Holds News Conference After Meeting with His Transition Economic Advisory Board (Chicago)," transcript, *CQ Transcriptions*, November 7, 2008, http://www.cq.com (subscription required). For press coverage, see David Cho, Michael D. Shear, and Michael S. Rosenwald, "Obama Calls on Congress to Act Fast on Stimulus," *Washington Post*, November 8, 2008, p. A1; and Jeff Zeleny, "Obama, in His New Role as President-elect, Calls for Stimulus Package," *New York Times*, November 8, 2008, p. A16.

4 Office of the President-elect (Obama), "2.5 Million Jobs," November 21, 2008, http://change.gov/newsroom/entry/ 2_5_millionjobs/. See also Jackie Calmes and Jeff Zeleny, "Obama Vows Swift Action on Vast Economic Stimulus Plan," *New York Times*, November 23, 2008, p. A1.

5 "Vice President-elect Biden Delivers Remarks Before Briefing on the Economy," transcript, *CQ Transcriptions*, December 23, 2008, http://www.cq.com (subscription required).

6 Office of the President-elect (Obama), "American Recovery and Reinvestment," January 3, 2009, http://change.gov/ newsroom/entry/american_recovery_and_reinvestment/.

7 "President-Elect Holds Media Availability Following Meeting with His Economic Advisers," transcript, *CQ Transcriptions*, January 6, 2009, http://www.cq.com (subscription required).

[8] CBO, *The Budget and Economic Outlook: Fiscal Years 2009 to 2019*, January 2009, "Preface," http://www.cbo.gov/ doc.cfm?index=9957. CBO's website links to the agency's testimony before the Senate Committee on the Budget, which held a hearing on the report on January 8, 2009, http://www.cbo.gov/doc.cfm?index=9958. The latter website also links to a C-SPAN Webcast of the hearing.

[9] U.S. Congress, Senate Committee on the Budget, *The CBO Budget and Economic Outlook*, 111th Cong., 1st sess., January 8, 2009, http://budget.senate and http://budget.senate NewHearings&Testi.htm.

[10] Ibid., p. 1. For more information and CRS reports on the topic of the "Economy, Recession, and Financial Sector," see http://apps.crs.gov/cli/level_2.aspx?PRDS_CLI_ITEM_ID=4.

[11] CBO, *The Budget and Economic Outlook: Fiscal Years 2009 to 2019*, p. 2.

[12] Ibid. Economic forecasts typically are subject to considerable uncertainty. CBO noted several sources of uncertainty in the present case that "make it particularly difficult for analysts to use historical patterns to forecast the near future." Ibid., pp. 4-5.

[13] See **Appendix A** for CBO's graphical display of a GDP gap, which is included in this chapter to aid with visualizing oversight issues related to the stimulus law's impact on the economy.

[14] CBO, *Testimony, The Budget and Economic Outlook: Fiscal Years 2009 to 2019*, prepared statement of Robert A. Sunshine, acting director, before the Senate Committee on the Budget, January 8, 2009, pp. 31-32.

[15] Amit R. Paley, "Stimulus Provision May Inhibit Watchdog Investigations, Critics Warn," *Washington Post*, February 28, 2009, p. D1.

[16] U.S. Congress, Senate Committee on Homeland Security and Governmental Affairs, *Nominations*, 111th Cong., 1st sess., January 14, 2009, http://hsgac.senate b0ac-4edb-a9bf-1 18eb55 19984. A transcript is available at http://www.cq.com (subscription required).

[17] He continued, "One of the difficulties in existing financial—federal financial management payment flows is that the time between when a contract is signed and when the information shows up on federal government websites is so long that we didn't want to allow that time lapse to occur. So we would propose that the contract officer ... fill out a simple template, basically to create a faster flow of information, at least at an aggregate level, on specific contracts." PDF stands for Portable Document Format and refers to electronic files that replicate paper documents.

[18] This language was posted at the new website, http://www.recovery

[19] It is possible that some oversight provisions may have been informed by experience with implementation of the Emergency Economic Stabilization Act of 2008 (EESA, Division A of H.R. 1424, P.L. 110-343) and the Troubled Asset Relief Program (TARP). For more information about oversight provisions in that law, see CRS Report RL34713, *Emergency Economic Stabilization Act: Preliminary Analysis of Oversight Provisions*, by Curtis W. Copeland.

[20] U.S. Congress, House Committee on Appropriations, "Summary: American Recovery and Reinvestment," press release, January 21, 2009, http://appropriations

[21] The measure has been referred to as "the stimulus legislation," the Recovery Act, and ARRA.

[22] Peter Baker, "White House Offers New Details on Recovery Plan," *nytimes.com*, January 25, 2009, http://www.nytimes.com/2009/01/25/us/politics. This online press report linked to an undated Obama Administration document: White House, "The American Reinvestment and Recover Plan—by the Numbers," [no date], http://www.whitehouse.gov/assets. Several days earlier, an early presidential memorandum appeared to presage more general Obama Administration plans regarding transparency, beyond the stimulus. The memorandum announced broad policy priorities to make government "transparent," "participatory," and "collaborative." In addition, the memorandum directed that recommendations be developed within 120 days (i.e., by approximately May 20, 2009) for an eventual "open government directive," which would be issued later by OMB. See U.S. President (Obama), "Transparency and Open Government," memorandum for the heads of executive departments and agencies, January 21, 2009, printed in 74 *Federal Register* 4685-4686, January 26, 2009, http://www.whitehouse.gov/the_press_office/Transparency_and_Open_Government/.

[23] Robert O'Harrow Jr., "If Spending is Swift, Oversight May Suffer," *Washington Post*, February 9, 2009, p. A1. Related to the issue of workforce capacity, the George W. Bush Administration's initiative to improve management of federal agencies, the "President's Management Agenda," established criteria for agencies to receive scores on things such as their workforce planning (e.g., to ensure the workforce is adequate to an agency's needs). According to the Bush Administration's criteria and final grades in December 2008, eight of the 15 cabinet departments received the highest rating of a "green" score for "management of human capital," while the other seven departments received the middle "yellow" score. See White House, "Executive Branch Management Scorecard," December 31, 2008, http://georgewbush-whitehouse.archives.gov/results/agenda/scorecard.html.

[24] Senator Claire McCaskill asked then OMB Director-designate Orszag about this issue in one of his confirmation hearings. See U.S. Congress, Senate Committee on Homeland Security and Governmental Affairs, *Nominations*, 111th Cong., 1st sess., January 14, 2009.

[25] Steven Mufson and Lori Montgomery, "Economists Agree Time Is of the Essence for Stimulus," *Washington Post*, February 8, 2009, p. A1.

[26] For a comparison of general oversight provisions in the House and Senate versions, see CRS Report R40215, *General Oversight Provisions in the American Recovery and Reinvestment Act (ARRA) of 2009: Brief Comparative Analysis of House and Senate Versions*, by Clinton T. Brass.

[27] U.S. Congress, Conference Committees, *Making Supplemental Appropriations for Job Preservation and Creation, Infrastructure Investment, Energy Efficiency and Science, Assistance to the Unemployed, and State and Local Fiscal Stabilization, for the Fiscal Year Ending September 30, 2009, and for Other Purposes*, conference report to accompany H.R. 1, 111th Cong., 1st sess., February 12, 2009, H.Rept. 111-16 (Washington: GPO, 2009), pp. 780-781.

[28] For a more comprehensive overview of ARRA's legislative history and non-oversight provisions, see CRS Report R40537, *American Recovery and Reinvestment Act of 2009 (P.L. 111-5): Summary and Legislative History*, by Clinton T. Brass et al. The White House released "state by state numbers" and several fact sheets about ARRA-related economic and policy objectives. See White House, "White House Releases State by State Numbers; American Recovery and Reinvestment Act to Save or Create 3.5 Million Jobs," press release, February 17, 2009, http://www.whitehouse.gov/the_press_office/White-House-Releases-State-by-State-Numbers-American-Recovery-andReinvestment-Act/ (website provides links to various fact sheets).

[29] P.L. 111-5, Section 4.

[30] Appropriations that were provided for a purpose of carrying out provisions in Division A, for example, would not be available for other purposes. However, appropriations that did not specify a purpose related specifically to Division A (e.g., some appropriations for GAO and IGs) also would be available for oversight of activities outside of Division A, including activities associated with Division B.

[31] Laws often leave room for interpretation regarding specific purposes and bases for judging "success." In addition, there may not be consensus on precise objectives or definitions of success among majority coalitions of Members of Congress, or between Congress and the President.

[32] CBO, Letter from Douglas W. Elmendorf, Director, to Senator Charles E. Grassley, Ranking Member, Senate Committee on Finance, March 2, 2009, http://www.cbo.gov/ftpdocs/100xx/doc10008/03-02- Macro _Effects _of_ARRA.pdf, also located at http://www.cbo.gov/doc.cfm?index=10008.

[33] Ibid., Table 1 (unnumbered pp. 5-6 in PDF file).

[34] Ibid., Table 2 (unnumbered pp. 7-11 in PDF file).

[35] Ibid., Table 2 (unnumbered p. 11 in PDF file).

[36] CBO indicated that discretionary spending totals included "estimates for changes to mandatory programs contained in Division A," ibid., Table 2, footnote "a" (unnumbered p. 11 in PDF file).

[37] Other terms have been used to differentiate this kind of statutory provision from appropriations provisions. Some examples include "substantive," "non-appropriations," "legislative," and "provisions that change existing law."

[38] The provisions were distributed among 12 titles in Division A and 1 title in Division B. A single appropriation to the Office of Inspector General of the Department of Health and Human Services was included in Title V of Division B. ARRA also contained numerous appropriations set-asides for oversight within specific accounts and programs. As noted earlier, these set-asides and other agency- or program-specific oversight provisions are not included within the scope of this chapter.

[39] In the appendix, IGs are listed in alphabetical order of their parent departments, followed by IGs located within independent agencies. GAO and RATB are listed at the table's end. The table indicates the division and title of ARRA in which the appropriation was included, the funding amount, the period of availability for the funds, and whether appropriations language specified that resources be used to oversee ARRA-provided funds.

[40] In contrast, the Emergency Economic Stabilization Act of 2008 made \$50 million available to the Special Inspector General for the Troubled Assed Relief Program (SIGTARP). For discussion, see CRS Report R40099, *The Special Inspector General for the Troubled Asset Relief Program (SIGTARP)*, by Vanessa K. Burrows. For more information about statutory IGs, see CRS Report 98-379, *Statutory Offices of Inspector General: Past and Present*, by Frederick M. Kaiser.

[41] Without specification of a purpose, appropriations could be used for purposes authorized by law that are not necessarily related to ARRA oversight. In addition, funds provided by Division A without a specification of purpose could be used for oversight of activities and funding associated with Division B.

[42] Division A, Title XV, Section 1524(f).

[43] U.S. Executive Office of the President, Office of Management and Budget, "Initial Implementing Guidance for the American Recovery and Reinvestment Act of 2009," memorandum for heads of departments and agencies from Peter R. Orszag, Director, M-09-10, February 18, 2009, http://www.whitehouse.gov/omb/assets 10.pdf.

[44] U.S. President (Obama), "Ensuring Responsible Spending of Recovery Act Funds," memorandum for heads of departments and agencies (contained in press release), March 20, 2009, http://www.whitehouse.gov/the_press_office/ Memorandum-for-the-Heads-of-Executive-Departments-and-Agencies-3-20-09/.

[45] U.S. Executive Office of the President, Office of Management and Budget, "Updated Implementing Guidance for the American Recovery and Reinvestment Act of 2009," memorandum for heads of departments and agencies from Peter R. Orszag, Director, M-09-15, April 3, 2009, http://www.whitehouse.gov/omb/assets

[46] See White House, "Vice President Biden to Oversee the Administration's Implementation of the Recovery Act's Provisions," press release, February 23, 2009, http://www.whitehouse.gov/the_press_office/Vice-President-Biden-toOversee-the-Administrations-implementation and U.S. Recovery and Accountability Board (hereafter RATB), "Recovery Accountability and Transparency Board Announces Membership," March 18, 2009, http://www.recovery. A Web page was established later to identify RATB members, http://www.recovery.gov/?q=content/recovery-accountability

[47] A classic framework for understanding oversight activity is the dichotomy between "police patrol" and "fire alarm" oversight. The former concept is more resource intensive, because it involves episodic, relatively in-depth searches for possible problems. The latter concept refers to ongoing, relatively less resource-intensive systems of rules, procedures, and practices that allow observers to "flag" issues of potential concern.

[48] For an expression of concern in the context of ARRA implementation, see U.S. Department of Energy, Office of Inspector General, *Special Report: The Department of Energy's Acquisition Workforce and its Impact on Implementation of the American Recovery and Reinvestment Act of 2009*, IG-RA-09-02, March 2009, http://www.recovery.. With respect to program evaluation, GAO has "found limited (and diminishing) resources spent on ... program evaluation" and "reason to be concerned about the capacity of federal agencies to produce evaluations of their programs' effectiveness." U.S. General Accounting Office, *Program Evaluation: Agencies Challenged by New Demand for Information on Program Results*, GAO/GGD-98-53, Apr. 1998, p. 1; and *Performance Budgeting: Opportunities and Challenges*, GAO-02-1106T, Sept. 2002, p. 16. See also U.S. Government Accountability Office, *Program Evaluation: OMB's PART Reviews Increased Agencies' Attention to Improving Evidence of Program Results*, GAO-06-67, pp. 15-16, 28.

[49] See heading entitled "Making and Measuring Progress" in CRS Report RL32388, *General Management Laws: Major Themes and Management Policy Options*, by Clinton T. Brass.

[50] U.S. National Commission on Terrorist Attacks Upon the United States, *The 9-11 Commission Report* (Washington: GPO, 2004), p. 344.

[51] For example, the advantages and disadvantages of legislating on the subject of enterprise risk management (ERM) might be explored. ERM is a process that focuses on bringing discipline to an organization's choices about how to deal with uncertain events that, in turn, might affect the organization's ability to accomplish its mission. More specifically, ERM refers to a process for dealing with or avoiding things that might "go wrong," or, alternatively, dealing with things that might "go better" only if they are appropriately handled. See Committee of Sponsoring Organizations of the Treadway Commission, *Enterprise Risk Management—Integrated Framework*, "Executive Summary," September 2004, http://www.coso.org/Publications/ERM/COSO

[52] CRS Report RL30240, *Congressional Oversight Manual*, by Frederick M. Kaiser et al.

[53] P.L. 111-5, Section 3, subsections (a) and (b), respectively.

[54] For macroeconomic analysis of the stimulus law and related issues, see CRS Report R40 104, *Economic Stimulus: Issues and Policies*, by Jane G. Gravelle, Thomas L. Hungerford, and Marc Labonte. Also see **Appendix D** for visual representations of early CBO projections of ARRA's potential macroeconomic impacts.

[55] For coverage of many discrete policy areas in CRS reports, see CRS Web page "American Recovery and Reinvestment Act," http://apps.crs.gov/cli/cli.aspx?PRDS_CLI_ITEM_ID=3405&from=3&fromId=4.

[56] In a March 9, 2009, article, RATB Chairperson Devaney was attributed to have multiplied a potential rate of fraud of 7% against the $787.2 billion value of the stimulus package, resulting in potential fraud of $55.1 billion. (See Neil King Jr., "Watchdog Over Stimulus Spending Toes a Delicate Line," *Wall Street Journal*, March 9, 2009, p. A4.) The 7% rate apparently was drawn from a report by the Association of Certified Fraud Examiners (ACFE), which suggested "the typical U.S. [private or public sector] organization loses 7% of its annual revenues to fraudulent activity." The ACFE fraud rate figure was based on a survey distributed to 16,606 certified fraud examiners, of whom 959 submitted usable responses (i.e., a 5.8% response rate, which may provide useful information but also is at high risk of nonresponse bias in resulting data). See Association of Certified Fraud Examiners, *2008 Report to the Nation on Occupational Fraud and Abuse*, 2008, pp. 8-9, 66-67, http://www.acfe.com/resources

[57] Existing agency general goals, performance goals, performance indicators, and program evaluations required by the Government Performance and Results Act of 1993 (GPRA) (P.L. 103-62) may cover some of ARRA's purposes and principles, but not others.

[58] RATB issued an announcement in April 2009 warning the public of potential frauds and scams that could be perpetrated on citizens and nongovernmental entities. RATB, "Recovery Board Issues Update on Recovery Act Frauds and Scams," press release, April 1, 2009, http://www.recovery. RATB encouraged people who come across suspected scams to notify relevant law enforcement or regulatory agencies.

[59] CBO, *Testimony, The Budget and Economic Outlook: Fiscal Years 2009 to 2019*, prepared statement of Robert A. Sunshine, acting director, before the Senate Committee on the Budget, January 8, 2009, p. 32.

[60] The term "impact" might be defined in this context as "an estimated measurement of how a program intervention affected an outcome of interest compared to what would have happened without the intervention."

[61] The program evaluation field refers to the concept of "what would have happened without the policy intervention" as "the counterfactual." Many methods may be used to evaluate programs and contribute to assessments of impact. For discussion, see CRS Report RL33301, *Congress and Program Evaluation: An Overview of Randomized Controlled Trials (RCTs) and Related Issues*, by Clinton T. Brass, Erin D. Williams, and Blas Nuñez-Neto.

[62] CBO, A Preliminary Analysis of the President's Budget and an Update of CBO's Budget and Economic Outlook, March 2009, p. 19, http://www.cbo.gov/doc.cfm?index=10014.

[63] Overall estimates of ARRA's macroeconomic impact may be approachable using econometric and other methods (Division A, Title XV, Section 1513), but it is not clear that impact analyses will be feasible for disaggregated methods (e.g., estimates of jobs created and saved submitted by funding recipients under Division A, Title XV, Section 1512(c)).

[64] Generally speaking, it is usually virtually impossible to simultaneously maximize the achievement of multiple objectives in a highly complex social and economic system. Wayne L. Winston and S. Christian Albright, *Practical Management Science: Spreadsheet Modeling and Applications* (Belmont, CA: Duxbury Press, 1997), pp. 337-388 (chapter 7, "Multi-objective Decision Making").

[65] CRS Report RL34718, *The Federal Funding Accountability and Transparency Act: Implementation and Proposed Amendments*, by Garrett Hatch.

[66] White House, "Remarks of Lawrence H. Summers, Director of the National Economic Council, 'Responding to an Historic Economic Crisis: The Obama Program,'" press release, March 13, 2009, http://www.whitehouse.gov/ thejress_office/Remarks-of-Lawrence-Summers-Director-of-the-National-Economic-Council-at-the-Brook/.

[67] CRS Report RL303 15, *Federalism, State Sovereignty, and the Constitution: Basis and Limits of Congressional Power*, by Kenneth R. Thomas.

[68] This overall "system" is arguably a product of the decision by the Framers of the Constitution to fragment governmental power both at the federal level (under a constitutional separation of powers) and between the federal level and states (in a system of federalism), in order to accomplish the varied purposes set forth in the preamble to the Constitution. Oversight entities may attempt to avoid duplication of effort and at the same time try to maintain autonomy to address their major concerns.

[69] See CRS Report RL30795, *General Management Laws: A Compendium*, by Clinton T. Brass et al.; and CRS Report RL32388, *General Management Laws: Major Themes and Management Policy Options*, by Clinton T. Brass.

[70] See, for example, 31 U.S.C. § 503.

[71] For some discussion about oversight of tax expenditures, see CRS Report RL33641, *Tax Expenditures: Trends and Critiques*, by Thomas L. Hungerford.

[72] For example, Division B of ARRA requires the Department of the Treasury to conduct studies of certain education incentives (Division B, Title I, Section 1004).

[73] With regard to RATB, its appropriations were made "to carry out the provisions of title XV of this Act" (Division A, Title V). In Title XV, RATB's functions are numerous, but most involve oversight of "covered funds" (Division A, Title XV, Section 1521). The term "covered funds" was defined in Title XV as "any funds that are expended or obligated from appropriations made under this Act" (Section 1501). Section 4 of ARRA states that references to "this Act" shall be treated as "referring only to the provisions of that division." Therefore, it appears that RATB's appropriations are provided predominately for the purpose of oversight of activities and funding related to Division A. However, some aspects of the board's activities appear to allow for the use of some discretion that could have implications for oversight of Division B (e.g., information that is included on the Recovery.gov website).

[74] At a congressional hearing, GAO indicated that it would dedicate some resources to evaluating the impacts of tax expenditures. Testimony of Gene L. Dodaro, Acting Comptroller General, in U.S. Congress, Senate Committee on Homeland Security and Governmental Affairs, *Follow the Money: Transparency and Accountability for Recovery and Reinvestment Spending*, 111th Cong., 1st sess., March 5, 2009, http://hsgac.senate Hearings.Detail&HearingID=bdb909ea-7e73-430f-a14d-a136aab767ab.

[75] White House, "Remarks by the President On Earmark Reform," press release, March 11, 2009, http://www.whitehouse.gov/the_press_office/Remarks-by-the-President-on-Earmark-Reform/.

[76] For example, concerns were expressed about how the Office of Juvenile Justice and Delinquency Prevention (OJJDP) in the Department of Justice (DOJ) used discretion in FY2007 for a competitive grant program. The concerns resulted in a letter from Chairman Henry A. Waxman of the House Committee on Oversight and Government Reform requesting information from the Attorney General. The inquiry cited a trade publication article that reported several "top-scoring" grant applications, as assessed by peer review, had been passed over for funding by the OJJDP administrator in favor of lower-scoring applications. See letter from Rep. Henry A. Waxman, Chairman, House Committee on Oversight and Government Reform, to Michael B. Mukasey, Attorney General, Mar. 13, 2008, http://oversight and Patrick Boyle, "For Juvenile Justice, A Panel of One," *Youth Today*, vol. 17, Dec./Jan. 2008, p. 1. See also coverage in Peter Cohn, "Justice Department Grant Process Gets Waxman's Attention," *CongressDailyPM*, Mar. 24, 2008. For broader discussion of the concept

of executive earmarking, see CRS Report RL34648, *Bush Administration Policy Regarding Congressionally Originated Earmarks: An Overview*, by Clinton T. Brass, Garrett Hatch, and R. Eric Petersen.

[77] U.S. President (Obama), "Ensuring Responsible Spending of Recovery Act Funds," memorandum for the heads of executive departments and agencies, March 20, 2009; and "Government Contracting," memorandum for the heads of executive departments and agencies, March 4, 2009, http://www.whitehouse.gov/the_press_office/economy_in_government_contracting/.

[78] For economic analysis of ARRA, see CRS Report R40104, *Economic Stimulus: Issues and Policies*, by Jane G. Gravelle, Thomas L. Hungerford, and Marc Labonte.

[79] CBO, *Testimony, The Budget and Economic Outlook: Fiscal Years 2009 to 2019*, prepared statement of Robert A. Sunshine, acting director, before the Senate Committee on the Budget, January 8, 2009, p. 31.

[80] For analysis of economic issues related to ARRA, see CRS Report R40104, *Economic Stimulus: Issues and Policies*, by Jane G. Gravelle, Thomas L. Hungerford, and Marc Labonte.

[81] Letter from Douglas W. Elmendorf, Director, to Senator Charles E. Grassley, Ranking Member, Senate Committee on Finance, March 2, 2009, p. 1, http://www.cbo.gov/doc.cfm?index=10008.

[82] CBO, A Preliminary Analysis of the President's Budget and an Update of CBO's Budget and Economic Outlook, March 2009, http://www.cbo.gov/doc.cfm?index=10014.

[83] Ibid., p. 21.

[84] Ibid., p. 19.

[85] Ibid., p. 21.

[86] Ibid., p. 19.

In: American Recovery and Reinvestment Act: History... ISBN: 978-1-61668-355-9
Editor: Paul G. Tellis

Chapter 7

ESTIMATED IMPACT OF THE AMERICAN RECOVERY AND REINVESTMENT ACT ON EMPLOYMENT AND ECONOMIC OUTPUT AS OF SEPTEMBER 2009*

Congressional Budget Office

Under the American Recovery and Reinvestment Act of 2009 (ARRA), also known as the economic stimulus package, certain recipients of funds appropriated in ARRA (most grant and loan recipients, contractors, and subcontractors) are required to report the number of jobs they have created or retained with ARRA funding since the law's enactment in February 2009. The law also requires the Congressional Budget Office (CBO) to comment on that reported number.[1]

Recipients report that about 640,000 jobs were created or retained with ARRA funding through September 2009.[2] Such reports, however, do not provide a comprehensive estimate of the law's impact on employment in the United States. That impact may be higher or lower than the reported number for several reasons (in addition to any issues about the quality of the data in the reports).[3] First, it is impossible to determine how many of the reported jobs would have existed in the absence of the stimulus package. Second, the reports filed by recipients measure only the jobs created by employers who received ARRA funding directly or by their immediate subcontractors (so-called primary and secondary recipients), not by lower-level subcontractors. Third, the reports do not attempt to measure the number of jobs that may have been created or retained indirectly as greater income for recipients and their employees boosted demand for products and services. Fourth, the recipients' reports cover only certain appropriations made under ARRA, which encompass only about one-quarter of the total amount spent by the government or conveyed through tax reductions in ARRA through September 2009. The reports do not measure the effects of other provisions of the stimulus package, such as tax cuts and transfer payments to individuals.

---

* This is an edited, reformatted and augmented version of a Congressional Budget Office publication dated November 2009.

Estimating the law's overall effects on employment requires a more comprehensive analysis than the recipients' reports provide. Therefore, looking at the actual amounts spent so far (where identifiable) and estimates of the other effects of ARRA on spending and revenues, CBO has estimated the law's impact on employment and economic output using evidence about how previous similar policies have affected the economy and various mathematical models that represent the workings of the economy. On that basis, CBO estimates that in the third quarter of calendar year 2009, an additional 600,000 to 1.6 million people were employed in the United States, and real (inflation-adjusted) gross domestic product (GDP) was 1.2 percent to 3.2 percent higher, than would have been the case in the absence of ARRA (see Table 1). Those ranges are intended to reflect the uncertainty of such estimates and to encompass most economists' views on the effects of fiscal stimulus.

CBO's current estimates reflect small revisions to earlier projections of the timing and magnitude of changes to spending and revenues under ARRA. In March 2009, CBO projected that in the third quarter of 2009, U.S. employment would be higher by 600,000 to 1.5 million people with ARRA than it would be without the law, and real GDP would be 1.1 percent to 3.0 percent higher.[4]

CBO's current estimates do not reflect any change in the agency's assessment of the effect that each dollar of spending increase or revenue decrease has on output and employment. Since March, CBO has continued to examine new research on the relationships between changes in government policy and changes in output and employment. To date, that examination has generated no significant change in CBO's assessment of those relationships. CBO has also examined incoming data on output and employment during the period since ARRA's enactment. However, those data are not as helpful in determining ARRA's economic effects as might be supposed, because isolating the effects would require knowing what path the economy would have taken in the absence of the law.

Because that path cannot be observed, the new data add only limited information about ARRA's impact. Economic output and employment in the spring and summer of 2009 were lower than CBO had projected at the beginning of the year. But in CBO's judgment, that outcome reflects greater-than-projected weakness in the underlying economy rather than lower-than-expected effects of ARRA.

Table 1. Estimated Macroeconomic Impact of the American Recovery and Reinvestment Act in the Third Quarter of Calendar Year 2009

	Change Attributable to ARRA	
	March 2009 Estimate	November 2009 Estimate
Change in Real Gross Domestic Product (Percent)		
Low estimate	1.1	1.2
High estimate	3.0	3.2
Change in the Unemployment Rate (Percentage points)		
Low estimate	-0.3	-0.3
High estimate	-0.8	-0.9
Change in Employment (Millions of people)		
Low estimate	0.6	0.6

High estimate	1.5	1.6

Source: Congressional Budget Office.

Note: These changes are relative to CBO's estimate of what economic conditions would be without the American Recovery and Reinvestment Act of 2009.

Measuring ARRA's Impact Using Recipients' Reports

ARRA requires primary and secondary recipients of more than $25,000 from appropriations made under the law to report a variety of information each calendar quarter. That requirement covers most grant and loan recipients, contractors, and subcontractors but excludes individuals. The required information includes the amount of stimulus funding received and spent; the name, description, and completion status of the funded projects or activities; the number of jobs created or retained; and, in the case of infrastructure investments, the purpose and cost of the investment. Recipients are instructed to count the number of employees working on funded projects, adjusted for the number of hours they work. Reports filed in October 2009 cover the period from ARRA's enactment on February 17, 2009, through September 30, 2009.

According to the recipients' reports, a total of 640,329 jobs—more than half of them in education—were created or retained with ARRA funds through the end of September.[5] However, adding up the reported numbers of jobs created or retained is not a comprehensive measure of ARRA's effect on overall employment, or even of the effect of those provisions of ARRA for which recipients' reports are required. The law's actual impact could, in principle, be significantly larger or smaller than the total reported number of jobs.

One factor that could make the reported figure too high is that recipients' reports may include some employment that would have occurred without ARRA. Some counted employees might have worked on other activities in the absence of ARRA—for example, firms might have bid on alternative projects if their resources were not committed to projects funded by ARRA. In the case of government employees, state or local taxes might have been raised in the absence of ARRA funding (or transfer payments might have been reduced) to maintain some of the jobs counted as created or retained.

A factor that could make the reported figure too low is that the reporting requirement is limited to primary and secondary recipients of funds and excludes lower-level recipients, such as subcontractors hired by the main subcontractor. Thus, if expenditures under ARRA led to increases in employment among such lower-level subcontractors and vendors, those effects would be missed by the reports.

Recipients' reports also do not incorporate indirect effects, which could either increase or decrease the impact on employment. Those indirect effects include potential declines in employment in other firms or economic sectors as demand shifts toward the recipients of ARRA funding—a phenomenon often referred to as the "crowding out" effect of government policies. Conversely, spending under ARRA could lead to higher employment at companies not directly connected to that spending—for example, because of additional purchases made by workers who are directly employed through ARRA funds and who would otherwise have been unemployed. CBO estimates that, under current conditions, the positive indirect effects outweigh the negative ones. In other words, taken together, indirect effects boost ARRA's impact on eco-nomic output and employment.

Table 2. Estimated Output Multipliers and Budgetary Costs of Major Provisions of the American Recovery and Reinvestment Act

Type of Activity	Estimated Output Multipliers[a]		Major Provisions of ARRA	Total Budgetary Cost of Provisions, 2009–2019[b]
	Low Estimate	High Estimate		
Purchases of Goods and Services by the Federal Government	1.0	2.5	Division A, Title II: Other; Title IV: Energy Efficiency and Renewable Energy; Title IV: Innovative Technology Loan Guarantee Program; Title IV: Other Energy Programs; Title V: Federal Buildings Fund; Title VIII: National Institutes of Health; Title VIII: Other Department of Health and Human Services	$88 billion
Transfer Payments to State and Local Governments for Infrastructure	1.0	2.5	Division A, Title VII: Clean Water and Drinking Water State Revolving Funds; Title XI: Other Housing Assistance; Title XII: Highway Construction; Title XII: Other Transportation	$44 billion
Transfer Payments to State and Local Governments for Other Purposes	0.7	1.9	Division A, Title VIII: Education for the Disadvantaged; Title VIII: Special Education; Title IX: State Fiscal Stabilization Fund; Division B, Title V: State Fiscal Relief Fund	$215 billion
Transfer Payments to Individuals	0.8	2.2	Division A, Title I: Supplemental Nutrition Assistance Program; Title VIII: Student Financial Assistance; Division B, Title II: Unemployment Compensation; Title III: Health Insurance Assistance	$100 billion
One-Time Payments to Retirees	0.2	1.2	Division B, Title II: Economic Recovery Payments, Temporary Aid to Needy Families, and Child Support[c]	$18 billion
Two-Year Tax Cuts for Lower- and Middle-Income People	0.5	1.7	Division B, Title I: Refundable Tax Credits; Making Work Pay Credit;[d] American Opportunity Tax Credit[d]	$168 billion
One-Year Tax Cut for Higher-Income People	0.1	0.5	Increase in Individual AMT Exemption Amount[d]	$70 billion
Extension of First-Time Homebuyer Credit	0.2	1.0	Extension of First-Time Homebuyer Credit[d]	$7 billion
Corporate Tax Provisions Primarily Affecting Cash Flow	0	0.4	Deferral and Ratable Inclusion of Income Arising from Business Indebtedness Discharged by the Reacquisition of a Debt Instrument;[d]Clarification ofRegulations Related to Limitations on Certain Built-InLosses Following an Ownership Change;[d] Recovery Zone Bonds;[d] Qualified School Construction Bonds[d]	$21 billion

Sources: Congressional Budget Office and Joint Committee on Taxation (JCT).

Notes: This table includes provisions estimated by CBO or JCT as having total budgetary costs of $5 billion or more over the 2009–2019 period. Certain provisions with lower total costs were included if the costs in the 2009–2011 period were large.

Provisions affecting outlays (including refundable tax credits) are identified by the same names used in Congressional Budget Office, cost estimate for H.R. 1, American Recovery and Reinvestment Act of 2009 (February 13, 2009). Provisions affecting revenues—all of which are included in Title I of ARRA—are identified by the names used in Joint Committee on Taxation,

Estimated Budget Effects of the Revenue Provisions Contained in the Conference Agreement for H.R. 1, JCX-19-09 (February 12, 2009), available at www.jct.gov/ x-19-09.pdf.

Some provisions include individual elements that have different multipliers, by CBO's estimate; in those cases, the provisions are listed with the multiplier used for the majority of the 2009–2019 budgetary cost.

The economic impact of three tax provisions with budgetary costs over $5 billion was analyzed using a different methodology, and their effects cannot easily be summarized by a multiplier. Those provisions were titled "Extend by Three Years the Placed-In-Service Date for Each Section 45 Qualified Facility" and "One-Year Extension of Special Allowance for Certain Property Acquired During 2009" in JCT's estimate and "Health Information Technology" in CBO's estimate.

a. The output multiplier is the cumulative impact on real gross domestic product over several quarters for each dollar of spending or reduction in tax revenues.

b. The costs shown here do not add up to the total budgetary cost of $787 billion presented in CBO's cost estimate for the conference report on H.R. 1 for two reasons. First, several provisions are excluded because CBO's analysis of them cannot easily be summarized by a single multiplier. Second, the costs presented here are translations of budgetary costs to categories of the national income and product accounts.

c. Most of the payments in this category go to retirees.

d. The budgetary impact of these provisions was estimated by JCT.

Finally, the recipients' reports reflect only about one-quarter of the total dollar amount of spending increases or tax reductions that resulted through September 2009 from ARRA's policies. The reports cover direct government purchases of goods and services, grants and loans to private entities, and grants to states and localities, but they do not cover tax cuts or increases in transfer payments (such as unemployment insurance payments) to individuals. The tax reductions and spending not covered by the recipients' reports probably had substantial effects on purchases of goods and services and thus on employment.

Measuring ARRA's Impact Using Economic Models and Historical Data

CBO estimates that the enactment of ARRA raised federal outlays by about $100 billion and reduced tax collections by about $90 billion through September 2009. CBO has used information from a variety of economic models and from analyses of historical data to estimate how output and employment have responded to those outlay increases and revenue reductions. CBO's assessment is that different elements of ARRA (such as particular types of tax cuts, transfer payments, and government purchases) have different effects on economic output per dollar of higher spending or lower tax receipts. Multiplying estimates of those per-dollar effects by the dollar amounts of each element of ARRA yields an estimate of the law's total impact on output. CBO combined that result with estimates of how changes in output affect the unemployment rate and participation in the labor force to produce estimates of ARRA's total impact on employment.[6]

CBO's Modeling Approach

CBO used the evidence from models and historical data to determine estimated "multipliers" for each of several categories of tax and spending policies in ARRA (see Table 2 on page 4). Each multiplier represents the estimated direct and indirect effects on the nation's output of a dollar's worth of a given policy. Thus, a policy's multiplier can be applied to the budgetary cost of that policy to estimate its overall impact on output.

Direct effects consist of immediate (or first-round) effects on economic activity. Government purchases of goods and services directly elicit economic activity that would not occur otherwise and thereby have a direct dollar-fordollar impact on output. For tax cuts, increases in transfer payments, or aid to state and local governments, the size of the direct effect depends on the policy's impact on the behavior of recipients. If someone receives a dollar in transfer payments and spends 80 cents (saving the other 20 cents), production increases over time to meet the additional demand generated by that spending, and the direct impact on output is 80 cents. Similarly, if a dollar in aid to a state government leads that government to spend 50 cents more on employees' salaries (but causes no other changes in policy), the direct impact on output is 50 cents.

CBO reviewed evidence on the responses of households, businesses, and governments to various types of tax cuts and transfer payments to determine the size of those policies' direct effects on output.[7] For example:

- A one-time cash payment is likely to have less impact on a household's purchases than a longer-lasting change to disposable income will, because the onetime payment has less effect on total lifetime disposable income.
- Increases in disposable income are likely to boost purchases more for lower-income households than for higher-income ones. The difference arises, at least in part, because a larger share of lower-income households would like to borrow in order to spend more than they do now but are unable to.
- Changes to corporate taxes that primarily affect after-tax profits generally have a smaller impact on output than do policies that alter the marginal return from economic activities such as investment.

Government policies can also have indirect effects that enhance or offset the direct effects. Direct effects are enhanced, for instance, when a government policy leads directly to higher income for workers who are employed because of the policy and those workers use their higher income to boost their consumption. Direct effects are also enhanced when greater demand for goods and services prompts companies to increase investment spending to bolster their future production.

In the other direction, substantial government spending can cause a shift in resources (including employees) away from production in other firms and sectors to government-funded projects. That indirect crowding-out effect could cause growth in employment among recipients of ARRA funding to be offset by declines in employment elsewhere in the economy. Increases in interest rates are one mechanism for such crowding out: Higher interest rates discourage spending on investment and on durable goods such as cars because they raise the cost of borrowed funds. However, that mechanism has not been an important factor this year because the Fed-eral Reserve has held short-term interest rates at very low levels. Activities funded by ARRA could also reduce production elsewhere in the economy if they used scarce materials or workers with specific skills, creating bottlenecks that hindered other activities. That effect, too, has been much smaller this year than it might be otherwise because of the high unemployment rate and large amount of unused resources (as well as the diversity of activities funded under ARRA). In estimating the size of such indirect effects, CBO relied heavily on estimates from macro- econometric forecasting models, informed by evidence from other types of models and from direct estimation using historical data. (For more details about those sources of information, see the appendix.)

CBO grouped the provisions of ARRA into general categories and assigned high and low multipliers to each category (see Table 2). The ranges between high and low multipliers are designed to encompass most economists' views about the direct and indirect effects of different policies. The multipliers indicate the cumulative impact of policies on GDP over several quarters. For instance, CBO estimates that a one-time increase of $1 in federal purchases of goods and services in one calendar quarter would raise GDP by a total of $1 to $2.50 over several quarters. That cumulative multiplier of $2.50 on federal purchases comprises increases in GDP of roughly $1.45 in the quarter when the spending occurs, roughly 60 cents in the following quarter, and roughly 45 cents in later quarters combined.

The multipliers are applied to outlays when they occur and to changes in taxes or transfer payments when they affect disposable income. CBO's estimates therefore account for the different rates of spending for various types of appropriations and, similarly, for the timing of different tax cuts or transfer payments. In some cases, when different elements of a single provision were estimated to have different multipliers, the total cost of a provision was divided among more than one category. In those cases, the provision is shown in Table 2 in the category to which most of its budgetary cost applied. Provisions that affect outlays (including refundable tax credits) are identified by the same names used in CBO's cost estimate for the conference agreement on ARRA.[8] Provisions that affect revenues are identified by the names used in the revenue estimate prepared by the staff of the Joint Committee on Taxation for the same legislation.[9]

The ranges for multipliers in Table 2 are the same ones that CBO used in its initial analysis of the economic effects of ARRA in March. Since then, CBO has continued to review research on the economic impact of various government policies, and some new research has emerged. Taken as a whole, however, the evidence continues to support the same ranges for multipliers, in CBO's judgment.

The estimates of ARRA's effects on output were translated into estimates of the effects on the unemployment rate and total employment in a series of steps. First, CBO calculated the impact on the output gap—the percentage difference between actual output and potential output.[10] Next, CBO calculated the effect of the change in the output gap on the unemployment rate using the historical relationship between those two measures.[11] Then, CBO took account of the effect of changes in the unemployment rate on the labor force. If unemployment declines and the economic environment improves, discouraged workers and people who have chosen to pursue activities such as schooling rather than work tend to return to the labor force. Together, the estimated effect on the unemployment rate and the effect on the labor force were used to estimate the impact on the number of people employed.

A key advantage of this model-based approach is the ability to provide estimates of the total effects throughout the economy of tax cuts, transfer payments, and government spending. By focusing on the net change in employment, this approach captures both jobs created and jobs retained as a result of ARRA.

A key disadvantage of this approach is that considerable uncertainty exists about many of the economic relationships that are important in the modeling. Economists differ on which analytical approaches provide the most convincing evidence about such relationships, and therefore they come to different conclusions about those relationships. In addition, each individual study involves uncertainty about the extent to which the results reflect the true effects of a given policy or the effects of other factors. For those reasons, CBO provides ranges of estimates of ARRA's economic effects that are intended to encompass most economists' views and thereby reflect the uncertainty involved in such estimates.

Updated Estimates of the Impact of ARRA

Because CBO's estimates of the relationships between government policy changes and employment changes have remained essentially the same since last winter, the slight revisions to CBO's estimates of the impact of ARRA result only from new information on the rate at which provisions of the law are being implemented. Initially, CBO projected that ARRA would cut taxes and increase outlays by about $185 billion between February 2009 and September 2009. Tax cuts through September turned out to be roughly $10 billion larger than initially projected, mainly because certain tax changes were carried out more quickly than anticipated.[12] Outlays for ARRA programs, as reported by government agencies, turned out to be slightly higher than CBO initially projected, but it appears that stimulus funds substituted for some spending from regular appropriations. On the whole, the net change in total outlays that can be attributed to the stimulus package was slightly smaller than CBO initially estimated.

Taking into account the slightly faster implementation of certain tax cuts and the slightly slower pace of outlays, CBO now estimates that in the third quarter of calendar year 2009, ARRA's policies raised real GDP by between 1.2 percent and 3.2 percent, lowered the unemployment rate by between 0.3 and 0.9 percentage points, and increased the number of people employed by between 600,000 and 1.6 million compared with what those values would have been otherwise (see Table 1 on page 2).

Appendix: Evidence on the Economic Effects of Fiscal Stimulus

The Congressional Budget Office (CBO) based its estimates of the economic effects of the American Recovery and Reinvestment Act of 2009 (ARRA) on information from a variety of sources: macroeconometric forecasting models, general-equilibrium models, and direct extrapolations of past data. Macroeconometric forecasting models incorporate relationships between aggregate economic variables that are based largely on historical evidence. General-equilibrium models, by contrast, are built on explicit assumptions about the decisionmaking of individuals and businesses. Another source of information on the economic effects of fiscal stimulus is research that makes projections for the future by directly examining the correlations between economic variables in the past or by evaluating the effects of specific types of policy events in the past.

Macroeconometric Forecasting Models

In analyzing the economic effects of ARRA, CBO drew heavily on versions of the commercial forecasting models of two economic consulting firms, Macroeconomic Advisors and Global Insight, as well as on the FRB-US model used at the Federal Reserve Board. Those models assume that the economy has an underlying potential output determined by the size of the labor supply, the capital stock, and technology. They also assume that actual output can change relative to potential output because of shifts in aggregate demand for goods and services from households, businesses, and the government. With those basic assumptions, the details of interactions between economic variables in the models are based largely on historical relationships, informed by theories of how those variables are determined (for example, the theory that total consumption depends mostly on disposable income, wealth, and interest rates).[13] Because they emphasize the influence of aggregate demand on output in the short run, the macroeconometric forecasting models tend to predict greater economic effects from demand- enhancing policies such as ARRA than some other types of models do.

Macroeconometric forecasting models of this sort are widely used, and they underlie most of the forecasts offered to paying clients of economic consulting firms. In addition, the models that CBO uses generally produce results that are roughly in line with the consensus of private-sector forecasters, as compiled in the *Blue Chip Economic Indicators*. However, some analysts criticize this sort of model for being based on historical relationships between aggregate economic variables, such as income and consumption, rather than being built up from clearly specified rules governing the behavior of households and firms. In particular, some critics argue that models based on historical relationships will not provide accurate predictions in the face of new policies or new circumstances. To address that concern and to reflect current economic conditions—in which uncertainty about the financial and economic outlook remains high, and interest rates are low and are expected to remain so for some time—CBO altered the models' usual formulation to reduce the extent to which interest rates respond to increases in output.[14]

General-Equilibrium Models

Some skeptics of the efficacy of stimulus policies have cited the results of an alternative class of models, which tend to imply more-modest economic effects for such policies. In those models, people are assumed to make decisions about how much to work, buy, and save on the basis of current and expected future values of the wage rate, interest rates, taxes, and government purchases, among other things. In the basic form of such models, stimulus policies tend to crowd out a significant amount of other economic activity, and multipliers tend to be less than 1—meaning that stimulative policies have less than a dollar-for-dollar impact on output.

Although some analysts favor the rigor of that approach to modeling behavior, other analysts view the assumptions underlying households' and businesses' decision-making in those models to be unrealistic and leading to unrealistic predictions. In particular, this type of model generally assumes that people are fully rational and forward-looking, basing their current decisions on a full lifetime plan. The forward-looking assumption implies that people expect to eventually pay for any increased government spending or reduced revenues in the form of future tax increases and that they incorporate those expected payments—even if far in the future—into their current spending plans. Thus, they are assumed to reduce their consumption when government spending rises, because their lifetime income has fallen by the amount of the eventual taxes. For the same reason, cash transfer payments and tax refunds have little or no effect on current consumption in such models. People in the models generally also have full access to credit markets, so they can borrow to maintain their consumption when faced with a temporary loss of income. This class of models does not typically incorporate involuntary unemployment: People can work as many hours as they choose at the wage rate determined by the market. Finally, in these models, monetary policy usually follows a fixed rule by which increased output or inflation implies higher real interest rates.

Recent research has shown that relaxing some of those modeling assumptions can result in much higher multipliers.[15] CBO has incorporated the results of that research into its view of the effects of government policies. However, the research results appear to be too dependent on particular assumptions for CBO to rely on them heavily.

Extrapolations from Historical Data

Another type of research uses historical data to directly project how government policies will affect the economy on the basis of how economic variables such as output and consumption have behaved relative to government spending and revenues in the past. However, estimates of economic effects from this research vary widely and are sensitive to the time period and estimation strategy used. Many estimates of this sort suggest that in the case of government purchases, crowding-out effects dominate, and the impact on output tends to be less than one for one and tends to fade over time. Some estimates, however, suggest multipliers higher than the range estimated by CBO. Estimated multipliers for tax cuts are generally higher than those for spending and tend to grow over time.[16]

One pitfall of this approach is that the direction of causation between policies and the economy is not always clear. For example, poor economic conditions can prompt the government to enact policies such as ARRA in an effort to boost economic activity. If weak economic performance led to such a policy, it would not be accurate to ascribe that performance to the policy, rather than vice versa. Likewise, if states and localities reduced purchases and laid off employees when their budgets deteriorated in a recession, it would not be accurate to blame the cuts in government spending for causing the recession. When causation runs in both directions in this way, the historical correlation between variables may not be a good guide for predicting the effects of a newly proposed policy.

A strategy that has been used to try to overcome that obstacle is to identify policies, such as wartime spending, that are arguably unrelated to other economic conditions and try to isolate their impact on the economy. Wartime spending, however, may not be indicative of the effects of other increases in government spending. For example, during World War II, the rationing of many goods may have reduced the indirect effects of government spending on private consumption. More generally, historical evidence shows the effects of policies under average economic conditions. Under current conditions—in which interest rates are apt to be less affected than usual by expansionary government policies, and there are high levels of idle resources—effects may be greater than they were, on average, in the past.

End Notes

[1] Public Law 111-5, sections 1512(c) and 1512(e); 123 Stat. 115, 288.

[2] The number of jobs and other information compiled from recipients' reports are shown at www.recovery.

[3] For a discussion of data-quality issues, see Government Accountability Office, *Recovery Act: Recipient Reported Jobs Data Provide Some Insight into Use of Recovery Act Funding, but Data Quality and Reporting Issues Need Attention*, GAO-10-223 (November 19, 2009), available at www.gao.gov/new.items/d10223.pdf.

[4] See Congressional Budget Office, letter to the Honorable Charles E. Grassley about the estimated macroeconomic impacts of the American Recovery and Reinvestment Act of 2009 (March 2, 2009).

[5] For the number of created or retained jobs that were in education, see Department of Education, *U.S. Department of Education American Recovery and Reinvestment Act Report: Summary of Programs and State-by-State Data* (November 2, 2009), available at www.ed.gov/policy/gen/leg/recovery/

[6] To measure the impact of a policy, it is sometimes possible to observe both people affected by the policy and otherwise comparable people not affected by it. For example, programs that help recipients of unemployment insurance look for jobs have been studied in exactly that way. The impact of ARRA is economywide, however, so there is no suitable comparison group of people who are not affected by the law.

[7] On household spending, for example, see David S. Johnson, Jonathan A. Parker, and Nicholas S. Souleles, "Household Expenditure and the Income Tax Rebates of 2001," American Review, vol. 96, no. 5 (December 2006), pp. 1589–1610; Sumit Agarwal, Chunlin Liu, and Nicholas S. Souleles, "The Reaction of Consumer Spending and Debt to Tax Rebates: Evidence from Consumer Credit Data," Journal of Political Economy, vol. 115, no. 6 (December 2007), pp. 986–1019; and Matthew D. Shapiro and Joel Slemrod, "Did the 2008 Tax Rebates Stimulate Spending?" American Economic Review, vol. 99, no. 2 (May 2009), pp. 374–379.

[8] See Congressional Budget Office, cost estimate for H.R. 1, the American Recovery and Reinvestment Act of 2009 (February 13, 2009).

[9] See Joint Committee on Taxation, *Estimated Budget Effects of the Revenue Provisions Contained in the Conference Agreement for H.R. 1*, JCX-19-09 (February 12, 2009), available at www.jct.gov/ x-19-09.pdf.

[10] Potential output is the amount that the economy is capable of producing given its labor supply, capital stock, and technology.

[11] Changes in the output gap affect unemployment gradually over several quarters. Initially, part of a rise in output shows up as higher productivity and hours per worker rather than reduced unemployment.

[12] That $10 billion change reflects the timing rather than the total size of the estimated impact on revenues. It is not possible to determine how close the actual 2009 revenue effects of ARRA were to initial estimates, because detailed data on 2009 tax collections are not yet available.

[13] The FRB-US model differs from the other two forecasting models that CBO used in that it explicitly incorporates the influence of expected future developments on current outcomes.

[14] Stimulative policies such as ARRA can lead to higher interest rates in two ways. First, if they increase economic activity, they can prompt the Federal Reserve to raise interest rates to combat inflation. Currently, however, that effect is likely to be smaller than usual. The federal funds rate (the interest rate directly controlled by the Federal Reserve) is near zero and is unlikely to rise until economic conditions have substantially improved. Interest rates on short-term government securities tend to move closely with the federal funds rate, so they are also unlikely to rise. For that reason, CBO estimates that expansionary government policies are likely to have less effect on interest rates now than under more-normal conditions, which implies less crowding out. (With the federal funds rate as low as possible, the Federal Reserve has used other policies to try to increase the availability of credit in order to stimulate economic activity. If ARRA caused the Federal Reserve to reduce those efforts, the law's effects would be offset to some extent even without affecting interest rates; whether the Federal Reserve would indeed respond in that way under current financial and economic conditions is unclear.) Second, stimulative policies can influence longer-term interest rates if they create expectations of higher interest rates or inflation in the future. Policies that imply steep increases in future deficits may lead to higher current interest rates to the extent that people expect that the deficits will crowd out private investment and result in a lower capital stock (which tends to imply both higher rates of return on capital and higher

interest rates). However, the policies in ARRA are temporary and thus are unlikely by themselves to have a major impact on the size of the capital stock or interest rates in the future.

[15] For examples of model estimates that incorporate a lower-than-usual response of interest rates to policy changes, see Lawrence Christiano, Martin Eichenbaum, and Sergio Rebelo, *When Is the Government Spending Multiplier Large?* Working Paper No. 15394 (Cambridge, Mass.: National Bureau of Economic Research, October 2009); Troy Davig and Eric M. Leeper, *Monetary–Fiscal Policy Interactions and Fiscal Stimulus,* Working Paper No. 15133 (Cambridge, Mass.: National Bureau of Economic Research, July 2009); and Robert E. Hall, *By How Much Does GDP Rise If the Government Buys More Output?* Working Paper No. 15496 (Cambridge, Mass.: National Bureau of Economic Research, November 2009). For examples of models that include liquidity-constrained agents, see Jordi Gali, J. David López-Salido, and Javier Vallés, "Understanding the Effects of Government Spending on Consumption," *Journal of the European Economic Association*, vol. 5, no. 1 (March 2007), pp. 227–270; and Marco Ratto, Werner Roeger, and Jan in't Veld, "An Estimated Open-Economy DSGE Model of the Euro Area with Fiscal and Monetary Policy," *Economic Modelling*, vol. 26, no. 1 (January 2009), pp. 222–233. For model estimates in which government spending can contribute to future production, see Eric M. Leeper, Todd B. Walker, and ShuChun Susan Yang, *Government Investment and Fiscal Stimulus in the Short and Long Runs,* Working Paper No. 15153 (Cambridge, Mass.: National Bureau of Economic Research, July 2009).

[16] See Olivier Blanchard and Roberto Perotti, "An Empirical Characterization of the Dynamic Effects of Changes in Government Spending and Taxes on Output," *Quarterly Journal of Economics* (November 2002), pp. 1329–1368; Andrew Mountford and Harald Uhlig, *What Are the Effects of Fiscal Policy Shocks?* Working Paper No. 14551 (Cambridge, Mass.: National Bureau of Economic Research, December 2008); Roberto Perotti, *In Search of the Transmission Mechanism of Fiscal Policy,* Working Paper No. 13143 (Cambridge, Mass.: National Bureau of Economic Research, June 2007); Valerie Ramey and Matthew Shapiro, "Costly Capital Reallocation and the Effects of Government Spending," *Carnegie–Rochester Conference Series on Public Policy,* vol. 48, no. 1 (June 1998), pp. 145–194; and Robert J. Barro and Charles J. Redlick, *Macroeconomic Effects from Government Purchases and Taxes,* Working Paper No. 15369 (Cambridge, Mass.: National Bureau of Economic Research, September 2009). In interpreting the results of this research, it is important to note that the reported multipliers are generally "peak" multipliers—that is, the largest effect on output in any one quarter of a dollar change to policy that persists consistent with historical behavior—rather than the cumulative effect of a one-time dollar's worth of policy change, as CBO defines its multipliers.

In: American Recovery and Reinvestment Act: History... ISBN: 978-1-61668-355-9
Editor: Paul G. Tellis

Chapter 8

AUTHORITATIVE RESOURCES ON THE AMERICAN RECOVERY AND REINVESTMENT ACT OF 2009 (ARRA)*

Kim Walker Klarman and Julie Jennings

SUMMARY

he following list of authoritative resources is designed to assist in responding to a broad range of questions and concerns about the American Recovery and Reinvestment Act (ARRA), P.L. 111-5. Links to the full text of the act, Congressional Budget Office (CBO) estimates, White House fact sheets, and federal, state, and municipal government websites are included, along with other useful information. This list reflects information that is currently available on the Internet. It will be updated regularly as other relevant material becomes available.

The following list of authoritative resources has been compiled to assist in responding to a broad range of questions and concerns about the American Recovery and Reinvestment Act of 2009 (ARRA), P.L. 111-5. Links to the full text of the act, Congressional Budget Office (CBO) estimates, White House fact sheets, and federal, state, and municipal government websites are included, along with other useful information. This list reflects information that is currently available on the Internet. It will be updated regularly as other relevant material becomes available.

FULL TEXT OF THE LAW

P.L. 111-5 (H.R. 1) was signed by the President on February 17, 2009.

---

* This is an edited, reformatted and augmented version of a CRS Report for Congress publication dated November 2009.

Conference Report (H.Rept. 111-16) was passed by the House and Senate on February 13, 2009. This includes the Joint Explanatory Statement.

Congressional Budget Office (CBO) Cost Estimates

Estimates of ARRA's impact on the budget and a detailed analysis of the budgetary impact by title. http://www.cbo.gov/ftpdocs/99xx/doc9989/hr1conference.pdf

White House Information

Fact Sheets

Provides general fact sheets on broad policy areas within the stimulus (e.g., education, energy, health, infrastructure) and estimates by state the number of jobs that will be created or saved. http://www.whitehouse.gov/the_press_ office/state_by_state_ employment

Recovery.gov

The Administration's website that is intended to be a repository for information related to implementation and oversight of the stimulus. It currently includes overview information about the legislation, a timeline for implementation, a frequently asked questions page, and an announcement page that will be regularly updated. The Administration's intent is to develop the site to encompass information about available funding, distribution of funds, and major recipients. http://www.recovery

Each federal agency receiving funds from the act will submit weekly cumulative reports on their recovery activities. Updated reports are submitted each Tuesday, and detail major actions taken by each agency and how much money has been spent.Weekly Agency Reports: http://www.recovery

Office of Management and Budget (OMB) Guidance

OMB issued a detailed guidance document on February 18, 2009, directing executive branch agencies to develop a dedicated portion of their websites for information related to the recovery. This document was updated based on input from the various stakeholders on April 3, 2009, and June 22, 2009. All three guidance documents are available on the recovery.gov website, in the featured news section:

Original document (February 18, 2009): http://www.recoveryInitial %20Recovery%20Act%20Implementing%20Guidance.pdf

Amended document (April 3, 2009): http://www.recovery

Amended document (June 22, 2009): http://www.recovery OMB+Final+Cover+Memo.pdf

OMB has created a nationwide data collection system for recipients of ARRA funds to use for submitting their required data. Only registered users may use this system. Data collected will be available to the public on the recovery site beginning October 11, 2009. http://www.federalreporting.gov/

Congressional Sources

The House Committee on Ways and Means provides instructions for requesting various benefits from the funding provided by the act. It also contains fact sheets on some of the tax provisions of the act: http://waysandmeans.house.gov/MoreInfo.asp?section=50

Government Accountability Office Reports

The Government Accountability Office (GAO) is required to conduct bimonthly reviews of selected funding recipients and to report on the use of funds. These GAO reviews currently include 16 states and the District of Columbia and are available on the GAO website at http://www.gao.gov/recovery

GAO has developed a website covering not only the above-mentioned fund recipient reviews, but also links to other GAO products and instructions for reporting fraud or misuse of ARRA funds. Following the Money: GAO's Oversight of the Recovery Act is available at http://www.gao.gov/ recovery/.

Other available GAO products include the following:

GAO-09-453T, American Recovery and Reinvestment Act: GAO's Role in Helping to Ensure Accountability and Transparency: http://www.gao.gov/new.items/d09453t.pdf

GAO-09-515T: American Recovery and Reinvestment Act: GAO's Role in Helping to Ensure Accountability and Transparency for Science Funding:http://ww.gao.gov/new.items/d09515t.pdf

GAO-09-580, Recovery Act: As Initial Implementation Unfolds in States and Localities, Continued Attention to Accountability Issues is Essential: http://www.gao.gov/new.items/ d09580.pdf

Federal Agency Websites

Corporation for National and Community Service: http://www.nationalservice.gov/about/recovery/index.asp

Department of Agriculture:http://www.usda.gov/wps/portal/arra?navid=USDA

Department of Agriculture – Plans: http://www.usda.gov/documents/FY09_Stimulus_Enacted.pdf

Department of Commerce: http://www.commerce

Department of Commerce – National Institute of Standards and Technology: http://www.nist.gov/ recovery/
Department of Defense: http://www.defenselink.mil/recovery
Department of Education: http://www.ed.gov/policy/gen/leg/recovery
Department of Energy: http://www.energy
Department of Energy – Energy Efficiency and Renewable Energy: http://apps1.eere. energy.gov/ news/daily. cfm/hp_news_id= 156
Department of Energy – Western Area Power Administration: http://www.wapa.gov /newsroom/ sec402.htm
Department of Health and Human Services: http://www.hhs.gov/recovery
Department of Health and Human Services – state Medicaid funding: http://www.hhs.gov/ recovery/statefundsmap.html
Department of Housing and Urban Development: http://www.hud.gov/recovery
Department of the Interior: http://recovery
Department of Justice: http://www.usdoj.gov/recovery
Department of Labor: http://www.dol.gov/recovery
Department of Labor – Employee Benefits Security Administration (COBRA information): http://www.dol.gov/ebsa/COBRA.html
Department of State: http://www.state.gov/recovery
Department of Transportation – Federal Transit Administration: .http://www.fta.dot.gov/ index_9118.html
Department of Transportation – press release regarding distribution and monitoring of economic recovery funds: http://www.dot.gov/affairs/dot1409.htm
Department of Transportation: http://www.dot.gov/recovery
Department of Treasury: http://www.ustreas.gov/recovery
Department of Veteran Affairs: http://www.va.gov/recoveryImplementing _the _Recovery _Act.asp
Environmental Protection Agency: http://www.epa.gov/recovery
General Services Administration: http://www.gsa.gov/Portal/gsa/ep/contentView.do?Content Type=GSA_OVERVIEW&contentId=2576 1 &noc=T
Internal Revenue Service: http://www.irs.gov/newsroom/article/0,,id
National Aeronautics and Space Administration (NASA): http://www.nasa.gov/recovery
National Endowment on the Arts: http://www.nea.gov/recovery
National Institutes of Health: http://www.nih.gov/recovery
National Institutes of Health (NIH), Director's statement: http://www.nih.gov/about/director/ 02252009statement_arra.htm
National Science Foundation: http://www.nsf.gov/recovery
National Science Foundation, Director's statement: http://www.nsf.gov/news/news_ summ.jsp? cntn_id= 1 14277&org=OLPA&from=news
Small Business Administration: http://www.sba.gov/recovery
Small Business Administration – press release: http://www.sba.gov/idc/groupssba_homepage/news_release_09-10.pdf
Social Security Administration: http://www.ssa.gov/recovery

STATE GOVERNMENT WEB SITES

The list below reflects states that currently post ARRA information on the Web.

Alabama: http://www.stimulus.alabama.gov/
Alaska: http://omb.alaska.gov/10_omb/budget/IndexEconomicStimulus.htm
Arizona: http://az.gov/recovery
Arkansas: http://recovery
California: http://www.recovery
Colorado: http://www.colorado.gov/recovery
Connecticut: http://www.recovery
Delaware: http://recovery
Florida: http://www.flarecovery.com/
Florida-transportation: http://www.dot.state.fl.us/planning
Florida-Workforce:http://www.floridajobs.org/about%20awi/open_government ARRA_plans _reports _OEL.htm
Georgia: http://stimulusaccountability.ga.gov
Georgia-transportation: http://www.dot.state.ga.us/informationcenter/gastimulus/Pages/default.aspx
Hawaii: http://hawaii.gov/gov/recovery
Idaho: http://accountability
Illinois: http://recovery
Indiana: http://www.in.gov/gov/2985.htm
Iowa: http://www.iowa.gov/recovery
Kansas: http://www.governor.ks.gov/Recovery/default.htm
Kentucky: http://kentuckyatwork.ky.gov/
Louisiana: http://www.stimulus.la.gov/
Louisiana-energy: http://dnr.louisiana.gov/sec/execdiv/techasmt/programs/arra_2009/index.htm
Maine: http://www.maine.gov/recovery
Maryland: http://statestat.maryland.gov/recovery
Massachusetts: http://www.mass.gov/recovery
Michigan: http://www.michigan.gov/recovery
Minnesota: http://www.mmb.state.mn.us/stimulus
Mississippi: http://stimulus
Missouri: http://transform.mo.gov/
Montana: http://recovery
Nebraska: http://www.recovery.nebraska.gov/
Nevada: http://nevada.gov/recovery
New Hampshire: http://www.nh.gov/recovery
New Jersey: http://www.state.nj.us/recovery
New Mexico: http://www.recovery
New York: http://www.recovery
North Carolina: http://www.ncrecovery.gov/
North Dakota: http://www.nd.gov/recovery Ohio: http://recovery.ohio.gov/

Oklahoma: http://www.ok.gov/recovery
Oregon: http://www.oregon.gov/recovery
Pennsylvania: http://www.recovery
Rhode Island: http://www.recovery
South Carolina: http://stimulus
South Dakota: http://recovery
Tennessee: http://www.tnrecovery.gov
Texas: http://txstimulusfund.com/
Utah: http://www.recovery
Vermont: http://recovery
Virginia: http://stimulus
Washington: http://recovery.wa.gov/
West Virginia: http://www.recovery
Wisconsin: http://www.recovery.wisconsin.gov/ ‘
Wyoming: http://wyoming.gov/recovery

State Funding Allocations

Department of Education: http://www.ed.gov/about/ overview/budget/statetables/ recovery

Department of Health and Human Services-Community Health Center Grants: http://www.hhs.gov/recovery

Department of Heath and Human Services-Medicaid: http://www.hhs.gov/recovery statefunds.html

Department of Health and Human Services-State Funding: http://transparency.cit.nih.gov/ RecoveryGrants/

Department of Housing and Urban Development: http://www.hud.gov/recovery

Department of Justice-Justice Assistance Grant Program: http://www.ojp.usdoj.gov/BJA/ recoveryJAG/recoveryallocations.html

Department of Justice-Crime Victims Fund Compensation and Assistance Programs: http://www.ovc.gov/fund/recoverycvfa2009.html

Department of Justice-Stop Violence Against Women Formula Grant Awards: http://www.ovw.usdoj.gov/recovery

Department of Labor-Workforce Investment Act Youth Activities: http://www.dol.gov/opa/media press/eta/eta20090249-chart.pdf

Department of Transportation-Funds for Highway Infrastructure Investment: http://www.fhwa.dot.gov/legsregs/directives

Department of Transportation-Public Transportation Programs: http://www.dot.gov/recovery docs/E9-4745 .pdf

Environmental Protection Agency-Clean Water and Drinking Water Revolving Fund: http://www.epa.gov/water

State and Municipal Sources

The Council of State Governments has compiled information on executive orders and state legislation related to ARRA, as well as key deadlines and grants information: http://www.staterecovery.org/ and http://www.staterecovery.org/state-responses

The US Conference of Mayors has prepared a summary of the act, highlighting those provisions they consider to be important for cities: http://www.usmayors.org/recovery

State-by-State Breakdown of ARRA Dollars:http://www.usmayors.org/recovery report-stateprog.pdf

Key Program Summaries: http://www.usmayors.org/recovery/

The National Conference of State Legislatures has prepared overview summaries of selected sections of the package (e.g., Medicaid, transportation, labor and economic development, energy and water, broadband): http://www.ncsl.org/?tabid=16779

Non-Government Sources

The Onvia Corporation has created a site geared to the business community that is dedicated to tracking every recovery dollar in real time: http://recovery.org

Protiviti, a business consulting firm, has prepared a Q&A document that outlines the responsibilities of the recipients of ARRA funds, including reporting requirements: http://www.energywashington.com/ewblogdocs/april2009/ew04302009_arra.pdf

ProPublica, an independent, nonprofit investigative journalism organization, tracks the stimulus and its projects: http://www.propublica.org/ion/stimulus

INDEX

A

B

C

D

E

F

G

H

I

S

T